And Now More Voices From Prison Walls

by
WILLIAM CAWMAN

Author of
Voices from Prison Walls
More Voices from Prison Walls
Yet More Voices from Prison Walls
Still More Voices from Prison Walls
Even More Voices from Prison Walls
The Disease and the Cure
Testimonies from Prison Walls

SCHMUL PUBLISHING COMPANY
NICHOLASVILLE, KENTUCKY

COPYRIGHT © 2025 BY SCHMUL PUBLISHING CO.
All rights reserved. No part of this publication may be reproduced or used in any form or by any means—graphic, electronic, or mechanical, including photocopying, recording, taping, or information storage or retrieval systems—without prior written permission of the publishers.

Churches and other noncommercial interests may reproduce portions of this book without prior written permission of the publisher, provided such quotations are not offered for sale—or other compensation in any form—whether alone or as part of another publication, and provided that the text does not exceed 500 words or five percent of the entire book, whichever is less, and does not include material quoted from another publisher. When reproducing text from this book, the following credit line must be included: "From *And Now More Voices from Prison Walls* by William Cawman, © 2025 by Schmul Publishing Co., Nicholasville, Kentucky. Used by permission."

Published by Schmul Publishing Co.
PO Box 776
Nicholasville, KY USA

Printed in the United States of America

ISBN 10: 0-88019-679-3
ISBN 13: 978-0-88019-679-6

Visit us on the Internet at www.wesleyanbooks.com, or order direct from the publisher by calling 800-772-6657, or by writing to the above address.

Contents

	Foreword	4
1	God Answers Prayer	7
2	Open Doors in Adverse Conditions	24
3	God is Still on His Throne!	42
4	God is Still Moving On	61
5	Unpredictable	79
6	Working With the Way Things Are	97
7	We Must Work While the Day Lasts	114
8	God's Hand is Still Upon Us	131
9	New Inmates—Same Old Problems	149
10	"How Forceful are Right Words"	168
11	The Heart of Kings is Still in His Hand	184
12	Is a Chaplain's Life Boring? Never!	203
13	Encouraging Signals	220
14	God's Grace Continues to Overcome	238
15	God is Not Baffled by Man's Changes	255
16	"Great is Thy Faithfulness"	271

Foreword

If one should look back at the Foreword of volume five of these letters from prison, it would be observed that volume five was not expected to be written; that Jesus' coming would prevent that. Well, as you can see, He yet tarries, and so four more years have brought their triumphs and trials, and any comment on which outweighed the other will be withheld. Suffice it to say, that no matter to what extent trials last or intensify, one more soul gathered for the Kingdom above is definitely worth it.

I do not pay much attention to bumper stickers, and have never had one on my car, but some time ago I did see one that lit a spark in me down deep inside. It simply said, "One More For Jesus!" If the past four years (2021-2024) saw only one more for Jesus, heaven would rejoice over that one, and so should we. Trustfully, there have been more than that, because many of you, the readers of these letters, have prayed for us. Thank you!

You will see from the following pages that the ministry among men in prison has undergone a number of changes since the last volume of letters was published. Much has changed in many areas since the catastrophic upset of Covid. Not many of these changes could be viewed as beneficial, but changes they were nonetheless, and we have had to submit to whatever we could not correct.

The end of the year 2024 brings back memories from almost twenty-seven years of laboring among these precious souls in prison. There have been numerous occasions during those years when without hesitation I have looked into the face of Jesus and said, "Lord, this was Your idea!" He has never upbraided me for it either. However, in all of those years and up to the present time, I have never felt even the slightest indication that God was releasing me from the calling He so tenderly laid upon me.

About two years ago, another part-time chaplain younger than myself, turned in his retirement. My supervisor asked me if I planned to continue, and I told him that it was God who put me there, and I would stay as long as He kept the door open. He thanked me for it and so in the words of Paul, "Having therefore obtained help of God, I continue unto this day..."

Having never been granted, and having never claimed, any prophetic gift, I leave the future in the same Omnipotent Hands that have guided up until now, and raise an Ebenezer, and commit my all to the One I love supremely. Amen!

Daniel gives a most glorious promise to the very day we are now living in. He writes Dan 9:25— "Know therefore and understand, that from the going forth of the commandment to restore and to build Jerusalem unto the Messiah the Prince shall be seven weeks, and threescore and two weeks: *the street shall be built again, and the wall, even in troublous times.*"

Knowing that God's Word is sure, and that every promise not yet fulfilled will be fulfilled, we will do well to lift our eyes to the building of the wall and the street therein, rather than the troublous times. The latter we cannot ignore, but the former is our challenge, and that until Jesus returns on that white horse under the blazingly glorious name: *Faithful and True!*

And so we send forth this sixth volume of God's faithfulness to me in prison; and carry on still!

There have been disappointments for certain, but we commit those to Him and raise an Ebenezer of gratitude to God and you, His praying people, for all the victories recorded in this volume. To God be all the glory, both now and forever!

WILLIAM CAWMAN

May 2025

1
GOD ANSWERS PRAYER

January, 2021

WHAT A YEAR THE past one has been! Will we see the end of another one? God only knows that. But it has certainly been a year of changes. Just about the time I write and tell you what we are doing, we start doing something else! And it has happened again since the last letter.

We have had another surge of Covid-19 cases in our prison, and over eighty officers and nine lieutenants were out sick by mid-month December. And so when we reported in on Monday, December 7, our supervisor told us that they had again suspended all religious services as far as group gatherings. Then he proceeded to tell us what the orders from the central office in Trenton were.

Now, mind you, this is coming from the man who a year ago had me personally in his cross-hairs, leaving me with no certainty of continuing on. You prayed! God heard! He said that he was not going to suspend me again. He wanted us as a team to get together each day and pray. Then he wanted me to come in and prepare written sermons and send one out each week through the inmate mail system to all those who were enrolled in Protestant services. I sent out the first one on Wednesday, December 9.

So, in case you didn't quite get what is happening, let me put it this way. I have a very private office in one of the chapels which is now not being used because of no groups. I can go there and study and pray and print sermons and prepare them for distribution, and the State of New Jersey pays me for every minute of it. I never imagined when I first answered the call of God into His vineyard that I would be paid for answering by the taxpayers of such a state as New Jersey! So, to all who live in this state, please keep praying and please keep paying your taxes!

Now I just wrote the above on the seventeenth of December, and I can only wonder just how long the present arrangement will last. Will I need to update with a change of plans or methods even before mailing this letter out at the end of the month? Such is a small picture of our changing world! "For here have we no continuing city, but we seek one to come." Heb 13:14.

December is the month for the Jewish Chanukah which commemorates the cleansing of the Temple after the reign of the Maccabees during the years between the Old and New Testaments. The first night a candle is lit in the Menorah, and then each night for eight days an additional one until the last night when all eight are lit. Just before it began this year the state closed down all religious services, asking us to provide service material in their cells as I told above. We received orders from Trenton that this would also apply to the celebration of the Jews. We came down to Tuesday evening, December 15, and my supervisor was already on his way home when he received a phone call. A very influential Rabbi had notified the governor that the inmates in prison were not being allowed to light their candles. The governor called the commissioner and he called the assistant commissioner and a call then was made to our director in Trenton and then to my supervisor. The Jewish inmates WOULD be called together to light their candles.

My supervisor called and two chaplains had not yet left, so he asked them to see that it was called out. In facility one, no one came. In facility two, no one came. In facility three, guess who came? The troublesome black man who is trying to be a Jew, and him alone. He had no idea whatsoever as to what it was about, so he was sent back. The next day a snow storm set in and all workers were told to go home at one o'clock. We asked about Chanukah and were told it would be cancelled. The next night it was again called and no one showed up. Our would-be-black-Jew had been sent to detention. Then we received another call that since they had missed so many, it was to be extended through Friday. My supervisor called me and asked if I could change my schedule and stay for it and I told him I would. Once again it was called out and no one came.

I will leave that story without comment or commentary. The Scripture clearly teaches in Prov. 9:10: "The fear of the LORD is the beginning of wisdom: and the knowledge of the holy is understanding." Now would it not only be sensible to say that without the fear of the Lord, there is not even the beginning of wisdom? Well, let me give you a little sample from the smorgasbord of stupidity that is coming out with our national rejection of God and the loss of His fear. By the most recent figures, it costs well over fifty thousand a year to keep one single inmate in our prison system. They are clothed and fed. They are entertained and given tasks. They are given a bed at night in a warm cell. And our bankrupt government with a national debt of ????? + ????? is now sending each and every inmate in prison a stimulus check for $1200.

Don't ask me to comment on that either.

But, let's move on to brighter subjects, for in spite of all the dark, antichrist powers that are pressing upon us from every angle, God and His Holy Spirit are still intensely at work preparing a Bride for the triumphant Second Coming of the King of Kings and Lord of Lords. And—blessed be our wonderful

Savior—He does not require that His Bride be selected from off the padded pews of a church. He loves these broken lives in prison just as much as the little baby born into a holiness home of sanctified parents! What a Savior! I just now recall the precious words of a chorus:

> *"I will serve Thee, because I love Thee;*
> *You have given life to me.*
> *I was nothing before You found me;*
> *You have given life to me.*
>
> *Heartaches; broken pieces;*
> *Ruined lives are why You died on Calvary.*
> *Your touch was what I longed for;*
> *You have given life to me."*

Since writing the earlier part of this letter, I just returned from a day in the prison in which I printed and mailed out the fourth sermon to the inmates. I have found a way to do this quite effectively (thank the Lord), but it requires some technical aptitude without which I would have to spend many hours on each one. The men are being moved about within the three facilities of the institution because of quarantine needs over the virus, and so just before each mailing I have to go into the inmate roster; isolate the list of enrollments in Protestant religious services; transfer it from the program used by the prison to Microsoft Excel; and then go through it and move any inmates who have been transferred, and then use that as a mail merge into the heading of the letter. Today's mailing was, if I remember correctly, two-hundred and thirty-four.

Now, just in case God has such a thing as a sense of humor, just listen to this. Probably half of the inmates receiving these sermons would never come to my classes and Bible studies because of my teaching the "false doctrine" that a man can be so cleansed by the Blood of Jesus that he can live entirely free from sin. Instead, they would attend those volunteer teachers who would tell them that no matter what they did, they could never live free from sin, but neither could they ever lose their salvation. Now God has, for the time, entirely shut every other mouth and all they are getting is the glorious news of full salvation! Do you think I will take advantage of this? Yes, I certainly will, and I ask you to pray for divine anointing to make hay while the sun shines.

The other part-time chaplain is bilingual and so he is writing to all of the Spanish speaking inmates. Even though his number is much smaller, it takes him more time to get it all printed in Spanish without the feature for doing so on the State computers. He has not yet caught on to the method I developed of merging the lists of inmates into a mail merge onto the letter headings, so I am trying to help him with it. We have a very cooperative chaplaincy team, and it is a pleasure to work with all of them.

Our supervisor has been out for a week and a half and has a week at least to go over a minor surgery to his spinal column. We are hoping and praying that it will give him some much-needed relief from the pain he has been enduring.

Now for "a tale out of school" as the old saying goes. Numbers of times over the years I have written about our Muslim chaplain who comes from Nigeria and whose father is the head Imam of Nigeria. I have related how he seems to be such a discontented and unhappy person that it is hard to even try to converse with him.

A couple of weeks ago, one of our officers passed away suddenly. He was forty-three years old and had been out with Covid for a few weeks, but had recovered and returned. He went home one day, spoke to his wife, and then collapsed on the floor and was gone; probably from a heart-attack.

All five of us chaplains went to the viewing for him and then we went out to a restaurant to eat. The Muslim chaplain was hilarious! He has been so good-natured ever since the new supervisor came on board. On the way back to the prison from the meal, I was riding with my supervisor and the Catholic chaplain, who is also a Nigerian, and my supervisor said, "Has —— (the Muslim) always been that way?" I immediately responded, "Chaplain, I'm going to tell you the honest truth—you have transformed that man!" I think he felt unwanted by the former supervisor and this one has treated him just like everyone else. I tell you it has been a welcome change too, after over twenty years of the way he was. Now I would love to see him get saved!!! Pray for him if God lays him on your heart.

And now as we pass the threshold of another year, we face uncertainties and unknowns such as never in our lives before. But one thing we know, and know of a certainty—God is working out His purpose and He will bring us through all that lies ahead with total victory if we keep our eyes on Him and our love for Him red hot. Let's do so! Thank you for all your prayers through another year.

William Cawman

February, 2021

OUR MINISTRY IN THE prison changes so rapidly that we find it hard to plan ahead very far. We now have one whole unit of the three under quarantine as well as a few other cell blocks. I have had one or two inmates tell me they have now had the virus twice; that's encouraging, isn't it?

At the close of the year most of our modules for our classes and services expired. These have to be put into the system up in Trenton, and when I sent in our requests for new ones, they just told us to wait. Meanwhile those who send in requests to be added to the list of those receiving the weekly sermons by mail have to be listed separately or put on hold as there is no module in place in which to enroll them. Just yesterday, orders came from Trenton to go ahead and send our list of modules in to them. I was assigned the task of preparing them, and I will have to wait until after the next staff meeting on

January 26, to be sure all of the chaplains have listed what they want for the coming year.

I am continuing to send out weekly sermons to about 230 men, and I have started a series of messages to them entitled "The Disease and the Cure." That title came from an old Irish preacher by the name of Gideon Ousley, who when God called him to preach, informed the Lord that he did not know what to say. God asked him if he knew anything about the disease. Immediately he told the Lord he did and began to tell the Lord all about it. After a half hour was gone, God asked him if he knew anything about the cure. Once again, he started in telling the Lord all about the cure. When he finished his hour sermon, God said, "Now Gideon, go preach about the disease and the cure; all else is only talk." Please pray that the Lord will anoint these messages with clarity and soul saving virtue.

I am also still able to conduct one-on-one interviews with the men. A couple of days ago I met again with the man who after years of trying to get him to forsake his barren and sinful pathway and let Jesus come into his heart, still finds his spiritual wilderness familiar territory. When he entered the room, I said to him, "J——, you know me and I know you, and it will do nothing for you to hide; how are you getting along?" He evasively said, "Good; I think I'm doing good. I'm not getting involved in some things that I used to, and I am reading my Bible and praying more. I think maybe I'm there."

I said, "J——, when you actually let Jesus come into your heart, you know it! You don't have to add up a few merits and conclude that you are now a Christian. The Bible says that a Christian is a new creature; that old things are passed away. It also says that those who receive Him have power to live as sons of God." He began to squirm and said, "Yeah, maybe so. I know I'm not where I should be." I said, "So when are you going to take hold of yourself and settle it to mind God?"

"I want to do that now."

"Then use the will God has given you and begin to open

your heart to Him and shut it to everything that would displease Him."

He then said, "I don't know that I'm really doing anything wrong… well, maybe. I love peanut butter and so I've been buying it from one of the men who works in the kitchen and brings it from there. Is that wrong?"

"J——, you know that's wrong. It is wrong for him to steal it and it is wrong for him to sell it and it is wrong for you to buy it. You know that is all against the rules of the prison, and the Bible says that if we regard iniquity in our hearts the Lord will not hear us. Your prayers will go no higher than your eyebrows when you are knowingly doing wrong."

He thought about it and then said, "Then I will stop it and just give up my peanut butter, but boy do I love peanut butter." I said, "So are you going to sell your soul for peanut butter?"

Suddenly I saw it dawn on him how foolish he was acting. He said, "Could I pray?"

"Of course you can." He prayed and then I prayed and when he went to leave the room he was reluctant to go. He said, "Oh I feel so much better now. I can live without peanut butter. I feel goosebumps all over me." But nearly every time I deal thus with him and he prays, he gets a sort of spiritual rush and says he is going back to his room to pray. Then we go through this all over again, and again, and again… It makes the words of Jesus stand out with flashing, flaming red: "What shall a man give in exchange for his soul?" Esau gave away his soul for a bowl of soup. Will this man give away his for a few blobs of stolen peanut butter?

The very next Sunday morning our pastor preached a very anointed message taken from the account of Josiah's cleansing of the temple and the command in 1 Corinthians 3 about our body being the temple of the Holy Ghost, and that He expects us to clean out the rubbish so that He can move in. Suddenly he stopped and said, "What are you talking about, pastor? I'm talking about exactly that thing you are thinking about right now!" And my mind flashed back to our conversation with J—— earlier in the week. In the presence of the searching eye of God, J——'s face was suddenly smeared all over with unlawfully obtained peanut butter! And if he chooses to return to his wallowing in the mire, he will appear again before the Great White Throne with peanut butter all over him. I am not trying to be frivolous; I am trying to be faithful to the question of Jesus as to what a man will be willing to give in exchange for his soul. As you read this, what are you thinking about? Thank you, Pastor!

Oh God, please give me patience and love for this soul when I remember how long I too beat around every bush in my own spiritual wilderness. Thank God, there came an historical moment in my life when I turned away from that wilderness and started for Canaan, and by God's help and grace I have never looked back. I want this for him. I long to have him come down some day all vibrant with victory, shouting "I have found Him!" So, I will see him again soon, Lord willing.

For the last while, my supervisor has felt it on his heart to reach out more to the staff and officers, as some of them have lost family members, and others are suffering from the virus. So many officers have been out sick at times that it puts an extra strain on the ones able to work. He mentioned it to us and we all felt the same and so we had a staff meeting and invited a representative from the officers' union to attend. We presented our thoughts to him and he was very solicitous of us reaching out to them, saying that many of them are suffering various effects from all that is going on right now. I assured him that we felt for our police across the nation as they are facing such a loss of respect from this lawless generation, and he seemed to really appreciate it.

And so, what we plan to do is open up a conference call within the prison personnel at one o'clock each Wednesday afternoon, and one of us chaplains will take prayer requests and then pray together over the phone for the needs within the ranks. Also, the representative said he will see to it that any officers or their families who would desire a contact from a chaplain would be able to get that to us.

With now over one third of the entire prison under quarantine, and many officers and staff afflicted as well, it offers a whole new set of needs than what we have ever had to face before. Please pray that through this God will be able to help some souls that would never have applied for it had all continued on in our comfortable American dream.

Since we were instructed (isn't God amazing?) by the officials in Trenton that we were to get together as a team and pray together each day, we have been doing so as often as we can. We are not taking this lightly! We have not made an issue out of our differences in theological persuasions, but have just been praying around the members that God would enable us to be His voice to these men in this time of heightened susceptibility. And I am hearing one inmate after another as I meet them coming and going on the compound, say, "Thank you for those letters! They are really helping me." Isn't it just wonderful that God has chosen such "foolish" (He said that, not me!) means to carry on His work? He chose the "foolishness" of preaching. He chose the "foolish" things of the world to confound the wise. And—oh my! Listen to this! "Because the foolishness of God is wiser than men." That terminology, "the foolishness of God…" would constitute downright disrespect had not God Himself named it. So, whatever God has ordained by means of what He calls "foolishness" had better not be tampered with by one touch of humanity and all its embellishments to the ark. Yes, Paul cried out: "I fear, lest by any means, as the serpent beguiled Eve through his subtilty, so your minds should be corrupted from the simplicity that is in Christ." Let the labors be ours; let all the honors go to Him!

Ever since my volunteer status in the prison changed to a paid position, about twenty years ago, I have had the same provision of hours. I am not to put in over nine hundred and forty-four hours in a year, and I am not allowed to volunteer time in addition to that. So you see, God had from the beginning of this ministry arranged it with about half of my time available for His work in other places. God alone knows what this year will hold. I had cancelled nearly all outside meetings from August through the end of last year and was planning to continue with a dual schedule for the present year. We had one short meeting in January and then a camp in February which has now been cancelled due to the prevalence of the virus in the location. So, will I be locked up all year? Can I tell you something? I am perfectly at ease and as happy as I can be to know nothing about tomorrow! If Jesus tarries until tomorrow morning, I plan with all my heart to love and obey Him. How much do I really mean it when I sing, "Trust and Obey, for there's no other way…?"

What a privilege to be living in this very hour with a heart full of love for Jesus. I feel it burning like a living flame right now! "Tempt not my soul away; Jesus is mine!" Thank you, song writer!

And now let me tell you of a new open door accompanied by a prayer request. On Wednesday, January 27, I was just prayerfully finishing typing out a message for the men for the following Monday, when a message popped up on the computer screen from my supervisor wanting me to call him. I did so and this is what I heard: "Are you ready to go to Judea and Samaria and the uttermost parts of the earth?" I responded, "I had better be." Then he said that the supervisor in the Mountainview State Prison (the furthest one north, and the one he had been supervisor at before coming here) wanted us to send him the sermons we were publishing for the inmates here and that he would print them out and give them to the inmates in that prison. And so I sent him the last four; at which time I had begun a Bible study on the subject "The Disease and the Cure." So God is expanding the congregation of those being preached to.

Now for the prayer request: please pray that the anointing of the Holy Spirit will cover these messages with soul saving power and that the rage of the enemy which is certain to be unleashed, will be covered by the Blood. These messages are not today's new age agenda designed to comfort sinners in their present sinful state. They are teaching the Biblical confession and forsaking of sin; the reality of the new birth; and the cleansing of the human heart from all inward sinful nature. If the chaplain at that institution does not agree with what he is being sent, you and I both know he will not likely just let it pass on to the men. Please help us pray that God, since it would appear He has opened this door, would cover it with His Precious Blood until it can reach those He is wanting it to reach. And then pray that there will be many who will open their hearts to Him through it. Did He not promise that His Word would not return unto Him void? Let's claim that promise. Time is short, and may God help us all to work while the day lasts.

William Cawman

┼┼┼

March, 2021

WHAT A RAPIDLY CHANGING world, life within this prison has become! Just yesterday I was working from the office right next to my supervisor's office and he came in and said, "Well, I just received word from Trenton that they want us to start having religious services again March 1. Can we be ready?" I said, "Well, when I turned in the new modules for this year I anticipated opening up again somewhere in the year, but what restrictions are we going to be under? Will we be limited to a certain number, and will they want it during the day on a weekday instead of Sundays? All of that will make a big difference in whether we can be ready that quickly." He said he would have to call and get some particulars.

I am currently right in the middle of sending a weekly Bible study on the subject "The Disease and the Cure." Even if we do open up for services, I will continue to send the studies until we get to the cure! How can I possibly leave them with only a partial cure? Please pray for us to know how to cope with the fast-changing requirements being made of us!

It might interest you and also help you to understand how to pray to have an update of our census within this prison. Since moving inmates between prisons and county jails has been limited because of the pandemic, our population has dropped from our limit of approximately 3500 to 2463. The Central Reception and Assessment Facility up north has been closed down and one tier in our prison has been cleared out to receive inmates from there. With all of that here is the latest census report:

Race: Asian, 15; Black 1451; Am Indian 2; Hispanic 441; White 548; other 6; Total 2463

Religion: Protestant Christian 380; Christian-nonspecific 64; Baptist 36; Jehovah Witness 33; Christian Science 18; Seventh Day Adventist 5; Pentecostal 4; Reformed 1; Muslim 535; Roman Catholic 220; No preference 106; other (not listed) 70; Buddhist 29; Jewish 25; Wicca 7; Native American 3; Eastern Orthodox 1.

Total listed 1537. So you see that 2463 minus 1537 leaves us with 926 inmates with no religion at all. Don't you think we have work to do, and don't you think you have something to pray about? Thank you for remembering us to the Lord of Harvest!

I have been earnestly praying for fresh oil in both the mailed-out messages and the one-on-one visits, and God has been helping in both. Several younger men have visited with me with tears in their eyes as I try to point them to a life worth living in God. It so pulls on my heart that I wish I could just gather them into my arms and try to lead them to Jesus; then I remember that He feels that way too, and He can do it so much better than I can. However, inasmuch as He is counting on me to reach them, I fervently crave His anointing.

We have had at least four staff members die of Covid, and I don't know how many inmates, but it does seem to be slowing down finally. None of us chaplains have contracted it.

I will let you in on a bit of humor between my supervisor and myself. After I write my message for the week, I go to a state computer and bring up an updated report on the men assigned to Sunday night services (which are suspended as of now) and then convert the list over into a mail merge and print the messages addressed to the individual inmates with their current location. This helps the prison mail room and saves them work. Since I do that for my messages, my supervisor has me print and address his also. His printer will not print double sided, where mine will, so last week I told him to just email his message to me in my office and I would print them from there with the addresses on them. He did, and then called and I told him I got it and saved it to my computer. He said, "Good, you might want to sanctify it as well!" He has a very healthy sense of humor, but has no time for chaplains who do not perform, and I really appreciate that. He is proving a blessing to the whole department and is very appreciative and encouraging.

In visiting one-on-one with numbers of inmates recently, I have been so aware of the lethal Satanic weapon of despair. The sooner Satan can drive a person over the edge of whatever the particular wages of sin are for him, into the deep devouring valley of despair, the more effectively he has him paralyzed and chloroformed. No matter the fact that there is a God in heaven whose promise is that "... if from thence thou shalt seek the Lord thy God, thou shalt find Him..." Satan's blindfold is quickly thrown over it and he beclouds every promise in the Bible with "It's no use. You've tried before. You'll never be any different. It's just safest to be like you are."

Here sits a man before me that I have tried over and over to help for nearly twenty years. He slouched into the chair provided for him and I asked him if he and the Lord are getting any closer. He shook his head and said, "I'm trying." I looked at him and said, "____ __," is that what you want written on your tombstone?" He burst out laughing and said, "Chaplain, you always know what to say to me," and then he laughed and laughed. Finally he said, "No, that isn't what I want there." I said, "Then it is going to take something more than what you are doing, isn't it?"

"Yes, you are right it will."

There have been times in the past when it seemed he would make some feeble progress out of his bondage, only to fall victim to it again. Twice, if I remember correctly, he was released on parole. He has a good wife who would do anything to see him get straightened out, but he again makes the choice to company with whores and drug himself up. Twice at least he has been mangled in fights. And with all of that history one would think surely he would be ready to welcome a new life by letting God take control of him.

Here are his words to me: "When I think of my past and the life I am familiar with, I feel somewhat comfortable to just be that way. I know that life. When I think of changing and becoming a responsible husband to my wife and providing for her, it scares me. I can't help it; it's just that way."

The old invitation hymn says: "When the living well is so near by; oh, why, will ye die?" And the answer to the loving invitation echoes back from the bottomless valley: "Despair! Despair!"

Another precious soul sits down across the desk from me. "How are you getting along?" His head shakes slowly from side to side; he adjusts his face mask; then looks up and says, "I'm not. Sometimes I think I'll just give up. I look back to the past when I thought I had it all under control and things were going so well for me, and now I think I'll never know that again and I just want to give up."

I looked at him squarely and said, "You know that is not the answer."

"Yes," he said, "I know it's not." I then began to point him to the One who could lift him out of that despair and start his life all over again. He listened and at least a bit of the dark gloom began to lift from his countenance. He said, "Chaplain, I'm so glad you called me down here to talk to me. I am going to go back to my room and get down before God and seek Him." I said, "If you do, you will be amazed at what you will find; if you don't your life will never be better than right now."

"Thank you, Chaplain, and thank you too for the messages you are sending to us."

No country on earth, no hellish scientist, can form a nuclear weapon more deadly than the dark monster of despair! How ghastly must be the never dying worm of that lost world that reminds the damned soul over and over, "You could have, but you despaired!" What on earth was so effective that it stopped your arm from reaching for the Arm of the Almighty to Save? And again the horrid word rings out, "Despair!" Thank God that it will be among those things which will never be heard in God's new heaven and new earth. But for now?!

It has been three days now since I told you that my supervisor related to me that the state office wants us to start holding group services again. This morning I asked him if there was any further word on it. He said, "No, nothing; but a new bombshell has hit their office." I said, "What is that?" He said, "They are closing Mountain View Prison." That is the one he had come from to come here.

Now, as I told you, we are down from 3500 inmates to 2400+ and they have closed down CRAF and now they are closing Mountain View. Do you suppose that crime is decreasing that much and that we are perhaps being ushered into the Millennium? Please don't throw me out of the window: I am not a Pre-Millennialist! I think perhaps I could come closer to the truth by suggesting that evil is so rapidly taking over our once God-fearing country that no longer is it necessary to consider sin as sin. We have by and large endorsed and legalized drugging ourselves up with marijuana; we have taken the Bible out of the courtroom and the schools and the news media, and so what constitutes infractions of any remaining moral code of behavior is pathetically negligible.

In the face of that, God's commission for His people still shines bright and clear: "But ye are a chosen generation, a royal priesthood, an holy nation, a peculiar people; that ye should show forth the praises of Him who hath called you out of darkness into His marvelous light..." I have been reading a recent publication (a very large book) entitled: "The Rise and Triumph of the Modern Self." What a history of the demonic philosophers, who with minds darkened by the entire indwelling of Satan, have brought the world about us to where we are today. Shall we succumb to such and become desensitized to demon-controlled disregard for the ethics we once held sacred? No! Let us rather echo with the Psalmist in that precious 119th Psalm: "It is time for Thee, Lord, to work: for they have made void Thy law." And the song-writer pled; "Oh Thou, Who changest not; Abide with me!" And so as long as God keeps this door open, I am committed by His help and your prayers to do my best to glean a few more souls for Jesus and the Kingdom of God.

In His love,

William Cawman

2
OPEN DOORS IN ADVERSE CONDITIONS

April, 2021

LET ME GIVE YOU a refreshing note from a man now out of prison for about a year. He spent several years in the Bible studies and classes and was always an inspiration. Every time he received new light he immediately and humbly walked in it and came out the better. He was a witness to all around him and was unashamed of his Lord. The last few years of his incarceration he used a wooden cane to stabilize his steps. One day he was sitting on the edge of his bunk softly singing a hymn when his devilish cell mate suddenly snapped: "Why are you singing and praying to that white Jesus? You're a racist!" Then he grabbed our brother's cane and whacked him right across the face, almost destroying his eye. In self-defense the brother threw him down and got on top of him and with that the officer, hearing the commotion, opened the cell and broke it up. They were both sent to lockup, except that our brother was first sent to the hospital on the outside to put his eye back together.

I went to lockup to see him and there was no ill will; no unforgiveness; and no revenge. He just said that God had a purpose in it all and he was witnessing to those in lockup.

About a year later he was released, as his time was up. A year later yet here is his report: he went in to see his parole officer and he told him that he could see he was a changed man. He said they had sent a spy out to check on him and found him on the street passing out tracts and witnessing. The parole officer said he need not report back in any more. Thank God for jail house religion that works outside of jail!

I have certainly been meeting many needy souls during this time when we can only meet them one-on-one. God surely has His way in the whirlwind, doesn't He?

Just today a man had submitted a request to talk about some spiritual concerns. I welcomed him to have a chair and he told me he was fifty years old and had been in prison since he was twenty. He had submitted several requests to be able to speak with the Islamic chaplain, but had gotten no response, so he asked for another. He told me that the Islamic community felt like sheep without a shepherd. They were getting no prayer schedules and no opportunity to gather for prayer, etc. I asked him if he would want me to ask the Imam to visit with him and he said he really would.

That being said, he then told me that he had another issue he wanted to talk with me about. He said that he had been born into the Islamic Nation, and that he had always been a Muslim. But then he looked at me and said, "But I am struggling with my faith. I feel like I want a real relationship with God." I asked if he had ever had one. He said that when he was in his teens a friend invited him to go to a church with him. He went, and the second time he went he got saved. He said it was wonderful and he could feel God's presence. He wants to feel that again.

I told him that it was definitely God knocking at his heart's door, for the devil would never make him want to feel the presence of God. He readily agreed. I told him that when he stands before the Judge on that final day, he will not be judged by what community of religion he was part of, but by whether he really had the relationship with God that his heart was desiring. I advised him to lay aside for the present the thought of whether he was Muslim or Protestant or Catholic, and just answer the One knocking at his door. He let me know with no uncertainty that he really wanted to do that. I told him I could call him down again in a little while to see how he was doing and he said he wanted me to.

Now, if all was going as usual, and the Muslims were allowed to congregate and practice their prayer times, etc., he may never have come and opened up his hungry heart like that. Do you see what I mean? God has his way, according to His Own Word, in the whirlwind (Na. 1:3).

And then I visited with a twenty-six-year-old for the second time. I asked him how he was doing since we last talked. He just shrugged his shoulders. I asked him if he was finding anything in prayer. He said he wasn't because he wasn't praying. He told me he just has no interest in anything or anybody. I asked about his past and he told me that he has no feelings for anyone, man or woman. He said he is not like most people who want a girlfriend; he is not interested at all. I began to probe around to find out some interest in his life to start with.

He finally told me that this life is not real. He had been introduced into books of magic and videos of magic and that was all that was real. They really fix things in those videos and life is real in them, but when he turns away from them nothing is real at all. I silently prayed, "Lord, help me with this one!"

I asked him if he believed in a life after this one. He did. I asked him if he knew that there were only two places of abode after this life—heaven and hell. He did. He said that he really wouldn't want to go to hell. I told him if he does not want to go there, he will have to do more than what he is doing, and he agreed. But he said he just exists through the day and doesn't think about praying or reading his Bible. I then told him that no matter what his emotions felt like, he knew that he would spend a forever eternity either in heaven or in hell, and he agreed with that. So I asked him if he wouldn't think it wise to use that knowledge and the intelligence God has given him to come before God and begin to ask Him to help him out of such confusion and into truth.

Twenty-six years, and already on the precipice of damnation over videos and satanic books. Thank You, Jesus, for saving us from what might have been!

Do you remember the Muslim man who had the dream about Jesus and turned immediately to Him? Well, I haven't been able to visit him for quite a while because the minimum unit has been closed due to Covid. I was glad to see him come in when I called for him and we sat down together. I asked him if he was still loving Jesus. He replied: "Oh I love Jesus so much! I love Him for coming to me when I wasn't looking for Him. When He came to me, He spoke such words of love that I just wanted to follow Him."

With that I began to tell him about the other Muslim man that I just wrote about above, who was not at all satisfied without knowing he had a relationship with God.

After I related this to the man who had the dream, he pensively said, "Did you say he went to a church?"

"Yes, before he ever came to prison." He said that in the Muslim religion it is a grave sin to ever attend a Christian church except in the case of the death of either father or mother, and then only if accompanied by two other Muslims. I could just feel the eagerness in him to be able to visit with the other man, but of course being in separate units, they cannot.

Please pray for both of them. Both are recipients at this point of a glorious opportunity, viz., "Behold, I stand at the door, and knock: if any man hear my voice, and open the door, I will come in to him, and will sup with him, and he with me." Don't you just feel like bowing down and worshipping and adoring a Savior who is still knocking, in spite of all that men have done to drive Him away?

I thank God over and over for my supervisor and how God definitely answered your prayers in sending him to us. I was leaving the area and would be gone for a few days in a meeting and he called me aside and said, "Chaplain, I want you to know that I really appreciate you and all you are doing for us. If I ever come across as demanding or quick, please be assured that I really do appreciate you." And I am not sure if he is capable of sounding demanding. He is not a stranger to the message of holiness at least as a doctrine, and he definitely makes no effort to suppress or counteract it. We have not conversed at large upon it, but he has let me know he does not agree with the Calvinistic doctrines. Thank you for praying and please continue, as he is a key figure in keeping the door open to this ministry.

Also, thank you for praying for the man I wrote about who has so long played around with God and different doctrines; has made a good start over and over and then fallen back into the wilderness bondage again. The last time I visited with him he had a much better report of making some real spiritual progress, and I felt he was not just trying to bluff me either. Please keep him in prayer. I see such a duplicate pattern of my own spiritual struggles in him that I cannot give up on him, for God and others did not give up on me. Regarding those years and the deliverance from them I have sometimes preached from the first few verses of Psalm 107, but rearranged the statements in the following order: "They wandered in the wilderness in a solitary way…Then they cried unto the Lord in their trouble and He delivered them out of their distresses….Let the redeemed of the Lord say so!!!!" Once more, I say, "Thank You, Jesus!!!"

Just today I had scheduled another visit with the fifty-year-old Muslim man who has been desiring to feel God's presence again as he did when a boy. For whatever reason he did not come down, even though I called the unit and asked the officer to send him. Please pray that he will not back down or give place to fear to seek God, even though he knows what it may cost him. I will try to schedule him again.

Word came from Trenton again that they wanted us to resume group services, but with only ten men at a time. In a prison this large with four different areas to cover and well over two hundred men who want services, we could see no way to comply until they open up completely. We had a staff meeting and all of us agreed that we could see no way to accomplish what they are asking, so we are sending a request for reconsideration and we will wait for their answer. If they insist, we will have to comply, but we are totally at a loss to know how. What ten men out of each facility do we allow to come? What will be the reaction of the rest of them? I think you can see the quandary we are in, so please pray for us. Meanwhile we will continue to send out the printed sermons.

We had another of our officers die of the virus. I think that makes either four or five. I'm not sure how many inmates were lost to it, but it does seem to be slowing down now.

Thank you each one again for your prayers for us. God is hearing them and answering in ways we never dreamed of. That's our God!

In His love,

William Cawman

┼┼┼

May, 2021

How thankful we should be that we love and serve a God who changes not. In an age of unprecedented change in everything else, our God changes never; bless His Holy Name! We will be able to depend entirely upon Him no matter what the future holds or doesn't hold.

I told you last month of a fifty-year-old Muslim man who has been in prison for thirty of those years but is now questioning his faith and remembering how he felt God's presence in a church in his youth. He told me he is wanting that again. I urged him to simply lay aside all names of religion and seek and ask the God who was giving him that desire to reveal Himself to him.

In a couple of weeks I scheduled him for a follow up visit, but he didn't come. I waited two more weeks and did it again. This time he did come, but only a few minutes before their count time. As I asked him if he was finding an answer in prayer, I could sense he has been counting the cost of changing from a lifetime of being a Muslim. You and I have no idea how weighty a matter that is. All of his family and friends; all of his former hopes and associations; all of his security however great or small; must needs go on the altar if he is to make the choice to open up to that Presence he once felt in his youth.

I did not try to pressure him, but I begged him to consider that someday soon he will stand all alone before the Great White Throne and will there be judged by what he did with the Voice that is calling him. He acknowledged that with a very thoughtful expression. I asked him if he wanted me to follow up again with another visit and he asked my name and said he would call for me if he feels the need.

Please pray for this man. I long to reach out to him, but then I remember that Jesus reached out also to a man steeped in counterfeit religion and the man counted the cost and went away sorrowful. I so hope and pray he will not do the same. Oh the tragic and traumatic disappointments and regrets there will be on that awful day for the rejectors of such loving mercy.

And then I want to ask you to pray for another young man. I answered a request from him just yesterday. He is terribly marked with tattoos, even on his eyelids. He told me that he is very confused between the Old Testament and the New, but that he really wants to know that all of his sins are forgiven and he just wants a whole new life. I assured him that such a desire was coming from God and that consequently God would not turn him down. But he said he had tried to ask God to come into his heart and received no answer. He then related how he is struggling with voices and other disturbances and that he goes from darkness to light. If he closes his eyes, he sees a bright light, then when he opens them, he sees darkness.

I asked him if he had ever become involved with the occult or with any type of witchcraft. He said he hadn't but that his father had. I told him to pray and ask God to remove his confusion and all of that darkness, and the very fact that he was wanting to be forgiven showed that God wanted to do it. I then had prayer with him and he was responding with tears as well as verbally. I told him that I would call him down in just a few days and see how he was getting along, and he wanted me to do so.

Today, my supervisor told me that one of the physiatrists wanted to talk to me about him. I went to her office and she asked me if he had said anything that would have alarmed me as to his mental state. I told her I didn't recollect being startled as to his mental condition, but that he did seem very burdened over his spiritual state and wanted to find forgiveness and deliverance from the things that were haunting him. She said he had told her some things that had her very concerned and that she was going to call him down again as she was afraid for him. I told her I planned to see him again soon also, and would let her know if I detected anything disturbing.

Now with that brief an encounter with him, I do not know if there is a mental problem or if he is simply under deep conviction for his past life. Will you please pray that God will give me wisdom to know how to help him find what he needs more than anything else?

We have been instructed to start having services again, but with a limit of thirty minutes and twenty-four men. When we were sending out printed sermons, we were sending to well over two-hundred inmates. With trying to have services in the daytime hours we were only getting about sixty of them prison wide. The director came down from Trenton today to see how things were going, and I explained this to him, so he said to keep sending the printed sermons as well until we can allow volunteers back in and open up Sunday night services.

I guess I will share a bit of the lighter side of chaplaincy with you. The Islamic Imam, who I told you some time ago is a changed man from what he used to be, is a very popular man throughout the prison. He steps into the offices of the administration and accuses them of milking their jobs. This has become such a well-known stunt of his that one of the sergeants found a picture of someone milking a cow and used photoshop on a computer and put the Imam's face on the person. Then he took a string of beads (probably a rosary) and put the picture on it and presented it to the Imam as his identification badge. Needless to say, it evoked measurable levity from all who saw it.

The men in the prison are now getting their $1400 stimulus checks. I guess it would be interesting and maybe disheartening to know where all that money is going. Let me slip in a comment as to the direction we are going as a nation. The Bible says that "the fear of the Lord is the *beginning* of wisdom." Wouldn't that imply that with no fear of the Lord there is no wisdom? Intelligence and wisdom are two very distinct things. Satan did not lose his intelligence when he fell out of heaven, but he lost his wisdom. Never have there been such manifestations of intelligence exercised by the human mind and its inventions of artificial intelligence, but what an exhibition of the misuse of that intelligence when it proceeds from God-forsaken minds!

There is another bright spot in a man in his mid-forties. He has been steadily seeking the Lord for some time and is about to be released. He will be sent up north where he came from to start with, but he says as soon as he can he intends to come down and attend our church, for he has found from our people something he has not found elsewhere. He tells me that He has promised God that his third act will be entirely God's. He means by that: first act—his way; second act—prison way; third act—God's way. He says this with utmost sincerity and I do believe his intentions are good. Please do pray for him that nothing will stop him from pursuing God with all his heart.

The other day he came in and told me that all was going

well except for one very troubling factor. His cell mate is a young Muslim who berates him and makes life very difficult for him. He told me it is causing him to find things inside that would like to react unlike Jesus. I told him that God was giving him a merciful opportunity to face what he is on the inside and help him to get the victory over it before he gets out. I took him to the words of Peter where he speaks of the trial of our faith being much more precious than of gold. I told him that God gave the three Hebrews victory in the fire before He brought them out. His whole countenance picked up and he said, "I hear you and I needed that! I will go and ask God to give me complete victory over him and I will resist the devil who is trying to press my old trigger points."

He has a golden opportunity to let God set his life straight from this point on. He is not involved in any marital tangles as he has never married, and he has very meager family connections. I let him know we are counting on him, and that God is counting on him too. He says he wants desperately to be completely filled with the Spirit and cease from his own ways.

An inmate came up to me after a service this week and asked if I could do anything to help him get a vegetarian tray instead of the regular one. He told me he had asked another chaplain (it was my supervisor) and he told him that state rules required it to be a recognized part of a religious belief; otherwise, it was not available to him. I told him that we do not make the rules; they are established in the state government offices and that the other chaplain was correct.

He said, "But I can't eat meat; it's not good for me." I said, "There is a fairly simple solution to that; don't eat the meat." He, like the rich young ruler, turned away sorrowful. I told my supervisor what I told him and he really laughed.

You might be interested to know also that we not only have men as prisoners, but Canadian geese as well. We have too many of them inside the prison and sometimes when we go in in the morning the compound will have one grand mess where they camped overnight. I suggested to the captain at one point that we serve them up for supper. He agreed, but had no solution as to how to go about it. Right now they are nesting in various places and hatching out little goslings. Sometimes the officers break the eggs to try to keep the population under control, but nevertheless, we still have way too many. I have never liked geese (as if you needed that knowledge), and I think just one of the reasons for that is the obvious distortion of taste they manifest in lodging in a prison compound when there are such beautiful lakes all around there. Just today I looked out a window at the dilapidated Indian sweat lodge and right in the middle of the fire pit where the rocks are heated to produce the cleansing steam for their ceremony, a mother goose was sitting on a nest of eggs. I wondered just what the American Indian would glean from that as an omen for good or evil? Sorry for that diversion.

I did not feel it to be the Lord's will to continue to cancel all outside meetings for this year, so we have worked it out that I preach in the services the weeks I am here and my supervisor does it when I am gone. I thank God and I thank all of you who prayed for the request I made a while back as my first supervisor retired and another took his place. God answered! Our new supervisor is a blessing to the whole department and to the inmates as well. And then you will remember the request also regarding the oversight from the State department. God has surely answered that as well, and in a brief visit with him a couple of days ago, he heartily approved all that we are doing and encouraged us to continue to send printed sermons as well as conduct the services. The door is still open; please help us pray that we will not disappoint our Great God who is keeping it that way.

I have asked five men who have given clear evidence that they have found and are walking in the beauty of holiness to write their testimonies. Every one of them has or is doing so with great humility and unworthiness. None of these are recent converts; each of them has proven himself in walking the pathway of holiness without a spot for a number of years.

I then want to have them published in a book to the honor of Redeeming Grace. Their united song would be:

> Worthy is the Lamb that was slain to receive power, and riches, and wisdom, and strength, and honour, and glory, and blessing... Thou art worthy to take the book, and to open the seals thereof: for thou wast slain, and hast redeemed us to God by thy blood out of every kindred, and tongue, and people, and nation; And hast made us unto our God kings and priests: and we shall reign on the earth.

Thank you each one again for your prayers,

William Cawman

June, 2021

THINGS ARE CERTAINLY DIFFERENT in so many ways from when I started ministering here in the spring of 1998. Our prison population for all those years until last November ran around 3500. Now it seems to have stabilized at about 2400. Just today I was getting ready to mail out another weekly message to the Christian inmates and as I walked in, I saw a whole line of inmates obviously moving to another location. I stopped and spoke to the sergeant and asked what was going on and he said they were moving about sixty-some men around in the prison. I said, "Well, that will certainly give the post office more work as I have already addressed my letters."

He just smiled and said, "Yep!"

There is a fairly large church not far from the prison which quite a few of the prison staff members attend. A couple of weeks ago they scheduled a retreat somewhere and they came back from it with the Virus. Our volunteer services coordinator and her husband were among them and had to be sent to the hospital. However, within the prison itself, there seems to be a quieting down of it and starting next week we will only have to be tested every other week.

I received a request from a man who wanted to attend church and talk with a chaplain. I went to see him and he was a thirty-three-year-old who didn't look a bit like a criminal. I asked him what his life had been and he said, "Well, just a drifter." He had been married but had lost his job and went to drinking which cost him his marriage and about all he had. He said both he and his wife had been Protestants, but that he hadn't been going to church much. As I talked to him about a better life than that, he evidenced no knowledge of a real Christian life or understanding of it at all. I wonder again and again just what many churches even exist for.

Oh the tragedy of a young wasted life. I will certainly follow up with him as he wants me to. I went from there to my supervisor's office and he took the paper work I was returning to him and said, "How did you find ——?" I said, "As heathen as could be," and then told him about him. My supervisor said, "Chap, do you know that in this ministry we have some very rare opportunities?" I agreed. God help us to lead them to Him.

Ramadan having ended on May 12, the final feast was scheduled for Friday, May 14. I was in my office next to the chapel where they were having Jumah prayer, and the man I told you about a month or so ago who has been a Muslim for fifty years but is questioning his faith, came into my office at the close of it. "My name is ——, do you remember me?"

"Sure I do, how are you getting along?"

"I want to talk to you again, can you schedule me for a visit?" I promptly did so and will see him next Tuesday. I do believe God is knocking at his heart's door and that just really pulls on my heart. He is the one who went to a church before coming to prison thirty years ago and the second time he went he says he got saved. Now he so wishes he could feel God's presence like he did then.

Several months back, in fact probably a couple of years ago, you might remember me writing about a man who is deeply entrenched in Calvinism and who tried his best to persuade me that he is just as fully Biblical as the doctrine I am teaching. He became so aggressively demonic in class a few times that the men were relieved when he stalked out in anger.

I only catch a glimpse of him now and then as he was not attending any classes I taught anyway, and then Covid stopped the services. Now that we are starting up services again, he has come about three times as it is the only service they have. In the first service he was back to, he came up to me after I had preached to them on obedience and said with anything other than the joy of the Lord on his countenance, "Do you know what you taught these men today? You taught them that we are saved and get to heaven by our works. We are not under the law but under grace."

I said, "You may go now."

The other day I was preaching from the words of Jesus, "For what is a man profited, if he shall gain the whole world, and lose his own soul? or what shall a man give in exchange for his soul?" I mentioned several things that men are going to give in exchange for their immortal soul. One of them was forbidden fruit. I told them about a service I was in where a man was all broken up with tears of hunger, but could not get clear with God because he had divorced his wife and was living with a young girl. We tried to pray with him, but could get nowhere. He finally looked up with tears and said, "I want to serve God, but I want to do it with her."

After the message, here he came again, bearing all the significant marks of one whose authority was beyond question. "Could I ask you a question?"

"Yes, go ahead."

"Didn't David sin with Bathsheba and then get forgiven and kept her as wife and God even blessed their son as the next king?" I said, "Sir, we are living under the New Testament standard, not what was allowed under the Mosaic law. Jesus annulled that whole provision of divorce and remarriage and set the standard back to what God designed in the beginning.

Furthermore, David was not married to Bathsheba while her former husband was still living."

I could easily see that what I said hit a brick wall of purely demonic self-righteousness. Oh how I would love to see him humble himself and have the demons of Calvinism (and I mean it exactly that way!) cast out until he could sit clothed and in his right mind before Jesus, but God only knows whether he will ever see himself in that light????

The Bible prophesies of the day we are now living in: "Now the Spirit speaketh expressly, that in the latter times some shall depart from the faith, giving heed to seducing spirits, and doctrines of devils; Speaking lies in hypocrisy; having their conscience seared with a hot iron..." And, mark this well: it is not speaking in figurative language. The doctrines of Calvinism are a direct product of the father of lies, and more souls are being led astray with a false hope through those teachings than through all the errors of Roman Catholicism combined.

We have some interesting discussions in chaplain staff meetings. Muslim Ramadan, the major Islamic observance, ends with the feast of Id-al-Fitr. The exact timing of Id-al-Fitr is determined by the sighting of the new moon in Mecca. It celebrates the beginning of the revelations of the Quran to Muhammed. That took place this past Friday. The Islamic chaplain was reporting to us about how things went this year and he said he asked some of the men why they were gaining weight if they were fasting. We all started laughing at him and then the supervisor said he had just gotten a note from a Muslim inmate stating that the chaplain got the date wrong for Id-al-Fitr. I spoke up and said he is probably in a cell where he can see the street light out of his window and thought it was the moon. We shared another laugh.

Then the Catholic chaplain was going over the dates of each chaplain's birthday so that we could celebrate accordingly. The supervisor said his was Dec. 27. I tapped the Catholic chaplain on the arm and pointing to the supervisor said, "His mother got him at an after Christmas sale." He started to laugh and then told us that he had found the receipt for his birth among his father's things and he had cost his parents twenty dollars for his delivery.

Perhaps such discussions prevent discord between our various colors of the cloth!

Well, a few days later: I again placed the hungry Muslim on the visit list, but he did not come down. I called his unit and they said they would send him, but still he didn't come. My heart aches for him. I fully understand the struggle he is going through. Fifty years a Muslim with but one break in the clouds in the time he has told me about as a teenager, when he got saved and felt God's presence in his heart. But now—all he has known, his family, his friends, his lifestyle, his way of viewing God, etc., and so much more pulls heavily on the one side while Jesus the Savior stands knocking on the other side. Oh, how I wish I could make the choice for him; that I could just for a moment transport him to the other side of this awful valley of decision; but I can't—but I am praying. Will you help me? I want this dear soul with a passion. Cases like this make me think how Jesus must have felt as he spoke with the woman at the well, "If thou knewest the gift of God, and who it is that saith to thee, Give me to drink; thou wouldest have asked of him, and he would have given thee living water." Don't you sometimes just wish, as you look over the crowds today in their mad infatuation with the trinkets of time, that you could almost scream at them, "If you only knew…!"

There is another subject I would love to ask you to help me pray about. A number of books have been written in years past about the miraculous conversions within the Salvation Army. They are certainly worth reading and are very honoring to the Savior of sinners. Then one undertook to write a book about the failures of the Salvation Army; the ones that slipped through their fingers and were lost in spite of all they tried to do for them. It is indeed a very moving account.

The battle for souls is a battle such as none other. It has

many and many a heartbreaking disappointment, and these have at times so overwhelmed me that I could easily give place to discouragement. Recently I felt a desire to magnify the grace of God that has so successfully kept some spiritually alive and sound up to the present day. I asked five men to pray and ask God to help them and then to write their story, both before and after. Two of these men are now out of prison and three are still in. They are all walking in the beauty of holiness and have been for some time. Two of them have sent me their stories and two are working on them and one is still struggling over the idea. I want to print them in a book to be published to the glory of the Savior of sinners and to the honor of the keeping power of the grace of holiness. Would you help me and them in prayer as they try to mind God in this? As you can imagine, Satan has no appetite for this to be published. If it can be done, it will be with no thanks to him! Please help us pray about it and I will certainly let you know if it becomes available.

I see more and more that if a soul is to "endure unto the end..." (Jesus' words), it will be done only by the keeping power of the Spirit of God dwelling within the heart in all of His fullness. One little tidbit of the DNA of the carnal mind will derail the person somewhere, and probably sooner than later. God certainly knew what we needed when He commanded, "Be filled with the Spirit!" And just as appalling as is the inevitable left turn that remaining sin brings, so glorious it is to watch a soul who is filled with the Spirit walk down through the very stumbling blocks that catch the carnal off guard, and bring them out on the other side with shining victory over all sin. Thank you, Jesus, for providing that "double cure" that John saw flow down from Your pierced side!

We are doing our best to get some of the restrictions moderated until we can increase the numbers in our services. Then we want to hold them in the evenings instead of afternoons, so that more of the men can attend. During the daytime hours there are so many work details, school classes, and appointments of various kinds that hinder the men from being able to attend. But in the evenings they are free from all of those other appointments. We want to take one facility each evening from Tuesday through Thursday at 5:30 for the service. This time works well as it still leaves most of the evening free and also enables getting to our church prayer meeting on Wednesdays. Please help us pray that this will be approved by the administration and state government. I will take these three services each week when I am home, and then when I am gone in meetings outside my supervisor will take them. However, let me add with a touch of experience, just about the time we get that all going smoothly, it will probably be time for another change. We sometimes refer to the DOC (Department of Corrections) as the Department of Change!

Thank you again for your prayers,

William Cawman

3
GOD IS STILL ON HIS THRONE!

July, 2021

THANK YOU SO MUCH for every prayer that is going up for us here in this little spot. God is working on hearts in answer to those prayers and even many times beyond what we can see. Every once in a while, a man will come out of the shadows and we find that God has been faithfully working with him even though we were unaware of it. I really believe this is the case worldwide. We may never know this side of eternity all that God is doing in this our generation, but because He is not willing that any should perish, and therefore is delaying His return, we can safely believe that He is carrying on His wonderful work of preparing a Bride for Christ.

One of the men that I have asked to write his testimony, wanted to talk with me. Now, I would have had utmost confidence in this man's testimony and life, and I still do. But he said when we had a chance to talk that there was something holding him back a bit and that is that he is still struggling with an area of anger. Injustices are all around him and it causes him to feel an anger toward others who are mistreating those he is trying to care for. He says he wants that totally gone out of his heart until it is not there. I honestly do not know whether he is actually experiencing remaining sin within or if he has not learned how to resist the fiery trials of temptation. I will do my best to guide him through this, but I will not for anything get in the way of the Holy Spirit and His work. God can show him just what it is.

Anyway, regarding writing his testimony, I said to him, "Now, brother, here's what you ought to do; start writing as God brings things to your mind and as you do, expect every moment that God will finish whatever needs to be done in your heart." He almost shouted. He said, "Oh, I needed to hear that! Hallelujah! I will do just that!" I instructed him that if there is unfinished work within him, that work will only be done by asking for more of the infilling of the Holy Spirit. I will have to say that there is never anything except a perfect agreement with any part of God's way or will manifested in him. Pray that God will make all things clear to him, whatever that needs to be. He is a precious brother indeed, and I find far more fellowship with a man who is flat out honest and hungry hearted than one who makes a high profession but feels no need of more of God. I need more of Him myself! I do, and I mean it!

We are now changing over to having our worship services in each area in the evenings instead of in the afternoons. We are just not getting the men out in the afternoons because of so many other assignments. Because of that I am continuing to send out messages by mail as well.

I think when I tell you this you will not blame us chaplains for having a laugh over it. A man was sent to our prison recently from another one of our prisons, and along with him a note came to us from his former chaplain that we might need to be wary of him. He is a wiccan who feels entitled to something more than prison can provide. Our supervisor, according to state protocol, asked him what he needed for the practice of his religion. In case you wondered, wiccan is actually Satan worship. Well, he sent a list of what he would like to have in the line of diet. Here it is in his own words and spelling: "I can have Stuffed peppers, Stuffed Cabbage, Stuffed shells, Baked ziti, Ravioli, Lasagna, Veggie Lasagna, Eggplant Parm, Fresh cheese, Fresh lettace, Fresh tomato, Fresh onions, Fresh peppers, Baked Maccaroni and cheese, Cakes and cookies, and Grape and Orange juice." Prison isn't all that bad, now, is it?

Oh, Hallelujah! One week later than what I wrote above about the brother struggling with what he termed "anger" toward injustices being done to others around him, I visited with him again. I felt the urgency to be sure Satan did not get advantage of him in any way. He came in bubbling over with more victory than ever! He said, "Chaplain, ever since we talked about that I have had total victory over it." Then as he began to explain how it all came about; I knew that what I had suspicioned was the case. I could not see how a man could be living with such continuous victory and still have the carnal nature within. He was not discerning a fiery temptation to allow anger from anger itself. I explained to him the Scriptural diagnosis of such a temptation. When we see the actions of sin and wrong doing around us it is totally Christ-like to feel a reaction of righteous anger over it, for God Himself is angry with it every day. But the Bible says: "Be ye angry and sin not...neither give place to the devil!" Never is the right use of the emotion of anger quickened but what Satan tries to offer his carnal anger through it. This leads to ill-will, and even to hatred. Not knowing how to "possess his vessel in sanctification" as yet, he thought that it was coming from his own heart, and consequently was allowing Satan to trounce him over what he himself was instigating.

Don't you just hate the devil and all of his rotten tactics? Now, in cases like this, I never want to play God and either excuse some element of remaining sin on the one hand or condemn a person who has not yet learned that area of spiritual warfare. It is best to just give the Scriptures pertaining to it and then allow God to make it clear. He did! The atmosphere around his vibrant person testified clearly that there was *no condemnation!*

What a delight it is to watch a soul who has walked in the light until all sin has been removed, then watch them learn how to navigate their vessel through the temptations and snares laid by Satan for their particular soul. An old preacher used to say to the sanctified, "Some of you people need to learn how to come down off the mountain without breaking your neck!"

Now the other day I witnessed a scene that had some attachments that I will relate to you. In the prison compound we have way too many Canadian geese. They are so used to us walking past them that they do not even move over unless you are headed right for them. And are they ever messy! They have tried various things to try to discourage and chase them, but to no avail. It reminds me of all the efforts I put forth in my lifetime to try to get rid of my own carnal nature, and that to no avail either. First, they tried cutting out plywood dogs and placing a few of them on the compound. That worked for a few weeks at the most and then the geese discovered that they were fakes and returned. So, they put plastic bags on the dogs' tails so that it gave them some motion. That didn't work at all, so they put the dogs on stakes so that they would rotate in the wind. Failure! They just nested there and came off with batches of goslings all over the place.

The other day I was walking down the compound and the recent rain had left a shallow puddle in the middle of the blacktop driveway. The puddle was perhaps four feet in diameter and was teeming with dirt, goose feathers, goose feces, etc., and was definitely where no one would want to step. A pair of geese were at one side and their goslings were trying to exercise the goose nature in the inch-deep puddle. As I passed by, both parents raised up their arched necks at me and hissed very threateningly. "Don't take away our puddle!" I thought to myself, "You geese, don't you know that there are very nearby some beautiful lakes and ponds where you could do your goose things? Why do you want to spend your life in that puddle?"

Then I thought of how similar the goose nature is to the carnal nature. We have ever so many men who, if they only knew it, could walk out into the sunlight of God's great will for them and never return to prison life, but instead they are repeat offenders who even hiss at the preacher who would tell them that there is a better way! The old song writer wrote so feelingly, "When the living well is so nearby, oh why will ye die?" When the Bible tells us that Satan is the "father of lies," it is anything but an overstatement!

In what I am now about to tell you, I feel no check of God to not declare plainly and bluntly that the teachings of Calvinism are not simply erroneous doctrine, they are exactly what the Bible labels "doctrines of devils!" 1 Tim. 4:1,2 "Now the Spirit speaketh expressly, that in the latter times some shall depart from the faith, giving heed to seducing spirits, and doctrines of devils; Speaking lies in hypocrisy; having their conscience seared with a hot iron…" If the Word of God by which all will be judged on that Great Day calls such "doctrines of devils," then I feel perfectly clear to stand right there.

At least four men in the past twenty years in the prison have been so deeply entrenched in such that I am convinced they were demon possessed. Every one of them that I have had to deal with has left me literally trembling and shaky. The devil is no plaything; he is no farce; he is no myth; he is real. What is his doctrine? Go back to the moment he defected from the high and holy archangel state in which he was created. What came from his lips? "I will be God!" Listen to this spirit infused into the dwellers at Babel. "And they said, Go to, let us build us a city and a tower, whose top may reach unto heaven; and let us make us a name, lest we be scattered abroad upon the face of the whole earth." In other words: "We don't need God's method; we can do this ourselves. We'll show God that we can disregard His clear Word and still make it into heaven."

Now, having said that, I am again encountering the man I wrote about several years ago who became so rancorous in his contradictions of the truth being taught that he walked out and never came back. Now since we have only one service that he can attend, he is having to hear me again. The other day I was preaching to them on obedience and how essential it is to our redemption. I used the illustration of a boy just out of grade school who asks his father for a ten-speed bike. His father makes a bargain with him that if he will keep the yard work all done and in order for the summer, he will then get him a ten-speed bike. I went on to describe how the boy was very obedient at first, but then as the summer went on, he became more and more careless and his father had to fill in for him over and over. Then I asked the question: "Do you honestly feel that the boy had any valid confidence that his father was going to buy him a ten-speed bicycle by fall?"

As most shook their heads "no" the Calvinist from the back yelled out, "Yes, absolutely Yes!" I stopped and looked at him and asked, "What makes you say that?"

"Because his father loves him so much that he will get him the bicycle anyway!" I said, "That is not true!"

"Yes, it is!" There it is in all of its manifestations — the doctrines of the devil — I can live anyway I want to and God is so good that He will take me into heaven anyway! Isn't that an atrocious distortion of love? I won't elaborate any further. Not every Calvinist is demon possessed by any means, but when a person insists on such false teaching in the face of God's truth, they willingly give themselves to a lying spirit which is none other than the spirit of the devil. Please pray that this man will not become any more of a disturbance than he has been already.

On the way out of the service that evening, a man who has been searching for help from God stopped and asked me this: "A lot of people are saying that once we are saved, we can never lose it; is that right?" I said, "If it is, then you can expect to meet Satan in heaven, for he was once saved." He looked at me for a moment, and I could literally see the light sinking in, then his face changed and he said, "I got it!"

Thank God, truth makes sense! The God of truth is the One who created our brain in the first place, and consequently error just doesn't ring that bell within that is only rung by truth! When we embrace the truth and the whole truth a clearness comes within and without that just rings true through and through! God is not the author of confusion, and I'm at war with confusion—but I had better stop preaching and affix my unimportant name.

William Cawman

┼┼┼

August, 2021

Please permit me to start this letter with a very urgent prayer request. I am sure many of you will remember the Muslim man in the minimum camp who wanted to talk to me and told me that a few weeks before, Jesus had appeared to him in a dream and he had immediately forsaken Islam and began to follow Him. Over the next few months, I watched and listened as he became mentally aware of what had happened in his heart. I won't go back and repeat that story as it is a long one. But then with the closures due to the Covid, I had not had a visit with him for almost a year. When I began going out there for the weekly service again, he was faithful in coming and a few times I had a chance to ask how he was doing and he always said he was loving Jesus.

Finally, yesterday (July 14) I went out and called for him to come see me. He immediately came in and was so glad that he could sit down with me again. I asked him how he was doing and he said he was praying much and really did love Jesus, but that he was struggling with something. He then dropped his head for a few moments and then said, "Chaplain, I need to keep this real, don't I?"

"Oh yes, for sure," I said. Then he dropped his head again and then looked me in the eye and said, "Chaplain, I have not stopped loving Jesus for a moment, and I am praying to Him a lot, but I have been hooked on K2 for a long time and I know that God doesn't want me to be, but I don't know how to get the strength to quit."

I instantly felt the desperate need of divine help. Then I said to him, "I will tell you what I believe I would do. I would go to whoever is supplying you with it and tell them that you are quitting, and beg them not to offer you any more even if you ask for it. Then get down before God and begin to plead the Blood of Jesus and the promise of God that He will not suffer you to be tempted above what you are able to bear. Then set your will to quit even if you die. You see, God will keep His promise; do you believe that?"

"I sure do!"

"Then He will, but you will have to do your part too." With that he looked at me squarely and said, "I will do my part."

I prayed with him and told him we would pray for him in our church prayer meeting that night. He seemed glad and said he really wanted to be free and please God. Will you help us pray that he will come out of this a living, shining testimony to the power of the Blood? K2 is one of the most vicious of drugs, but none of them are beyond the power of Jesus' Blood.

Then I asked him where he would be going when he gets out in a little over a year. He put his hands over his face and started to laugh. I didn't know what was coming, but soon he said, "You might think it's funny that I am laughing until I tell you. For a long time, I was estranged from my family, but when you started visiting me and Jesus came into my heart, I said, 'Jesus, I really would like to be restored to my family.' He said to me, 'Isn't that something included in My promise to give you whatsoever you ask for?' Then my brother called me. He is a retired Navy commander, and he began to connect me again with my family. I am restored to them! I have been praying with my mother over the phone, and I really believe my brother is praying too."

He also told me that Jesus continues to come to him in his dreams and it is always so precious.

Now two weeks later, since we were away: I went out to the minimum camp and called his name on the intercom. In very short order he came upstairs and was so happy to see me. I asked him how he was doing and he immediately said, "Good; everything is hunky-dory!" I said, "Has God then delivered you from that chain that was binding you?"

"Yes, He has!" I said, "You had a lot of people praying for you." He looked at me with great surprise and said, "Really?"

"Yes, you did."

"Oh, please tell every one of them thank you for me!" Thank God, He has answered prayer and set the captive free. And He answered prayer for this dear man before I could even get the request sent out to most of you. Do you see, sometimes God may lay a weight on your heart and you may not know what it even is, but God does. I just read a statement from A. B. Simpson a while ago in our family devotions that instantly struck both my wife and me at the same moment. He said that whenever you feel a sense of weight come over your spirit, consider it a call to prayer.

They have put us back on Covid tests every week instead of every other week as several staff members have been testing positive. God only knows what the future holds on every front as well as here in the prison.

This week I started having Bible studies again for the first time in about a year and a half. I handed out copies of the Tree of Jesus' Life and the Harmony of the Gospels taken from the Thompson Chain Reference Bible and told the men we were going to study in depth the life and teachings of Jesus. I think one thing that inspired this is that it is said of the early church more than once, "They preached Jesus." What a thrilling Life to study! Please pray that the cry from many of their hearts will be, "Oh to be like Thee!"

At the close of one Bible study, one of the men looked just like an excited boy over a new bicycle as he pointed to the lesson plan and said, "Chaplain, this is great! This is something we really need."

And so, as of now my schedule is a worship service at 5:30 on Tuesday, Wednesday, and Thursday; a Bible study in each facility on the same days at 1:00, and then a service in the minimum unit on Wednesdays at 2:30. That makes three full days for sure, but it is so good to be able to be back at it after so long.

This week I preached a message in all four services on coming to God through the Blood. God definitely honored the truth and more so with every service. The last service was unusual with God's presence and the men were greatly moved by it. It was probably one of the best services I have ever witnessed in the prison. If God honors so definitely the lifting up of the Blood here on earth, what will it be when that host that no man can number of all tribes and kindreds shall sing in perfect harmony and unity:

> Thou art worthy to take the book, and to open the seals thereof: for thou wast slain, and hast redeemed us to God by thy blood out of every kindred, and tongue, and people, and nation; And hast made us unto our God kings and priests: and we shall reign on the earth....Worthy is the Lamb that was slain to receive power, and riches, and wisdom, and strength, and honour, and glory, and blessing. And every creature which is in heaven, and on the earth, and under the earth, and such as are in the sea, and all that are in them, heard I saying, Blessing, and honour, and glory, and power, be unto him that sitteth upon the throne, and unto the Lamb for ever and ever.

I had told you in a previous letter that our population was down since they released so many men during the Covid ordeal. Due to not wanting to move men around, our population has been at about 2400 for nearly a year. Now they have moved men around until one whole housing unit was empty, and then for five weeks they brought in one hundred men each week from the county prisons where they had been held for the state. Now the prison is getting pretty full again, and yet they are continuing to release men on an average of nine months early. The newcomers in that housing unit are being held for a time in quarantine as most of them had not been regularly tested. Apparently, this was not a bad move because several of the officers in that housing unit then tested positive. The last couple of days I have received requests from some of them to be enrolled in church services and Bible studies, but the sergeant told me to just hold them for a while yet as they could not move out of that unit.

Because of all these moves, I have had a lot of extra clerical work, removing men from programs in one facility and re-enrolling them where they moved to. This takes a lot of time that could be better used. Yesterday my supervisor came up with a brilliant idea. He suggested we have a new module created up in Trenton for each program for the whole prison, rather than separate ones for each facility. I called a secretary in Trenton to be sure it would work and then sent up the new modules. This way when men move, we won't have to make any changes as they will automatically appear on the appointment sheets where they presently are. Thank you! Supervisor! What a help you are! Now as soon as I get all the names transferred into the new modules, I can devote more time to one-on-one visits instead of looking at a computer screen! By the way, have you ever thought upon this—there will be no technology in heaven! Isn't heaven looking better all the time?

We were supposed to be in Malawi for a good part of August, but the borders are closed to non-citizens, so back to prison I will go. There are times when I get my work caught up with scheduling, etc., and yet it is not a time when I can visit with the men personally, so it gives me a perfect prayer time in one of the chapels. I have had some precious moments alone with God there. Today was one such time and I was reminding God that my being in prison was His idea, and that since He has seen fit for now to lock the men in with me to a great extent without contrary voices, I wanted to offer myself to the fullest to help Him accomplish all that He yet wants to do here in this prison.

A man just told me this week that his coming to this prison has been the salvation of his life. I have heard a number of men recognize that very thing. Sometimes the infinite mercy and love of God has a rough hand at the outset. When the Scripture admonishes us, "Behold therefore the goodness and severity of God…," it would be very untrue to God's nature to attribute that severity only to judgment upon the ungodly. It is often a merciful wakeup call.

Recently, a twenty-seven-year-old has started coming to the Bible study and to church service. He does not have the look of a criminal, but looks like he would fit better in a Bible school. I had a chance this week to talk with him a bit more and I asked him about his family life. He told me that his mother is an alcoholic and did not really provide for him, and his father was for the most part absent from his life. I began then to understand why his life had gone bad. I so often try to put myself in a life like this and wonder if I would be in the same shape had I been raised in the same fashion. Certainly, we have nothing to be proud of, do we?

What little contact I have had with him so far, and by the questions and comments he has offered so far, I can tell that he is just about as heathen as an American can be. And, this you probably also have discovered, Americans today are almost totally Biblically ignorant. But let me tell you a little amusing statement of his. After the first Bible study and after introducing the subject that we would be looking into the life of Christ, he said to me on the way out, "You know when Jesus fed the five thousand and they had twelve baskets full of fish and bread left over?"

"Yes."

"Well, I often think it would have been wonderful if those

twelve baskets were full of potato chips!" I laughed and told him I would not disagree with him about that.

Thank you again for praying.

William Cawman

┼┼┼

September, 2021

ON AUGUST 5, MY wife and I and another couple were scheduled to embark for Malawi, Africa, for a ministerial conference. This trip had originally been scheduled for the Spring of 2020, and then rescheduled three or four times due to the Malawian borders being closed over the pandemic. Each time we were told that Ethiopian Air does not give refunds, but simply reschedules. As of August 5, the borders were still locked down except for Malawian citizens, so once again I had to cancel. My wife and I made it a special matter of prayer to God that morning, telling the Lord that with such uncertainties ahead and so much money tied up in those tickets, we really needed to get a refund instead of another reschedule. After prayer I called a travel agent and explained in detail our situation. He said, "Let me see what I can do for you." He held my little flip phone in steady service for around two hours until my battery was down to 10%. Suddenly he announced, "I have gotten a refund through for you!" We just thanked God for one more evidence that He still answers prayer! "What a mighty God we serve!" He can just as easily still handle Ethiopian policies just as effectively as He can baptize a eunuch of its queen by sending an evangelist by air without even a ticket or passport to get it done.

Anyway, you might wonder just what I will do with the time that was to be allotted to Africa? You got it! I will be sent to prison for it. And right now, there is such a need of being there. I delight to tell you that from the bottom of my heart I sing the song, "My times are in Thy hand, Oh Lord; My God, I wish them there."

Our supervisor was in Trenton at a supervisors' meeting and the assistant commissioner was telling the chaplains that there is a police chaplaincy that would love to take over the work that we are doing as civilians. She said that we had better be proving our worth, or it could happen. My supervisor spoke up and said, "You have made it a point that we are there not for just inmates, but for staff as well. Why isn't there being a record kept of ministry efforts to staff?"

She immediately took him up and added that category to our reports. The next day our supervisor told us about it and urged us to keep an alertness for any opportunity to minister to staff. That very afternoon, since I was going to be staying into the early evening for a service, I went to the officers' dining room to get a bite of nourishment. (I would prefer to leave the menu and the quality undescribed except to say that at least it enhances my appreciation for my wife's good cooking).

When I entered, I noticed our prison dentist at one of the tables all by himself and so I went and got my food and sat down with him. I have met and spoken only briefly to him over a number of years and have known that he is a Messianic Jew. When I sat down, he had his Bible open beside him and he seemed glad for company. I again asked him if I had remembered correctly that he was Jewish and he confirmed it. I then told him I thought that was wonderful, that as a Jew he had embraced the Messiah. We talked for a bit on the deplorable conditions of true Christianity in our present age, and then he said to me, "For about a year now, I have been seeking a deeper and closer walk with God." I began to open up the way of holiness to him and he listened with good attention. For about twenty or thirty minutes we visited about the reality of a walk with God and freedom from sin as the Bible defines "sin." We then had prayer together and he thanked me from his heart for the visit. Please pray for him also, that he will find that which he is seeking for. I recorded a staff encounter on my daily record.

That same day I had received a written request from an inmate stating that he wanted to talk with me about his spiritual health. He is a quite young black man with what I immediately sensed was a heart door being knocked on by the faithful Holy Spirit. He told me that he had grown up in churches where there was much emotion and praising and shouting and speaking in tongues and that he had been told in the churches and by men in prison that he has the Holy Ghost in him. "But, Chaplain," he said with deep feeling, "I know I don't have the Holy Spirit in me because of the way I'm living in sin. I have done so many bad things in my life, and I want to get rid of them. I just want to get things right and have an assurance that the Holy Ghost is in me." I began to gently point to the false worship he had known in the past and begged him to lay it all aside and simply ask Jesus to come into his heart and make him what He wanted him to be, and give him the assurance he was seeking for.

As we talked and prayed together his eyes flooded with tears and I told him he was not far from finding peace with God if he would just believe and obey Him. I promised I would call him down again very soon, and I will, but cases like that pull my very heart out. I believe I can actually feel some of what Jesus felt when it says: "Then Jesus beholding him loved him..." I just feel like I want to reach out and wrap him up in my arms and heart and pull him right over into the kingdom, but then I have to remember what else Jesus told the man, "...and said unto him, One thing thou lackest: go thy way, sell whatsoever thou hast, and give to the poor, and thou shalt have treasure in heaven: and come, take up the cross, and follow me." Only Jesus can save; it is my business to "...bring him unto Me." It is early in the month as I am writing this and I am quite sure there will be more to follow.

Yes, there is, about two weeks later. You see, I scheduled him about a week after first seeing him, but he didn't come. Then when I scheduled him again, he came in and looked very upset. I said, "How are you getting along?" He said, "I'm really upset; as soon as I started really seeking God, they took my good job away and then moved me over to this facility and now I have to start all over again at the bottom wage." (Then I understood why he had not come for the time scheduled the week before.) As soon as he had blurted it out, I said, "Now let me talk to you about this. You should know that Satan wasn't one bit happy about you seeking God for a new life. Jesus warned us that if we follow Him, we can expect trials and persecutions even. You ought to just take courage that you are doing the right thing in seeking God since the devil is so upset over it! Now, what you need to do is to just take all of this to Jesus and look up into His face and say, 'Lord, no matter what happens to me, I will not turn back. I am going to love and obey You.'" With that I saw the anxiety release from his face and he said, "I want to do that; I can't go on with the same life I've known; I want to be right."

I said, "Then you need to pray until you break clear through into the smile of God, and then all these other things will seem so unimportant. Life is so short and so uncertain, but eternity is forever and forever." He said, "Can we pray now?" As I prayed for him, I could hear him repeating after me and then he continued for a while after I said, "Amen." He then looked up with teary eyes and said, "I believe it's going to work." I said, "I know it will if you don't give in to Satan and back up. You'll soon have no regrets that you started out after God and His favor." He said, "I am going to do that." He then thanked me so much for seeing him again and I told him I would follow it up next week and would be praying for him. Will you help pray too? I know you will. Thank you!

The pressures are mounting, as you well know, over this unprecedented government takeover with COVID vaccines. We were informed this week that when we take our weekly test this coming Monday, we will have to report as to whether we are vaccinated or not. I can just see the momentum developing for a mandate that requires it. I called Liberty Council and got some direction and then took a sealed envelope to

Human Resources ahead of being asked. I protested the breach of privacy in being asked and then stated that I would not be taking a vaccine, regardless, and gave the reasons why. We need to pray earnestly that God will either halt this overreach of our government or else give us the promised grace to pass under the rod as many other people in the world are doing. We belong to Him, don't we?

Just about the time I tell you what we are doing for classes and services, we are told to do something else. I guess a few COVID numbers rose somewhere on the planet and so after we had just stepped up to 50 men for hour long sessions, we were told to go back to 24 for only a half hour. All of these changes require so much clerical work that it is very time consuming. These policies are made for the whole state, and many of the prisons can make the changes much easier than we can with three prisons in one, plus a minimum-security facility outside the wall. I sometimes wonder, "How long? Oh Lord?"

Our former Muslim in the minimum camp who had the dream about Jesus and began following Him and then faced a long-standing addiction to a very serious drug, testifies that he is continuing to have victory over it. I tell him many people are praying for him and he begs me to thank each one. He is getting excited about our church on the outside where he wants to come when his next few months are over.

When I started having Bible studies again about a month ago, I felt like I wanted to study the life of Christ. This past week we were going through all the Old Testament prophecies of the coming Christ, and my how it did come alive to all of us. I had read all of those prophecies before, but I do not remember ever taking the whole list of them and reading them through together. The men were getting excited and so was I at how every minute detail of Jesus' life was prophesied clearly hundreds of years before. The internal evidence of the veracity of the Word of God is overwhelming! If you want to get in on the blessing, go to the Harmony of the Gospels in the Thompson Chain Reference

Bible and read the 37 OT prophecies of Christ in order. It will be well worth your time.

Different times over the last few years I have brought up a man who, deeply entrenched in Calvinism, comes for a while, and then becomes a disturbance and hindrance that we have to handle with firm discipline. Recently he has returned to all that I am teaching in his unit, and so far, he is being very constructively cooperative. Oh, how I would love to see him really humble himself and really get born again. He feels so sure of himself and so able to teach others and win souls, and yet as long as he does not contradict the clear teachings of God's Word, I allow him to contribute and hope that God can yet get through the deception of the "doctrines of devils" that he has been immersed in. After all, Saul of Tarsus with a head full of intellectual dexterity was a pretty hard nut to crack too, wasn't he? Yet the love of Jesus did not pass him by.

For several years now, for the memorial of the 9/11 tragedy in our country, the chaplains and administration have wanted me to play the National Anthem and then the Taps on my trumpet as they lower the flags as part of the memorial. The last couple of years my wife has accompanied me on the keyboard and now they do not want anything else. This year we plan to be away in a camp meeting over that date, so they have asked us to pre-record it for them to play for the memorial. We will try to comply. Recently, in one of them, our Catholic chaplain gave a speech and he did an excellent job of it too. He made no attempt to be politically correct. He said that our Lord had taught us to love our enemies and forgive them. I heard no objections either.

The Odinists, Wiccans, and Jews all have sacred holy days coming up, and all provision is being made for them to be able to practice their "faith." Even though no volunteers are allowed in as yet, two Rabbinical students are being allowed to come in to celebrate these with the Jewish inmates. Eyebrows are raised, as you can imagine; I will comment no further except to say that I would love to see our country and our government place as much emphasis and value on the one true religion as they do on all the false ones. But—our God is not defeated, is He? It will not be long until "every knee shall bow and every tongue shall confess!" Lord, hasten the day!

With much Christian love,

William Cawman

4
GOD IS STILL MOVING ON

October, 2021

SCRIPTURE RECORDS THREE DISTINCT times that the Father in heaven spoke audibly while His Son was on earth. The first was at the baptism of Jesus, the second on the Mount of Transfiguration, and the third shortly before Jesus finished His work here on earth. Listen to what He had to say that third time, which, by the way, is the last time that God spoke audibly from heaven. Jesus had just prayed; "Now is my soul troubled; and what shall I say? Father, save me from this hour: but for this cause came I unto this hour. Father, glorify thy name. Then came there a voice from heaven, saying, I have both glorified it, and will glorify it again." What a promise! Thank God He is still doing it too. And He will continue to do so no matter what men or devils come up with next. Thank God!

Two men who were long in my classes and Bible studies in the prison have now gotten out and are starting to come to our church. What a blessing it is to us all to see their hunger for God. Please pray for them that they will go all the way with God. One of them went into prison at the age of eighteen and has been there for thirty-five years! Pray especially for him as none of us can imagine the adjustments and shock reentry brings after all that time. He says he is being ever so careful and wants to obey God in everything.

The third generation Mormon that I have written about over the years and who is keeping the blessing way up in a prison in another state is one of five I have asked to write their life testimony which I want to put into book form when they are finished. Recently they put provision in his prison that they can make phone calls out, so here while I was away at a camp in KS last week, he called me. We had a wonderful visit and he told me that he had gotten his story all written and that he had made arrangements with a fairly well-known minister to type it out for him and get it ready. When he mailed it to him, the minister called him and told him he should not publish it as it was false doctrine. Isn't it strange indeed that a man would think what has turned a former Mormon into a sanctified saint is false doctrine?

Anyway, our brother dropped that arrangement and found someone else. I thanked him with rejoicing in my heart that he did not flicker under such charge, for he knows full well in Whom he has believed and what He has done for him. I have two of the stories complete now and am waiting for the other three. His should be in my hands soon.

The man I wrote about last month who seems so hungry for clearness with God is still struggling. He told me a couple of days ago that he knows he does not have yet what he is seeking for, but that he still wants it. Please pray that he will soon enter in and that the devil will not discourage him. Why some struggle more than others God only knows, but reading recently the autobiography of Adam Clarke, he tells at length the prolonged struggle he had in praying through to God's forgiving favor. He then says that in the years afterward, God definitely used those struggles in his helping other struggling souls. I am thankful that he is not content to just profess something like so many do. He feels keenly the need of a real change of heart.

Now let me tell you something about the dear man in the minimum unit who was a Muslim and then Jesus appeared to him in a dream and he has been growing in grace ever since. I told you last month that he had come face to face with a serious addiction to a powerful drug and after talking to me about it, he faced it and God brought a marvelous deliverance. He has had victory over it ever since. But the other day he told me that he wanted to share something with me that God used to jolt him as to his need to be cleansed of the addiction. Here is what he told me.

One day he had taken the drug and it almost did him in. He was standing on a concrete floor and went out and fell over backwards and cracked his head hard on the concrete. Several other inmates ran over and brought him to and got him up and mopped up the pool of blood on the floor and cleaned off the back of his head. They said he had a gash in the shape of a Y in which they could see the inner flesh, and when they pulled it back they could see clear into his skull. Two days later, the officers heard about it and came to examine him. They looked and looked at the back of his head and there was no scar or wound there. He feels, probably rightly, that God was being merciful to him and healed it so that he didn't get into trouble. God certainly knew He was about to cleanse him of the addiction. He is one of those cases that you can literally see him growing in God.

It seems that Satan has really been fighting our services and Bible studies. Over and over, the men do not come for the session and then say afterwards that they never called it out or unlocked their cell doors. Finally, it got so bad that I went to visit with the Major. He welcomed me in and listened to my complaint. I told him we were trying to do our job there but that it was almost an impossibility to conduct a meaningful teaching with such sporadic attendance, etc. I told him that we have to report our numbers to the office in Trenton and if numbers drop, they want to know why. What were we to tell them — that they would not call it out or open their doors? He said that he would immediately take care of the situation and that he wanted me to report to him if it did not get fixed and he would fix it.

That day they called out both of my services clearly and I had a record attendance. The next week I was gone in a meeting and my supervisor said it was terrible. This past week was also. They cancelled two days of classes to give Covid vaccines and didn't even tell us they were doing it. Please pray that we can get this back on track as it has been very discouraging both to the men and to us as well.

Years ago, and for some time, I wrote things about an inmate who had committed two murders at the age of eighteen and was committed to prison for thirty to life. He prayed through to a genuine case of salvation and sought to be sanctified, but before he found it, they moved him to another prison. He was only there for a few months, but men coming here from that prison told what a positive influence he had on them spiritually. He was then moved on to yet another prison. After almost two years, if I remember correctly, he wrote to me and told me that he had been back peddling and not in earnest to be sanctified. He then said that Satan was telling him that if he really gave all to God, He would ask him to get up on a table in the courtyard and shout. He also told him that God would then make him witness to everyone he met.

These bluffs had intimidated him for a long while. Before I had a chance to write back to him, I received another letter. He started it out with the words: "Well, Praise God! The old man is dead!" Then he went on for a whole paragraph, shouting and praising and rejoicing. Finally he said, "Now I need to stop and tell you about it—no, I can't!" and another paragraph of shouting and praising followed.

They sent him on a court trip and he testified to everyone on the van. They put him in a cell with thirteen other inmates and he testified to them all. They sent him to court and he testified to the sheriff and the judge.

I got so amused that I wrote to him and said, "I thought

you were afraid that God would make you shout and witness; now it seems that you are enjoying it!"

How long he retained that experience I do not know, but somewhere since he stumbled and lost that joy and that clearness and was seeking it again. Just this week I received two requests from him and found he was sent back to this prison after all these years. His request stated that he wanted some good holiness books to read. I will have to tell you more about that in the next letter, as this one will be printed the day before I am scheduled to see him. Pray for him!

It has been a couple of weeks since I wrote the first part of this letter and told you about the struggles in getting men out for the services. The remarkable change that took place right after talking to the Major lasted one brief day. Since then, they have been calling the services much more clearly, but so many things are going on that interfere with our service times, such as codes for disruptions, Covid vaccinations and testing, commissary, etc., and so we really need prayer for the situation that we can get back to at least part of a normal procedure and be able to have effective times for religious services. It is so difficult to be able to have a structured Bible study with such erratic attendance of the men.

Now, after saying that, today was a delightful change. The two services were called out right on time and I had a good attendance of men. I have told the men in Bible study that although we do have a particular subject that we will study, they are welcome to interject any subject that they feel the need of help in. The Bible study today was such a blessing as the men kept responding and asking questions. For several years after I graduated from college, I taught classes in the college in math, Bible history, and a few other subjects that don't come to my memory right now. In all of those classes and with all of those students, I never remember such enthusiasm being evidenced as is among these men in prison. It is invigorating to teach them and to learn from them as well. Come join us sometime and you will enjoy it too.

I am still putting in more hours than I did before the Covid shutdown as we still have no volunteers allowed back in. The months that I was suspended due to Covid gave me more time to use now, so it is all working out for the best for the present need. I am praying and asking God for fresh anointing and passion that will help bring revival and awakening to the many who still are living so far below what God has for them. I preached to them this week from the grant that God has offered, viz., "that ye might be filled with all the fullness of God." I believe it as sinking into some of their hearts, and I pray God they will really dig in for more.

I received a written request from a man who wanted both a Bible and a Koran. I thought about that dear woman in a Muslim country who laid the Bible and the Koran on the kitchen table and went back and forth until she said, "When I read from the Bible light comes into my heart; when I read from the Koran, darkness comes out of it." I surely hope and pray that it will be the same with this man.

No matter the darkness that is developing around the world, Jesus is still preparing a Bride, and that makes my heart rejoice. Let's ask afresh to be filled with His Spirit that we might work with Him.

William Cawman

✝✝✝

November, 2021

LET ME TELL YOU something that really warmed my heart, and I'm sure it will yours too. The former Muslim man out in the minimum unit who had the dream about Jesus a little over a year ago, and who I wrote more about last month, has been really growing in his walk with God and his understanding of the Christian life. The other day I asked him to open the service with prayer. He started off as you would expect, but then paused and said, "Jesus, it seems like we ask You for a lot of things, but I just want to tell You that I love You!" I thought to myself, "I doubt that he ever prayed that to Allah or his prophet Mohammed!"

On Saturday, October 9, at about 11:30 am, a dryer belt caught fire in housing unit two. It immediately caught the lint on fire in the vent that had probably never been cleaned out in the twenty-five years of the prison's existence. It shot up the vent and out onto the roof, burning a hole in the roof even though it was a metal roof. Four fire companies were called in and after they tore a gaping hole in the roof and soaked the building with water, it was totally unusable. They had to evacuate the men into the gym and chapel until they could move them to other locations in the prison. Fortunately, the prison has not been up to capacity ever since they released several hundred men last November, so they were able to house them all without busing any out to other prisons.

As soon as they got the men temporarily located, they called a prison wide standup count to be sure none of them were missing. Then they began moving them into any vacancies in other parts of the prison.

This, of course, necessitated my having to go into the records and move men around on the appointment sheets in order for them to attend the classes and services, and even that caused many absences until the records of where they are catches up with the appointment sheets.

Last month I told you about a man who had left this prison a number of years ago (actually it was seventeen years ago), and now has been sent back. I placed him on the visit list and when he didn't appear on time I went searching and found he was one of the ones who had been moved from the burning building. I tracked him down and had them send him down to me. What a rejoicing visit we had after seventeen years. He seems to be presently enjoying a bright walk with God and is in full harmony with the way of holiness. He told me how barren the places were where he had been and how he longed again and again to be back here. Now he is thrilled that he can spend his last year back under the teaching that he knows and is fully persuaded of.

He told me that when he gets out, his father and mother and sisters want him back home again and that the home is not far from our church where he definitely wants to come. Pray that he can win his whole family for God. He says he would love to go back into his boyhood neighborhood and tell those he once knew about what God has done for him. I told him that was certainly a noble desire, but to keep it totally in the hands of God. He is agreed that such is the only way.

He is such an inspiration as he sits with a huge smile of hunger and appreciation on his whole face. It is very obvious that he is back under the teaching that he has been hungry for. Whether or not he is presently fully sanctified I have not yet discerned, but he is certainly very conspicuously eager and bright.

On a Monday morning, I walked into my supervisor's office and noticed an unusual expression on his face. He said, "Would you please read this?" He then handed me a written request from an inmate who identifies as an Odinist*. I am quite sure you might like to read it too???? Just in case, and so that you can obtain a taste of some of today's Mar's Hill gods, here it is as written.

> "PLEASE TAKE LEGAL NOTICE that this institution is in violation of the Religions Land Use and Institutionalized Persons Act of 2000 and 10A, for failing to follow the IMP for Asatru, provide equal callouts and services, post all holidays, and provide me with religious literature. I request again to be provided with print outs of the Poetic Edda and the Prose Edda, which are in public domain, and free literature that can be printed out for prisoners from the TROTH. I request to be provided with the blot offering of animal shaped crackers or cookies, and the Sumbel offering of honey, spring water, and fruit juice in lieu of

---

*A follower of the pagan religion of the ancient Scandinavians. —Ed.

mead, and all the listed items in the IMP necessary for performing rites. I ask again to be given my approved religious diet, for there to be equal time for services instead of only once a month, for study groups, and for holiday meals that are equal in number to the holiday meals and Date-fruit offerings and other non-line tray foods give to Muslims yearly, spread."

After some incredulous head shaking, my supervisor said, "I don't want to interview him about this alone; can you be with me when I call him down to visit?" I told him I would.

Do you recall the god that Isaiah talks about that is carved from part of a tree, the rest of which is burned for warmth? Such a god as he pictures actually makes a whole lot more sense than the ones we are encountering in this day! Isn't it almost unbelievable as to how far away from any spark of common sense the grasp for a god of our own comfort can take us? Isn't it also an amazing demonstration of the vitality of the sinful nature in man, that he can so offend the law that he is locked up and yet feel entitled to such special favoring of his every whim?

And so the arrangement was made and we both sat down with this individual. He was a very intelligent man of about forty-four years of age who was serving thirty years to life. He has been in prison for twenty-four years of the thirty, so still has a good while to go after which he is sure he will receive at least another fifteen-year hit. He does not expect to ever be released, so he wants to get all he can out of life while incarcerated. Now let me insert an observation here as to the statement I just made that he is a very intelligent man. Intelligence and wisdom are two very distinctively different items. Satan is very intelligent, but he lost all wisdom when he lost holiness. Hitler was very intelligent. And so just because a person has come into the world with above average brain cells, doesn't mean at all that those brain cells will be used wisely.

This man has already been before the judge with his case of religious rights, and accordingly he came to us with a background of coming out on top of any opposition to his religious needs. When asked what he really wanted of us, he stated that he really needed those animal shaped crackers or cookies to perform his daily ritual which was an emblem of how his forefathers practiced the sacrifice of animals and even humans. Then he also needed a mixture of fruit juice and honey as a daily drink offering. We instructed him to put in a request to administration to allow him to order his animal crackers from an outside source, since we had no such thing to give him while he is in prison. I asked him how long he had been practicing this religion and he said it had been since about 2008. We ended the hour long visit without a show of violence at least.

I must confess that ever since the shut-downs over Covid, it has been very frustrating and disappointing as to the attendance at our services. It is not only the Protestant ones; it has been the same for the Catholics and Muslims. Only a fraction of those who used to come out are now coming. We have tried to figure out what the reason for it is, but no ready answer has been found. I would ask that you pray for us, that whatever is hindering, we can again get the men out for services. We do know that many times the officers are not calling the services out or unlocking the doors of the men on the appointment sheet, but even when it does get clearly called out, only a few appear.

Because so few are attending the services our supervisor has urged us to continue to send printed messages through the mail system, and we do hear back from the inmates that they really appreciate the messages sent that way.

There is an old man in a wheelchair who has been faithful in coming and I always set up the piano for him to play for us. He knows nearly every hymn in the hymnal and plays very beautifully and worshipfully. However, he was in the house that had the fire and so they moved him to another of the facilities altogether. The first time he tried to come to service in that facility, he had no one as yet to push him, so he worked his own way down to the chapel, arriving after they had already shut the door. The men motioned to me that he was wanting in, and so I went to the window and motioned to the officer that he was out there. The officer just waved at him telling him to go back to his cell. I felt grieved for him, but did not want to make a scene in front of the inmates. Hopefully it will go better next time he tries.

In every way, we are definitely living in a different world than two years ago. Things may never be as they were before this tidal wave of demonic control struck our country and the world. Just what the future holds in regard to it all, God alone knows—but He knows! That is enough. It is simply up to us to obey Him moment by moment with an absolute trust. He most certainly is not finished getting His bride ready yet, or He would return before daybreak of another day. And as long as He tarries, there is work for us to do, for His closing words to us are these, "the Spirit and the bride say, Come!" Jesus, help us to carry so much of Your presence with us that the "Come" flows out of us just as it does from Thee!

Partly because of the sense of need within the prison itself over staff losing loved ones to the Covid, we have started a staff prayer time every Wednesday from 11:30-12:30. So far it has been only the chaplains who have gathered in the designated room, but hopefully others will respond as we send out invitations to all of the staff and officers. As soon as our supervisor in Trenton heard about it, he asked that we write up a notice about it and send a picture of it so that he could publish it in the Department of Corrections newsletter. Before we could get it done, someone objected to the room being called a prayer room, and so we did not take the picture as yet. I'm sure if we had called it anything else, even some other religious name, it would have been acceptable, but such is the strength of the antichrist era we are entering into.

The other day as we met together, we shared some burdens that needed prayer and then each one prayed in turn. I must tell you that when our Nigerian Catholic chaplain prays, one would never detect that he is Roman Catholic. He prays with earnestness directly to Jesus, asking his petitions straight from Him. Just what his personal relationship with God is, I do not know, but he openly expresses his love to me in front of all the chaplains, and it is very easy to testify to him, as I do not feel any resistance from him no matter what I tell him. You might just want to hold him up in prayer, and I will not, by God's help, miss any opportunity to share with him the goodness of the way of holiness. He actually left a much higher paying position to come to the prison because he felt he wanted to do something for God.

I love the unique way these men who are not versed in church culture have of expressing themselves many times. The other day after preaching to them, one of them who is always living in good victory shook hands with me and said, "Oh Chaplain, keep that fire burning!" By God's grace, I intend to obey him. When Jesus promised to those who obey Him that there would be rivers of living water flow from them, He did not mean that they were the source of the river; they are only the channels through which it flows. Lord, pour more in, and let it flow out!

William Cawman

December, 2021

AMONG THE MANY PRECIOUS and unfailing promises in God's Word there is one that says: "Cast thy bread upon the waters: for thou shalt find it after many days." Ec. 11:1. How many days am I now preparing to tell you about? Approximately 9490! No, I haven't lost my mind just yet! You see, something very exciting and rewarding has been happening in the chronicles of prison ministry. It was sometime in the year of 1994 that I visited, for the first time, a young man in prison. I did so in response to his answer in a letter I had written to him which said, "First of all, I want to thank you for caring about me."

Now—twenty-six years later, he has been coming to our church and sitting right beside me whenever I am there. Yes, God, You keep Your promises! Even if "many days" stretch into nearly ten thousand.

And so, even amidst the many, many disappointments that accompany a ministry such as this, there are definitely very precious rewards as well. How heart-warming are the words of the old song:

> "Shall I empty-handed be,
> When beside the crystal sea,
>   I shall stand before the everlasting throne?
> ...If no soul to me can say,
> 'I am glad you passed my way;
>   For 'twas you who told me of the sinner's Friend.'"

The attendance at our services continues to meet so many challenges, but after talking with chaplains from other prisons, it seems to be a widespread condition. In fact, it is not only in prisons, but across the world, that attendance in churches has dropped dramatically with the advent of Covid. Is there a reason why God so clearly admonished us in His Word, "And let us consider one another to provoke unto love and to good works: Not forsaking the assembling of ourselves together, as the manner of some is; but exhorting one another: and so much the more, as ye see the day approaching"? Heb. 10:24,25 While I am still mailing messages out to the population, it is not the same as having them gathered together any more than it is a healthy substitute in the outside world to have online or virtual services. It just is not the pattern outlined for the New Testament Church.

We are facing another unplanned-for situation. This prison was built twenty-four years ago and the State graduated approximately six hundred officers to man it. After twenty-five years of service the officers can retire with full benefits. So—guess what? This coming year well over a hundred are planning to retire, and they have not as yet trained any replacements. You see, our present communist government is handing out such glamorous benefits for doing nothing that they cannot find anyone who is interested in training to become an officer for forty-some thousand a year. There was even some talk of closing down one third of our prison, but that ran into so many complications that they tabled the idea for now.

One of the officers who has twenty-four years in and that with a very good record, contracted Covid this week and died. Everyone felt saddened that it happened so close to his finishing his time and going out on retirement, but that is just how uncertain life is.

It has been almost two years now since any volunteers have been allowed to come into the prison system; so as a consequence, the multiple voices that taught such a spurious salvation that sinning continues in the life have been absent. Not knowing how much longer this door will remain open if vaccines are required to work in the prison, I am trying to get the truth out to the men while the day lasts. Here is the latest sermon I put together for the men and will mail it out after Thanksgiving Day.

Are Christians Still Sinners? — Chaplain Cawman

I think you would agree that any teaching that contradicts the Word of God will be encouraged by Satan, the father of lies. If you want to believe that the answer to the above question is "yes," then you will find plenty of people who will encourage you to believe it, but that does not make it true. I heard a Bible teacher say these exact words: "We all know that after we are born again, we still continue to sin." 1 John 5:18 says: "We know that whosoever is born of God sinneth not; but he that is begotten of God keepeth himself, and that wicked one toucheth him not." So, who is correct: the Bible teacher or the written Word of God?

Now, let me pause here a moment and clearly define what sin is. If we have a wrong definition of sin, we cannot have a correct answer as to whether or not we commit it. 1 John 3:4 gives a very clear definition of sin: "Whosoever committeth sin transgresseth also the law: for *sin is the transgression of the law.*" Isn't that what we are looking for? Sin is not being tempted, or making a human error; it is a willful transgression of a known law. Having this definition of sin, who can believe that we can commit it and still be a Christian?

Now if Jesus Christ came for the express purpose of destroying the works of the devil (1 Jn 3:8), and if He came as the angel announced to save His people from their sins (Mt 1:21), what was He but a dismal failure if we cannot be so restored to His image that the sinning business stops?

Let me quote from a very sound Bible scholar: "Can a state of justification be retained while sin is committed? It cannot. 'He that committeth sin is of the devil.' The commission of sin negatives the justified state, and any professing Christian who lives in the commission of sin, is a sinner and not a saint. 'We know that whosoever is born of God sinneth not. Whosoever committeth sin transgresseth also the law. In this [committing sin or otherwise] the children of God are manifest and the children of the devil.' All sin is forbidden, and he who commits sin is 'of the devil.' No state of grace admits of committing sin. A state of justification implies freedom from the guilt of sin by pardon and freedom from the commission of sin by renewing, assisting grace. 'Whosoever is born of God doth not commit sin; for his seed remaineth in him, and he cannot sin, because he is born of God.' The lowest type of Christian sinneth not, and is not condemned. The minimum of salvation is salvation from sinning."

Another writer says: "Every voluntary violation of the known law of God is a realization of sin in its completeness. To assert that the Holy God has made sin necessary under the reign of grace is to slander the Father, and pronounce the redemptive plan a stupendous failure. There is no sin where perfect love reigns. This may consist with innumerable defects, infirmities, and theoretical and practical errors. To a superficial observer these may look like sins, but a deeper inspection shows that they lack the essential characteristic, namely the voluntary element. It follows that every sin sunders the soul from God and makes communion with him and sonship or assimilation to Him impossible. Sin is willful, and is utterly incompatible with fellowship with Him."

Now, no matter how good these writers may be, and no matter how contradictory to the Word of God some others are, if we really care about where we will be spending eternity, we had better listen to the inerrant Word that God has so faithfully entrusted us with. That sacred Word makes absolutely no promise that a person can continue in sin and yet enter a holy heaven. Every Scripture that some have tweaked and twisted to try to prove that Christians still sin, can be clearly shown wrong by numbers of other Scriptures that cannot be misinterpreted.

Eze 18:20 "The soul that sinneth, it shall die."

Eze 33:12 "Therefore, thou son of man, say unto the children of thy people, The righteousness of the righteous shall not deliver him in the day of his transgression: as for the wickedness of the wicked, he shall not fall thereby in the day that he turneth from his wickedness; neither shall the righteous be able to live for his righteousness in the day that he sinneth."

1 Jn 3:6 "Whosoever abideth in him sinneth not: whosoever sinneth hath not seen him, neither known him."

1 Jn 3:8 "He that committeth sin is of the devil; for the devil sinneth from the beginning. For this purpose the Son of God was manifested, that he might destroy the works of the devil."

1 Cor 6:9,10 "Know ye not that the unrighteous shall not inherit the kingdom of God? Be not deceived: neither fornicators, nor idolaters, nor adulterers, nor effeminate, nor abusers of themselves with mankind, Nor thieves, nor covetous, nor drunkards, nor revilers, nor extortioners, shall inherit the kingdom of God."

These and many other Scriptures make it so very clear that if we would make heaven our home, we must be fully cleansed and cured of all sin here below. Let's not argue about it; let's ask God for the cleansing Blood.

Will all of the men who receive this message believe it and take it to heart? I'm not professing that my faith is that strong, for I know full well the strength of sin and its interpretation of God's sacred Word. And there is something alarming about those who do not receive the truth in its purity: they become vicious opponents of it. John, in writing under the inspiration of the Holy Spirit, gave us a very clear way of discerning who is of God and who is not. After he had told us not to believe every spirit, but try the spirits, whether they are of God, he gives us a very definitive method of doing so. He says: "We are of God: he that knoweth God heareth us; he that is not of God heareth not us. Hereby know we the spirit of truth, and the spirit of error."

It is so much easier to see this demonstrated outwardly in a prison setting than in a cultured church environment. If a person is truly born of God, and then they hear that God has provided a deeper work yet, they immediately either say, "I want it," or "That sounds too good to be true." But if the Spirit of God is not dwelling in them, they immediately label the very heart of what Jesus came and gave His life for, false doctrine. Yes, John, "Hereby know we the spirit of truth, and the spirit of error."

And so please pray that as the men receive the message, they will at least ponder and think about it rather than immediately spit it out as the indwelling devil would have them do. There is not, in all of the disease germs that can attack the physical, a more violent reaction than can be seen in the disease of sin in its instantaneous rejection of the Light that comes from above. Satan knows full well that if reason is allowed to work, his masterpiece of deception will show up for what it is worth, and consequently he rises up within the heart controlled by him with lightning speed, to cast out as false doctrine the very truth of God. If it weren't so eternally serious, I would find it rather amusing that the very thing Jesus came to do is called false doctrine, but that is exactly what many in the prison say I am teaching, by standing by the Word of God.

Please pray for a renewed awakening among the men to the seriousness of the hour we are living in. It is a tragedy that living so near the end of all things, there is such a desensitization to the eternal. Satan has laid a terrible trap in getting our generation so addicted to entertainment that eternity never even crosses the mind.

William Cawman

5
UNPREDICTABLE

January, 2022

How the years are slipping by! As the old saying goes: "Time waits for no man." But time is quickly running out and soon that angel with one foot in the sea and one foot on the land will cry "Time shall be no more!" And time as we know it and are so tuned to it, will be no more: eternity will begin. Oh, Jesus, have I done my best for You this past year?

As I have told you, our service times are shorter than they used to be, and so our sermons have to be shorter also. (You don't need to say, "Amen!") The other day as the men were leaving the chapel, the man I've written about from time to time who has such a shining face, stopped and shook hands and said, "Chaplain, you were just getting warmed up: I still had three amens left." I laughed and told him I'd take a rain check.

The first few days of December were days of Chanukah for the Jewish inmates. Two of the nights I took my turn sitting with them while they burnt their candles. Oh, thank You, Jesus, for bringing in something better than the ritual and form without life. I do not know why, but one night two of the men had two candles each which burnt for a whole twenty minutes after all the others were burned out. Now of course they cannot blow them out; they have to wait until they burn out, so we all stood around including the officer and watched and wondered just what was really burning. After all visible trace of candle wax was gone, they continued to burn. I told the men that perhaps they had come across some of the oil that burned for eight days! Anyone who knows the story of Chanukah would recognize what I meant.

I was driving toward the prison the other morning when I received a call from the inmate in another state who was a third generation Mormon, but is now a sanctified lover of Jesus. It was so good to hear of his continuing victory and spiritual hunger. He told me something very interesting. He had a dream that the DOC came around and took Habakkuk out of all their Bibles and told them they could not have that book anymore. He said it really got him to thinking of what it would do to us if one book of our Bible was taken away, and it created in him a new appreciation for the Word of God.

I think I told you some time back that he has been training seeing eye dogs in the prison for people who cannot afford them. He told me that he wants to write a book of how that training is so essential also in our walk with God. He said that the very first command the dog must learn is "Come." I believe he said there are twenty-one commands altogether and every one of them relates to walking closely with God. Two more that he mentioned were "Drop it," and "Wait." Sounds like it will be a very good book, doesn't it?

The other morning, I walked into my supervisor's office and he met me with a very serious look on his face and said, "I need you to help me with something."

"All right, what is it?"

"I know you have a lot of experience and I really need your help with this." He stood looking at a page out of a catalogue for a moment and then said, "I am trying to get just the perfect Christmas gift for my wife, and I need you to help me pick out the best one." Then he handed me the page—a selection of snow shovels! As soon as I started to smile, he burst out laughing.

Please allow me to try to express something that is so foreign to me that I am baffled by it. It is this: I meet so many souls who seemingly have so little concern about what is next after this short life is over. To me, being certain that I am ready for eternity is of such paramount importance that it eclipses and minimizes every other consideration. I cannot understand how a person becomes so desensitized to that which matters most, that they can be staring eternity in the face and seem so unconcerned about it.

I met just such a person yesterday. He is a fifty-four-year-old man who has come to several of my services out in the minimum camp, but who I would judge to be what Jesus described as "dull of hearing." There is no evidence of any real divine life coming from him. He carries almost a sense of arrival as to any spiritual growth. Then I heard that he was in the prison hospital and so I went over to see him. He had not been feeling well for some time, but the doctors and nurses told him there was nothing wrong with him. A day or two after Thanksgiving, he was diagnosed with fourth stage pancreatic and liver cancer, and was beyond hope of treatment.

He seemed, that is apart from the obvious pain level, to be just taking it in stride. He said he just wanted to go home with the Lord. When I began to really probe deeper into his certainty of knowing that all was well, he just responded: "God is merciful." Sometimes I just want to scream at souls like this: "STOP! LOOK! LISTEN! Is it well with your soul?"

Then, knowing that God is faithful to every soul just as He was mine, I have to wonder where and what in this life brought about such a numbness to being sure about the forever hereafter. That baffles me; and it concerns me too. I pray, "Please, Lord, anoint me to be Your voice extended to this eternity bound soul!"

On Tuesday, December 7, I went into an office and opened my email to find that Trenton had finalized the decision to close down one third of our prison, due to a severe officer shortage. So the next two days I didn't even go in as they were limiting movements in order to ship over three hundred men out to other prisons and then disperse the remaining hundred plus within our other two facilities. Now I will have to pull up the lists of men enrolled in all of the classes and services and relocate them in order for them to show on the appointment sheets. The prospects for new officers are bleak due to the socialistic provision to pay more for sitting at home than applying for a job. Please pray!

Then on Wednesday, December 22, I went in and found that there had been a sharp rise in positive Covid tests in the whole DOC the day before, so they immediately called for us to cease the services and one on one visits again for the next thirty days. I was planning to leave the next day to visit our family in PA and OH and so I quickly typed up another message and sent it out through the inmate mail system to all of the men enrolled in our services. God alone knows just how long that will last this time, but please help us pray that it will not continue to spiral upwards.

My supervisor had a medical procedure on the twenty-eighth of December and has been out this week. He hopes to be back by Monday and we have been holding him up in prayer that the procedure will give him much needed relief from the pain in his back and hip.

Now, for a few reflections as we look back over the past and then into a most uncertain future. I am now writing this part of the letter on New Year's Eve. How well I remember this very evening, twenty-four years ago. I had gone down into the basement of the home we were living in at the time to pray. As I looked ahead into the unknown year before us, a prayer came from way down deep in my heart in these words: "Jesus, if there is anything I would like to ask of You for the coming year, it is that I could enter more fully into the heart of

Jesus." I meant it! I still mean it! I will not turn aside from it, no matter what the future holds or doesn't hold.

I did not know as that prayer was coming from my heart of love for Jesus, that within about eight weeks I would walk away from a fairly high-paying job and launch out into the clear leadership of God's call into the prison ministry. I had been visiting a few inmates in the visit hall for several years, and the pull was growing almost unbearable to be able to talk to many more of them. To my heart, they were not outcasts of society, but what I would have been too, had it not been for my Christian home and church and education—none of which had become mine by my own choice. Now I can tell you that a number of times across these twenty-four years God has renewed that call just the very same as He does what David prayed for Him to do— "He restoreth my soul." Many a day has not been emotionally fulfilling. There have been profound disappointments many. There have been discouragements that Satan has tried to use over and over. There have been enemies of truth that have opposed what God was wanting to do. But through it all, God has gathered a few more souls for His kingdom above.

Now: He has been able to do that because of your many prayers for us back across these years. I want to thank you for them, and Jesus thanks you too, as well as the men in prison. Because you have been faithful in prayer, God has accomplished good things in many hearts that gave us good news to write to you about. Thank you! Thank you!

As I look ahead, the future has never looked more uncertain, but I am perfectly comfortable with that because I know that He knows all that I don't know, and I have settled it to obey Him and follow Him. I love Him too deeply to fail Him now.

I distinctly remember another season in prayer at the turn of the year 2019-2020. Again, I was praying at the close of the year and this time, out of my heart, way down deep, came a prayer: "Guide me, oh Thou Great Jehovah!" I knew nothing at that time about the coming pandemic. I knew nothing about an upcoming catastrophic change in government. All I knew was that I needed Him to guide me into the unknown. That prayer comes back over and over and is only increasing in its fervency. I am not referring only to the ministry in the prison, but to life itself. I can tell you with a passion that I am not fearful or nervous about the future. I am the Lord's and He is mine, and I am gloriously content to leave every moment of the future in His hands. Will a government mandate force me out of the prison? Not if God still wants me there. Will I get in trouble preaching in a government facility truths that are Biblically commanded and politically offensive? Not unless God allows it. It is settled! No turning back! I am the Lord's, Hallelujah!

And so, to all of my dear brothers and sisters in the Lord who have labored with me in this corner of God's great harvest field, I promise that by your continued prayers I will stay where God has placed me until He calls me home.

Now, that's a retirement plan if I ever heard of one!

With much love and appreciation,

William Cawman

February, 2022

I VERY OFTEN WONDER when I start another of these prayer letters just how many more times the uncertainties of our present world will allow another letter to go out. God knows, doesn't He? And that is enough.

Let me tell you how the very first day of this year went in prison ministry. It was Monday, January 3, and we woke up to a white world. I started out to the prison around nine thirty and the roads kept getting worse and worse. I made it in without any real trouble and after going over plans with my supervisor I went to my office to catch up on the usual duties there. After a bit my supervisor called and said that the Islamic chaplain was down on rt. 49 and had a mishap and was waiting for the wrecker and needed someone to pick him up. I told him to give me his phone number and I would see what I could do.

After trying four times to get through to him, he finally answered, and when he did I heard a tone of voice I had never heard from him. He immediately said, "Oh Reverend Cawman, God is so good. Everybody was stopping to see if they could help me. This is a wonderful country! Finally an older couple came along and they pulled me out and I'm on my way to the prison. God is so good!"

I said, "Yes, chaplain, God is good, isn't He?"

"Yes, He really is, I'm about to cry." By then I was about to cry too. Now let me give you a bit of background to this. This chaplain is a Nigerian, born and raised there, but due to a school shortage his father, who by the way was the high priest of Islam in Nigeria, sent him to a Christian school for his early learning. His father had either nineteen or twenty-one sons, and there was not space for them all in Nigeria and that is why this one ended up in this country.

So with his knowledge of Christianity and his having been around us for all these years and watching our lives and hearing our testimonies, this show of kindness really spoke to him and he recognized it was God—no mention made of Allah!

Well, about one half hour went by and I got another call. Center command had gotten a call from him that he had been in an accident on Shoemaker Road and needed someone to come get him. My first thought was, "My, this is really a snow driver, if I ever saw one!" Anyway, my supervisor and I left and got in my truck and headed for Shoemaker Road, not far from the prison. When we arrived, we saw him and two state troopers looking over the situation where he had skidded off of a straight road and took out approximately thirty feet of someone's split rail fence, including the corner post. His car was pretty well shredded under the bumper.

I walked up to him and put my hand on his shoulder and

said, "Chaplain, you are making me think of a sign that used to be on a fence on Rt 40, which read, 'Here lies the body of Jonathan Tate; he drove through the fence instead of the gate.'" He immediately burst out laughing along with the two troopers and I think the bit of humor helped him relax. We stayed there until a rollback came to pick up his car and he told them to take it to the prison parking lot. Then my supervisor and he and I followed it back and when we got there, I got out a few tools and cut away the parts still hanging that were rubbing on the road or on his tire and told him I thought he could probably drive it home. But I told him to go slow as his tires were nearly worn out.

My supervisor and I then put our hands on his shoulders and prayed for him and thanked God for protecting him and helping us get it taken care of, and by that time he was definitely softened and touched by such overwhelming kindness. As we parted, my supervisor said to me, "Remember—witness wherever you go, and when necessary, use words." I then followed the chaplain part way home to be sure he was going to be all right.

Would you pray for this lifetime sixty-year-old Muslim?

A couple days later when I opened the prison email, I read this message from him. "Good morning everyone, due to my inability to safely control my car due to snow on the roads, I am working from home."

We started the year off with so many cases of Covid and so many units on quarantine, that all we can do is flood their mailboxes with written messages, which we are trying conscientiously to do. Once again, God knows what He is doing and He knows the way through this wilderness. At least many more are getting the messages than if we were giving them in person.

Let me tell you something that definitely bears truth to the Scriptural admonition: "And let us not be weary in well doing: for in due season we shall reap, if we faint not." For a number of months now, our chaplain department has been having a time of prayer every Wednesday from 11:30 to 12:30 in a room upstairs in the front house. We share our thoughts together and prayer requests and then pray around the circle. We have been very much encouraged in doing this by the supervisors up in Trenton. We have posted a notice of this prayer time on the bulletin boards, but so far it has only been us chaplains. To be honest, I believe God ordered it that way for a while, to bring us to know each other's concerns more. At one of the meetings, the Catholic chaplain opened up and shared his heart with us and it was good for him and us as well.

Recently, the chaplains decided to have each of us take a turn and give a short devotional before we went to prayer. They took a list of topics that had been sent to us from Trenton for subjects to discuss in the services in the restrictive housing units. All of the topics were worthy of consideration. They asked me to take the first one and the topic was "Forgiveness."

We gathered together right on time and even the Muslim chaplain came (he has a few times). When we entered the room, two ladies from classification were in the room eating their lunch. One excused herself but the other one said she would like to stay if it was alright. We assured her it was and so we began. As I started speaking on the subject of forgiveness, I told a few cases of men right there in prison whom God had forgiven. The Muslim chaplain was leaning forward with wonder written all over his face, and every so often he would exclaim: "Is that really so? My!" While he was thus responding, the young lady from classification began to tear up and soon was wiping her flowing eyes freely. Suddenly she burst out, "I really needed to be here today; I need God to help me; there are some people I haven't been able to forgive!" I tried to point out to her that forgiveness is not an act of emotion, but of our will, and that when we choose to forgive God will give us the power to forgive. I urged her to really pray to God, expecting Him to give her forgiving grace. Then I led in prayer for her. She then left saying she would most definitely be back next week.

When we left the prayer time, my supervisor and I went to the business office to order some materials we needed and when we stepped into the purchasing agent's desk, my supervisor said to him, "We have just come from a prayer meeting upstairs."

"Oh, really? I've heard about that and I want to come, but I wasn't sure just how it worked." We assured him that the door was open and he said he would come.

We don't have any idea what is ahead for all of this, but please pray that God will cover us with His Blood, as undoubtedly old Satan doesn't like it one bit. We started these prayer meetings expressly with the idea that in these uncertain times, there would be those who would feel a need that they may have ignored before. Of course, this prayer time is only for staff and custody; not for the inmates.

Then on Thursday morning, January 13, I awoke to discover that I had been long enough among the victims of the highly politically popular virus—it was my turn. Fortunately, I seemed to get off with a light dose and am much better now, but I had to quarantine for five days before returning. At the same time nineteen out of our twenty operating units were quarantined also, so maybe we'll all get this over with soon.

Then, while out, I received word that our governor, in his state of the union speech, mandated vaccines for state workers in congregate settings such as prisons. Thankfully, in point ten of his speech were these words: "The policies adopted by covered settings pursuant to this Order must provide appropriate accommodations, to the extent required by federal and/or state law, for employees who request and receive an exemption from vaccination because of a disability, medical condition, or *sincerely held religious belief, practice, or observance.*" Thank the Lord for answering prayer concerning that! Thank you to those of you who prayed about this situation.

Well, a few days later the paragraph above needs to be corrected. Light dose? NO! After a few more days I was overwhelmed with such weakness that I finally went to the emergency room and spent almost two days in the hospital. They were afraid I might develop blood clots in my lungs, so put me on blood thinner and I'll remain on that for a while. I came home on Monday and was so weak I didn't know whether I was "in the body or out of the body," but it was not heavenly like Paul's experience—not one little bit. I'm doing better, but am left with a deeper sympathy for anyone who has to take a turn with it.

And then something happened that I just must tell you about because it is so precious. For several days I bounced back and forth between feeling a bit of encouragement and then such overwhelming weakness that I didn't know if I would get over it. One late afternoon I was feeling anything but encouraged and anything other than spiritually blessed. It seemed I had not been able to hardly lift a word with feeling in it to the Lord in prayer.

I was reclined in the living room and my wife sat down at the piano and began to play, "Master, the Tempest Is Raging." It was! Suddenly—those words: "The winds and the waves *shall obey My will;* peace, be still; peace, be still! Whether the wrath of the storm-tossed sea, or demons, or men, or whatever it be... *they all shall sweetly obey My will;* Peace, be still!" Instantly, without an effort on my part, a gusher of perfect joyful resignation to whatever the will of God for my life should be just boiled up and ran over with tears all over my face. I said, "Lord, if suffering like this is part of what You see fit to allow me to pass through, I just simply love You for it!!!!" So what, tempest! So what, storm! So what, total wreckage of all desirable emotions! I belong to Jesus! He is nothing but love! He has my all, for time and for eternity, and I will not ask one thing outside of His perfect will for me. And now I am realizing it was more than a spiritual touch; I am feeling much better!

Oh the joy of full salvation! I wish everyone in the world

knew how precious my Jesus is! After days of spiritual wilderness, I suddenly found that open veil again into the sweet presence of Jesus. There was one time also, that I would want to tell you about earlier in the week before, when it seemed I did not have one bit of what it takes to actively pray. I sat down and looked up to heaven and all of the sudden the great loving arms of Jesus just reached down and enfolded me with the words: "I understand, my son, and I still love you!" No wonder the song writer penned the words: "Oh how could I this Friend deny, when He's so true to me?" What irresistible love!!

Then there was a knock at the door and here was a huge, beautiful fruit basket from the chaplains in the prison. I appreciated it so very much!

How long I will yet be out God alone knows, but He always knows best. Thank you each one for your prayers.

With more love to Jesus and you than ever before,

William Cawman

March, 2022

THANK GOD THAT BY His help and the prayers of His children I was able to resume activities in the prison on February 7, and have been gaining strength every day since. I returned to many greetings and thankfulness that I was back again; I guess it's good to be missed???

We then received word that we could resume having classes and one-on-one visits. I had a backlog of requests for visits and so I began to put the inmates on the daily appointment sheets, but most of them did not come at first. Then I found out that the officers still didn't think we were doing it, so they didn't allow them to come down. After a few days that difficulty cleared up, but I knew because of the same reasons, that if we immediately opened up services again hardly anyone would come. Then for the most of February my supervisor was to be on vacation, so he left me with the assignment to get out a posting to be sent to all areas as well as updated religious service calendars so that we could start up in March. Until further notice, we are only allowed to have nine inmates plus the chaplain, so we will have to have two services each week in order to provide for the men who will want to come. Please help us pray that with the reopening of the services, the men will feel the renewed interest in coming.

On Friday, February 11, quite a group of officers went to Trenton from our prison to protest mandatory vaccines. Such is the total insanity and demon power behind all this that such protests are simply ignored. February 16 was the deadline for us to either take the vaccine or send an exemption request to Trenton. I sent my request and we will see what happens with those. The largest percentage of the officers are simply ignoring it all.

I suppose we will never know all the reasons why some souls respond so quickly to the call of Jesus and some struggle so pathetically. For months now I have tried to help a very broken man get to Jesus. He never had a home of his own, but was bumped around in the foster system and found there nothing but examples and influences that drug him into every form of sin. The Book of Revelation speaks of those who have known "the depths of Satan." Here is one. He has been well acquainted with the entire warehouse of Satan's glittering offers and promises, and consequently all of his nature is awakened to its very depths by the dregs of sin.

I would have to go back and look up my records to see how many visits I have had with him over the past year or so, but every single one of those visits pulled my heart out after this most damaged vessel. Remember now that the old song says: "Heartaches, broken pieces, ruined lives are why You died on Calvary…" Oh how my heart has longed both in visiting with him and in private prayer that he could just once taste God's smile.

He has told me that there was a time in his early life when

he did find and walk with God. He knew it was real, and therefore he cannot be satisfied with anything less. Churches have told him that he has the Holy Spirit, but he tells me he knows he does not, for he has no power to stop sinning. He is experiencing an intense struggle between the desire to really know and live for God and the chains of gripping sinful habits and desires that have him so bound. He says that it is tempting to just give up.

A week or so ago I had another visit with him at his request. Again he unloaded his heart as to how he longed to be free to live right and forever be finished with the wages of sin. We talked for a while and then he said, "Do you think that it would be possible for me to find God right now?"

I said, "I know that it is possible; let's pray and ask Him for it." I prayed for him and then I asked him to pray. He did not pray in learned familiar phrases, but simply opened his broken heart up to God. Suddenly he stopped and exploded, "Whew! Thank you, God." I felt the very presence of Jesus reaching for him.

After a bit I said, "K——, did you feel the hand of Jesus touch you?"

"Yes, I did."

"Then if you will just hold onto that Hand and refuse to listen to Satan, He will bring you clear out into the power to live like He wants you to."

A few days later, I sent for him. He came in and said, "Chaplain, I almost didn't come, because I don't want to be such a disappointment to you. It seems I just can't live above sin."

I said, "K——, the other day Jesus reached out His hand and touched you; don't ever doubt that. Now you are going to have to take your will and rise up and say, 'Satan, I'm done with you and I don't belong to you. I am going with God.'" I told him if he would really do that, it would not be long until he would begin to find the power promised in God's Word to live right. Would you help me pray for this dear man? He needs your prayers.

One of the assignments which my supervisor left me while he is gone is to visit the men who send in requests for vegetarian diets to see whether they qualify for such by being actively practicing a religious belief for which vegetarian diets are recognized. Thank you, supervisor! Nice assignment! At least it makes me more sympathetic with his having to do it regularly. I will give you one example that I met with. The man came in and said that he needed a vegetarian diet. I had looked up his face sheet before meeting with him and he was not classified as any religion at all. So I asked him if he had any religious belief. He replied that he was a Christian. I told him that I could not put him on the list for a vegetarian diet as such was not a recognized element of the Christian religion. Then he told me that he has ulcerative colitis and the meat bothers him. I told him that was a medical issue that he would need to take up with that department. He said he had already tried that, but they did not consider his condition serious enough to warrant the diet. So then he asked me if he would become a Rastafarian, would he then qualify for a vegetarian diet?

I looked squarely at him and said, "I cannot tell you, according to the rules of the State, that you cannot do that, but I would not recommend it. Your religion should not be governed by your diet." With that I left him to ponder his next course of action. However, I believe I was correct to conclude that he was not a Christian. Such are some of the less attractive duties of a state prison chaplain.

Now about two weeks later, let me update regarding the assignment I was left with while our supervisor was on vacation. As I wrote above, we had received word from Trenton that we were to start having services again. So it was up to me to get together a plan for such and put it in a posting, along with calendars of activities for each facility and get them distributed. Now I really wanted to get this posting clearly stated and get it to all areas, because for two years now we have had to make so many changes and start and stop our services, that everyone was confused as to what we were or were not doing. To add to that confusion, so many officers are retiring and will be in the next few months, that often the tier officer is not a regular and does not know when the services are or what ones are being held.

I worked very diligently at making sure it was clear and accurate; then I had to call administration and get posting numbers for each item; then I had to take it up to administration and have it signed by the superintendent. Then I went back to the office and made copies for everyone who receives them (something like 40 copies of everything) and put them all in order for distribution. I was finished with all of that and was planning to start delivering them all within an hour, when I received an email from the supervisor in Trenton stating that we could now increase our attendance at services from nine inmates to twenty-five, and our time limit from thirty minutes to forty-five minutes.

I immediately forwarded the letter up to the superintendent and asked if he was agreeable to this, as the final call for each prison lies with the administration of that prison. He sent a note right back saying, "Hold up. I am forwarding this up to Trenton for approval." My first thought was, "It just came from Trenton!" But then my years of experience with government mindsets and methods overruled and I tried to force myself into relaxation over it, knowing all the while that we had only two more days in which to get it distributed.

Fortunately, the heads of state must have realized that we did not have time on our side and so they sent back their approval for the changes. Even though I was very happy about the changes, due to the fact that it would allow us to have them all in one service for each area, I had to start all over again. I had to revise the memo and the calendars, send them up front for signatures, print and collate them all again for distribution. I was praying for God's help, and I know He answered, and I had the distribution all made by Friday—March beginning on Tuesday.

Now, you may wonder why I told you all of that? It is so you know better how to pray for this chaplain! In case you think that my time is spent in nothing but winning souls for Jesus, let me be transparent enough to tell you that many hours are spent doing such duties as this in order to open the opportunity for preaching and teaching the Word. This ministry is no different from many mission fields where missionaries spend much time in elbow grease and mundane tasks in order to open doors for ministry. But whenever a sinner is transformed into a child of God, all of these hours of labor fade into non-remembrance for the joy of helping a soul to Jesus.

The man I have written about who was a Muslim and had a dream wherein Jesus appeared to him and he immediately began to follow Him, is rather overdue for release. I am not sure what is holding it up, but he is very eager to get out and come to our church. Please do pray for him that nothing will detour him. I have seen over the past twenty-four years, so many men that I had great hopes for, come out and almost immediately fall into a trap of Satan and be led away. You and I probably cannot even come close to knowing what it is like to have been locked up for a long period of time, then suddenly released into a world of dazzling temptations without having one's roots firmly fixed in the Rock of Ages. In Jesus' parable of the Sower, one of the enemies of fruit bearing was the fowls of the air that immediately snatch the seed from the ground and make off with it. Oh my! Jesus! What a painfully fitting illustration! I have seen this played out in living drama over and over and over, and still it hurts just as terribly as the first time it happened. Please help us pray for some more good soil to receive the seed.

A man who was released nearly two years ago stays in contact very often and comes way down from the northern part of the state whenever he can to church. He recently asked for some holiness books to study as he is trying to teach a Bible study to a few people in his area. All the while he was in prison, I never felt or saw this man resent or reject any light that came his way. Just how far he has gone personally I could be very mistaken to try to judge, but his spirit is so open to truth, and to this day he will not override the warnings and instructions of God to his own heart. His wife had died while he was in prison and he began to develop an interest in another woman near him. They had gone far enough that they were planning to be married, when God brought to his consciousness the fact that her being a divorced woman was a violation of God's Word. He prayed all night, but he came through clean and dropped her in order to stay clear with God.

Now, I will confess that it would be very agreeable to me if many more men would come to our church and join our loving church family. I thank God for those who are in His perfect will in so doing. But God knows where there are hungry hearts all over this state, and He can send men wherever He sees they will bring honor to Him. I love to feel that they are all "my boys," and God does not condemn me for enjoying that feeling; but really, they belong to Him, and so do I! I love it Your way, Jesus! Amen!

With love and gratitude,

William Cawman

6
WORKING WITH THE WAY THINGS ARE

April, 2022

THANK THE LORD, THIS month we are able to resume the weekly Bible studies as well as the church services. And, thank Him still farther, our only restrictions on numbers are that we have a space adequate to let them social distance.

To be very honest, I am not paying much attention to that detail since I see them bumping shoulders regularly on the basketball courts. But at least we are gaining some ground and the men are ever so grateful to be back in services.

As we came back together again, I preached to them from the words of Daniel before Nebuchadnezzar, "There is a God in heaven," and told them that whatever had been occupying their minds or disturbing their thoughts about all that was happening in the world, it was time to refocus on the reality that there is a God in heaven.

Last Sunday they released over one hundred more inmates, ten of whom were on our lists for Protestant services. There are strong rumors that the State is going to bring many of the inmates from the closest prison to fill up our facility which has been empty for almost a year, and that would also bring in more officers from that prison to replace ones that are retiring soon. If that happens, of course our work load would increase by one fourth as we would add services for that facility.

Do you remember the man I told you about who had been a Muslim for years and Jesus appeared to him in a dream and he immediately turned from Islam and began to walk with the Lord? It has been so precious over the past year or so to watch him learn about the ways of God and walk in them. I asked him a few weeks ago if Jesus still appears to him in his dreams and he said, "More often than not."

He wanted the address of our church and said he really wanted to come to it when he was released. He was released in early March and he called our pastor and said that he was maxed out but that they would not let him go unless someone came to pick him up. He called so close to service time that the pastor and another brother had to wait until after church to go get him. He testified to them of how Jesus had appeared to him and said he wanted to come to church. Being that he had nowhere to go, they took him to a motel and paid for a few nights of lodging until we could see what he would do.

The next day one of the brethren who has also been in the prison, went to see him and he was sitting on the curb outside waiting for a cab to take him to Atlantic City. He said he had a check from the State waiting for him there. The brother pled with him not to go to Atlantic City which is full of nothing but sin of all types, and even though he listened, he still insisted that he had to go. We have not seen nor heard from him since.

Sometimes I feel I cannot take one more heart-break, but then I remember how many times I also broke the heart of Jesus and yet He did not give up on me.

Several times when things like this happen, the Lord reminds me of the Scripture in Matthew 12, "When the unclean spirit is gone out of a man, he walketh through dry places, seeking rest, and findeth none. Then he saith, will return into my house from whence came out; and when he is come, he findeth it empty, swept, and garnished. Then goeth he, and taketh with himself seven other spirts more wicked than himself, and they enter in and dwell there: and the last state of that man is worse than the first."

It is a fact that cannot be denied, no matter how uncomfortable the thought is, that in the best of Christian churches, there are those who, having been raised in the culture of the church, simply live that culture without the transformation that comes with the indwelling Christ. Then one day, they are awakened as the rich young ruler—"What lack I yet?"—and they begin to earnestly seek the Lord and He is found of them. Everyone rejoices over the victory they are enjoying which they never had before. Then, little by little, the first glow of love fades, and they go back to the culture without the dynamics of the Power within. What happened to them? They went back to the house they came out of.

From God's perspective, there is no difference when a man comes from the dregs of the low life, responds to the call of God and begins to walk a new pathway, but then lets that glow of new life slip and goes back to the house he came out of. Many a pastor, if he could see into the inner heart of people like God can, would be just as tempted to discouragement as I am when a man I was really counting on goes back into the swill barrel of Satan.

I will follow that with a thanks to God and your prayers for everyone who continues to keep the fire burning and is still running up the pathway to heaven. Oh that there were many more!

Another inmate who has been faithful in attendance and vocally supportive of all we have preached to him was to be released in less than a week. He wanted to talk with me and so we met together for a visit. He told me that he would be living with an aunt, his only living relative except for a divorced wife, and that he couldn't wait to come to our church. I told him of how many times my heart had been broken over men that I was counting on coming out and failing, and he looked me in the eye and said, "I tell you; I will not be like that. I am going to mind God!" Pray for him, for after years in prison, Satan has him in his crosshairs without a doubt.

One afternoon recently, I went over to facility three for the worship service and when I got to the gate, I quickly realized that the facility was in a code, which is not uncommon at all. It was a very clammy day with drizzle and chilly wind, and consequently I hoped I would not have to stand there long when I saw a group of about six officers come out of the door I wanted to enter with an inmate in cuffs. As they came around the inmate gate to escort him into the holding cell area, he was bending over at the waist and coughing violently, and after they had put him inside and closed the door, I could still hear him screaming in there.

Then the control center must have felt sorry for me standing out in that weather and so they clicked open the gate. I entered and as I passed through the next gate an officer standing by the door I was planning to enter said, "Chap, they just let you through a code." I said, "Yes, I guess so." He said, "Be careful because there's likely blood on the floor." There was, and as I stepped around it and went on in, I could still hear the inmate screaming. I read in the tour report a few days later that they had sprayed him in the face with mace and thrown him to the floor as he was resisting being cuffed.

I waited and waited and finally they told me we could not have the service as they were not finished documenting the incident. Everything has to be photographed and written up for the record. So I just left for the day.

Another incident happened on Monday, March 21, that was more amusing than the one I just related. Some officers were escorting an inmate down the main compound from having been out to an outside hospital and a goose flew right into him and knocked him to the ground. The geese are extremely active and noisy right now as they are preparing to raise more families of geese. What a mess they make! The inmates throw bread through the fence of the recreation yard out onto the compound, which I guess provides a diversion from the humdrum of cell life, and then the geese leave their tips all over where we have to walk.

About eleven o'clock on Tuesday, March 22, an email popped up on my computer, followed by one from our director in Trenton. The first one was from the resident ombudsman, stating that a family had called in, very concerned for their son who was in detention and was very disturbed and threatening suicide. The second email was from our director urging us to get right on it. I called my supervisor and told him and he suggested I come right up to his office and we would go over together.

When we approached the cell, the man was definitely in a livid state of being emotionally distraught. All we could do for about ten or fifteen minutes was let him vent his frustrations and anger. We then began to talk with him and I told him that every one of us is comprised of two parts: our emotions and our wills. I told him that he was letting himself be a victim of his emotions and that in essence meant he was a victim of Satan. I said that if he acted out what he felt like it would not be the answer and that he would regret it later. I told him to look up to God and ask Him to help him take ahold of his will, and then look at Satan's lies and tell him he didn't belong to him and would not do as he was wanting him to do. Then, by God's help, he could get through it and he would come out a better man for it. He listened and began to shake his head in the affirmative. My supervisor had prayer with him and told him that Paul the Apostle had been put in prison for preaching, but instead of reacting to it, he wrote letters to the churches and told them that he had great joy in his heart. When we left him, he seemed much calmer and more collected than when we arrived.

During the first part of the visit, he told us with a passion how he was being mistreated, and that everyone else in there was getting the same degree of torment. There were some verbal agreements coming from nearby cells. But as we continued talking to him, the cell block became quiet, and when we started walking down the row from his cell, which was all the way in the far end, men began asking us for Bibles. We decided that more good was done than just to the one inmate. Maybe it was another example of: "Surely the wrath of man shall praise thee: the remainder of wrath shalt thou restrain."

Please help us pray for the Good Friday services. We haven't had these for the past two years because of all the lockdowns, but we are trusting and praying for a very special anointing on them as we gather this year to remember the Lord's death. A man who is now out of prison tells us that the Good Friday services were the highlight service of the year to him. Pray that it will be for many others too.

Also, please pray for the effectiveness of the Bible studies as we resume them, beginning in April. In the past, I would say they have been more valuable than the worship services and I am looking forward to having them again.

Thank you for all your prayers for us.

With love, William Cawman

May, 2022

ARE YOU STILL PRAYING for our Muslim chaplain? I hope so, and if so, could I tell you that God is not leaving him alone? Last week at our chaplain prayer time he came, although he seldom does. As we were discussing the signs of the times all around us, he looked at me and said, "Rev. Cawman, sometimes I can't sleep at night because I am afraid. I just have to ask the Lord to forgive me." He is due to retire late this summer, but he is undecided whether to do so as he really does not have a life outside of the prison. Please do pray for him, for nothing is impossible with God; except, that is, for Him to turn down the earnest prayer of a troubled Muslim!

We had a very sad happening on Tuesday evening, April

12. A sergeant who had started his career here at this prison about the same time that I started, and had only a few months left until retirement, had lost his position when they closed down facility one. He wasn't very happy about it and had talked to me about it a couple of times, but said he would hold out until he retired. I think he must have begun to drink more heavily and suddenly we received word that he was in the hospital and that they had him in an induced coma to try to recover him. He didn't make it; his liver was too far gone. It has really affected many people as he was well liked and well known. We chaplains have been trying to walk around and speak to other officers regarding it and they seem to appreciate it.

Do you remember the man I have written about a few times who is struggling to get clear with God? Well, as usual when someone is struggling, there is some definite hang-up they are up against. Today, the man came down to Bible study and immediately said, "I have a testimony."

I said, "Well, it's about time!" He went on to tell how someone had given him quite a stash of drugs and he had it in his locker and his cell mate knew it and his cousin in the cell next to him knew it and they wanted some of it. He was in a battle royal. He knew he could make money on it, but he knew it was wrong. Finally, he went to his locker and put his head inside, almost crawling in himself he said, and began to literally bang his head against the walls. His cell mate called across to his cousin in the next cell and told him that he was praying. He said he kept hearing a voice, and he knew it was God's voice, saying, "I've got you; get rid of it!" All of the sudden he said, "All right, God," and he flushed it all down the toilet. Immediately he felt the smile of God on him.

I urged him to follow right on and seek after all God has for him and he said he would, but in just a few days the pressure of temptation and the influences all around him seemed more than he could bear and he fell back again. Please pray for him as you and I both know that while Satan hasn't given up yet, neither has the Hound of Heaven! Thank God for the persistent Holy Spirit.

I am writing this part of the letter on the eve of Good Friday, and I will sign off and tell you more of tomorrow after it is past. I plan to go in at nine o'clock and be there until probably seven-thirty. I will have to be present for the Islamic prayer time at 12:30 as they are in Ramadan right now. Then at 2:30 I have a Protestant service in Facility Two, then another in Facility Three at 5:30 and then I will have to be present for Passover for the Jews in Facility Three. Never before in the life of the prison have all the four major religions had a simultaneous holy day, because Ramadan moves about twelve days each year.

Well, this is now later. I will try to describe the events of Good Friday without any glamorization, for one purpose of doing so is that we really need your prayers for the continuance of the ministry here in the prison. I will try to outline the whole situation as it presently stands.

Before Covid ever struck, I was having classes of twenty or more and Sunday services with a total attendance of 250 to 300. Then for two years we were shut down from group services. When they started them back up, it was with severely limited numbers—for a while only nine inmates to a group and later twenty-five. Now we are not limited in numbers but we are supposed to be practicing some degree of social distancing. But the numbers have never come back up. We presently have somewhere around one-hundred fifty inmates enrolled in worship services and around fifty or sixty in Bible studies. We rarely exceed twenty in one service and most of the time not that many. Often for Bible study we have only a handful.

There are several reasons for this, some of which we may have to work through, and some of which are totally inexcusable. Due to the fact that the numbers are way down in all religious services, we observe that after a long time of not attending services, the men have grown accustomed to it. If that were the only reason, we could expect to see a rebound of interest as we continue, but here are some other factors that we really ask for prayer about.

The prison is now twenty-five years old, and all of the officers who were trained to staff it are now coming to retirement. No foresight or provision has been made for this and as more and more retire; we are severely short-staffed. Consequently, many of the housing units do not have a regular officer, but are being covered by floaters who are not familiar with the schedules. Added to this is the fact that one by one, the intercom systems on the housing units have gone down, and so there is no way to announce the services from the center. Instead, they depend on the officer on each tier hearing it announced over his radio and then just yelling at the top of his voice and expecting one hundred and twenty-eight men in their cells to hear it.

Unfortunately, I would have to add that it is too obvious to deny, that many of the temporary officers, just filling in for the day, do not care, and consequently just ignore the call for religious services.

So, on the last service for Good Friday, I had purposely gone to every cell block and kindly spoken to the officers, informing them of the services for the day so that they would be alert to them. When that service was called out, about two-thirds of the men on the appointment list showed up, and so we went ahead with them. Nearly at the end of the service, the rest of them appeared, and that not in the best of attitudes, reporting that they had been banging on their cell doors and asking the officers if it had been called out, and they told them it had not.

Now, let me interject an incident here which would accentuate that some of this is deliberate neglect. Several months ago, since this problem has been ongoing, I stopped in at the office of the Major of custody. I explained to him what we were experiencing. I told him that we were employed by the

State of New Jersey just as much as the officers, and that we had a job that we were expected to do, but that it was next to impossible to carry on an effective Bible study with such sporadic attendance. He told me that such was totally unacceptable and that he would do something about it. The next few classes and services, it was called out and we had record attendance. That lasted about one day and then it went right back to the way it was.

Just before Good Friday I sent a written complaint to the new administrator and the two majors about the broken intercoms and the failure to call the men out. The administrator asked me if anyone from chaplaincy had complained about it before and I told her we had been documenting it for two years. Then with all of that coming up to Good Friday, I thought it would certainly improve, but the result pointed definitely to a custodial unconcern as to whether the men get to their religious services or not. I understand that the issue is being looked at now, as administration knows full well that denying men their religious rights is cause for a law suit.

Now, I hope you know that I am not just venting frustration, although this is and has been very frustrating, but that we really need prayer that this situation can change; otherwise, we are being drastically limited in getting to the men. It is also very discouraging to the men to try for weeks on end to get out of their cells to come to church and not be able to.

Then there is another angle to this that we also need much prayer over. Due to the shortage of officers, men with short time left on their sentences are being released early to make room in this prison. Then they plan to close down two smaller prisons and transport those inmates and the officers to this one, filling it back up again. I am relatively sure that we will also inherit another part-time chaplain. All of this just adds to the upheaval and confusion for some time to come.

But, back to Good Friday. After holding two Protestant services I stayed into the evening to cover one of the facilities for the Jewish Passover meal. Outside Jewish vendors had sent in Seder plates and Matza bread and grape juice and little booklets of what they are supposed to say with each part of the Seder meal. We called them down at six-thirty in the evening, but of course they cannot partake of the ceremonial meal until sundown, so they just visited until seven-thirty. Then they began the ceremony by reading a section of the little booklet and then breaking off a piece of the head of lettuce. They then smeared a liberal plaster of horseradish and some brownish paste (I suppose that represented the roasted lamb) provided with the Seder plate onto the lettuce and ate it. Then they had to go wash their hands and proceed with the other items on the plate. When they opened the pre-packaged container of six boiled eggs, the appearance was anything but delicious, and they threw them in the trash! All in all, the ceremony lasted until about quarter till nine, at which time they had to go get locked in for the night. My supervisor and I each took a facility for these ceremonies, both Friday and Saturday nights.

As I watched and listened, I thanked Jesus for coming to save us from such a dead (could I say it respectfully—ridiculous) exercise as this. All semblance of life and even meaning had vanished from what I witnessed just as surely as had life-saving power from the brazen serpent. We need to pray for the Jewish people! Oh that they would just acknowledge their wonderful, life-giving Messiah! Rejecting Him has rendered all of their rituals and ceremonies vain to the point of being utterly ludicrous.

In both of the Protestant services, the men were very much wanting to make up for lost privileges in singing their favorite Easter songs from the hymnal. We sang several at their request and then I spoke to them from the sayings of Jesus on the Cross. God helped us and I wished there could have been many more there.

Recently I received a request from a name that I remembered asking for a visit. I didn't know whether he had been for a while in another prison and returned or just what, but when we sat down together, he began to open up his heart with tears. He told me that I had been so faithful to warn him about going back into the area he had come from and about keeping in touch with God, but he said that when he left prison, he left God too. He started a business and was doing very well, but after five years under a stressful circumstance he thought one dip into drugs would help relieve him. One dip lasted thirty days and he was violated and now is back in prison. He seemed to be thoroughly repentant over it and told me he now cares about nothing except getting right with God. He said he would now take my advice and never go back into his old life again, but stay where he could go to a good church. Please pray for him.

God is obviously dealing with a number of the men and is answering your prayers, so please continue for His sake and theirs. I would leave one more request. We have felt for some time the need of having some provision to help some of the men who get out and are really serious about going on with God. Thrusting them back into the societies they came from throws them into temptations as well as discouragements that are far beyond our comprehension. Pray that God will give us wisdom and knowledge as to what to do about it.

With love and appreciation,

William Cawman

June, 2022

THIS PAST MONTH WE had a very precious revival meeting in our church and our evangelist preached one night on being a slave to carnality. Just in case you would be tempted to think that the word "slave" is too severe regarding our relationship to the sinful nature within, you might want to follow my visits with a particular inmate over the past year or more. I have written some about him, and I'll not go back and try to make a connection, but when he first came to me, he seemed broken and sick and tired of a life of sensual sin. He never had a home life; he was bumped around in foster settings and even worse, and was introduced to unharnessed sin from his earliest recollections.

Becoming a total addict to women and drugs, he finally reached a stage of its wages that was more than he felt he could bear. He told me that he remembers a time in his early life when he really gave his heart to Jesus and was so happy and blessed, but he drifted away from it and literally spent years wallowing in the cesspool of Satan's choosing.

He told me he was finished with all of what he had been in, and just wanted to know once again that he was right with God. False churches had bolstered him up, telling him that he had the Holy Ghost, but he told me he knew he didn't for he was living deep in sin. Oh how one could wish that God's wrath would fall on these false teachers who tell a person he is filled with the Holy Ghost when he is filled with the devil.

Anyway, for probably over a year now, I have kept calling him down and trying to lead him to really forsake sin and open his heart to God. Some time back I told you how he came down to a Bible study and immediately told me that he had a testimony. He related how God had so convicted him of all the drugs he had stashed away in his locker that he finally yielded and threw them all away. Immediately he felt God's smile come over him. I encouraged him to go right on and ask Jesus to fill him completely with His Spirit.

I didn't get a chance to see him after that for about two weeks as I was away in a meeting, but he sent several requests in that he needed to see me. When I returned and called him down, he seemed very despondent while telling me that his good resolve had only lasted a day or two and that with all the temptations around him, he had fallen victim again and gone back to the drugs and to lusting after women. I tried to point him to a forgiving God and told him that if he would just rise up again to his feet and go after God, He would hear and forgive him and give him the power to stand.

About a week later, I called him down again, and when he came in the room, I could very easily sense that he was drugged up. I asked him about it and he confessed it. I tried again to point him to the remedy, telling him that eternity was so near ahead and that he could not afford to spend it in hell. Always before as I would talk to him, he would melt down with sorrow and remorse and say he really wanted to put an end to all this, but this time I sensed that he was so stupefied that he really did not care. I saw no repentant breaking in him, but he simply said, "Chaplain, I love you," and got up to leave.

Now, what do you call that if it isn't slavery? No iron shackles put upon an African, no ankle bands put upon a member of a chain gang, no brutal whip of a task master could be more enslaving than is this dear man to the passions of his lower appetites. Will I give up on him? No! I love him! But if he does not soon rise up in holy wrath against himself, he may give up on me. And then—worse by far, slavery for all eternity.

We are in the dead center of major changes in our population as well as our custody. I think I told you that the facility that has been closed up since they had a fire in it, is now being reopened, and they are bringing inmates from the nearest state prison as well as the officers from there, and then they plan to close that one down. We have in some degree decided to just go with the flow until all this settles down, and then we plan to address the injustices that are becoming more and more flagrant. For instance, when they call out Jumah prayer for the Muslim inmates, they announce it over the loud speakers that go everywhere and then even give another call ten minutes later. They call out very clearly for recreation, for school, for count time; but for any religious services apart from Islam, they will not call it out nor will they pay much attention to opening the cells of the men who are on the appointment sheets. Please help us pray that we can bring this chaos back to some degree of normalcy, for it is extremely difficult and disappointing to us as well as to the men to be so dysfunctional in our religious services.

Several weeks ago, I had noticed that a water treatment company on one of our main streets in Vineland, was being worked over, inside and out. All of the sudden in driving by, we noticed a line of people from the front door clear to the street, and a parking lot overflowing, with two policemen standing by. Then we noticed the sign "Cannabis" over the door. Then I remembered that our state has now embraced the sale of recreational marijuana. We have already seen such a tragic departure from the basics of sanity (let alone fear of God), that it would seem this is the last blow to it. You see, the Bible declares that the fear of the Lord is the beginning of wisdom. Doesn't that imply that without a fear of God there is none?

In a week or so, I noticed my prison email being flooded with requests for inmates to be expunged from all of our records. I couldn't help but wonder if these inmates had been imprisoned for the illegal use of marijuana, and now their records have to be deleted! I guess—forgive the irony here if you need to—that there are two ways to have your sinful record expunged. If you come to God through the Blood of Jesus, every sin ever committed can be expunged from your conscience for ever and ever. If you come to civil authorities who no longer call sin, "sin," you may have your civil record expunged at least in part. In case you think I am misjudging, please read the last verse of Romans chapter one.

I am encouraged for an inmate whose thirty-year sentence is nearing completion. He has fully embraced the teachings of heart holiness and sees that all else makes no sense. He has been shut away for three decades. Just think back a bit and you will realize that what you and I have witnessed as a developing (though ever so rapid) change, will for him be a Rip Van Winkle awakening. He says he cannot wait to be able to come to our church from which he has received so much help for years with our people going in to minister. Please pray that he will not be sideswiped by the trickery of the devil. His parents are worldly Catholics, but they want him to live with them and help his father in his business. It is dead certain that Satan has his plans all laid to knock him endwise immediately upon his release, so he really needs your prayers that he will not listen to any other voice than that of the Holy Spirit.

I am also going to share a disclosure with you as we so need prayer for this. For years we have seen the need for a place where we can give men coming out of prison a start in the right direction, rather than let the state place them in some half-way house right down in the pits of sin. I can look back across the years and think of several men who might have stuck with the right way had they been given such a chance. There are several right now. This is a need that the whole church is feeling deeply and as we have sought God's mind and put a few feelers out, we can see perhaps a bit of light in that direction. Please pray with us for this desperate need.

So that you can more fully understand this, let me explain a few things that I have learned over the years by watching others try it and also by being very familiar with the guidelines of parole, etc. First of all, if we can find a suitable property to accomplish this, we would need a qualified man (preferably single) who could serve as a mentor and overseer of the project. Secondly, if the property is owned by the church, it would be tax exempt, which would be a tremendous lift in this state, but it would also mean that we could not actually charge rent without violating our tax-exempt status. Thirdly, we would have to be very careful and selective as to who we allow to take advantage of it; we would have to discern how serious they would be in staying true to God. If the property was to be set up as a business, we could not discriminate, but if it is a church function, we can have a very specific set of rules, one of which would have to be that if they failed to attend church or in any way violated those rules, they would be dismissed. We would definitely appreciate any insights that anyone would want to share with us as to these parameters.

You can easily see that there are many factors to be considered, but that in no way outweighs the need we feel so keenly. It is nothing short of painful to see men pulled away to the environments they are sent into if we can do anything to help it.

Years ago, when I was first starting into this ministry, a very well-meaning minister who was volunteering on Sunday nights, saw this very same need and started up a home for men getting out. He made it known among the inmates and even opened the door for them to send monetary contributions to help with it. As soon as the state discovered what he was doing, they banned him from coming into the prison anymore. Even though I believe that was an over-reaction on the part of the state, our church versus the State of New Jersey might not be the most delicious headlines for you to hear. So, in light of that, I will approach the administrator and special investigations unit of the prison before getting deeply involved. Please pray for that also.

Now, if one would listen to the news and all the prophecies of pending doom that are available, perhaps even with some validity, it might be a thought that the end of all things is so near that it would not be wise to launch out into a new area of ministry. Since such a thought is totally unscriptural, we reject it hands down! If anything, the lateness of the hour and the colossal amount of unfinished business for the Kingdom of God, would demand increased efforts, not an abatement of them. I, personally, have no interest in Jesus finding me when He comes, huddled into a corner polishing my own robes, when the multitudes He died for as well as myself are still without Him. So, please Jesus, guide us by Thy Spirit into the future, however long or short, to yet gather as many souls as we can around the marriage supper of the soon coming Lamb.

With much Christian love and thanks,

William Cawman

7
WE MUST WORK WHILE THE DAY LASTS

July, 2022

How quickly the summer is passing us by! It's only another reminder that time will shortly be over, and oh how much work remains to yet be done. Please help us, Jesus, to not let one more soul slip through our fingers.

We are trying to bring order back to the religious department in the prison. Starting in July we inherit another part-time chaplain from the prison that closed down and sent the inmates here. We also get another full-time Islamic chaplain, and that in itself is creating some tensions as the two do not teach the same thing. Pray however God lays it on your heart concerning that!

Already requests are coming in from the recently re-opened facility, and we have started having services there as well. The very first Bible study was received enthusiastically, and the men left saying they were going to spread the word around that others needed to come. Yet, for all of that we are still struggling with having the services called out and the men's doors unlocked so that they can come. More and more the men are reporting that every other function is called out, including the

Islamic services; but never any other religious services. Please pray that as we address this issue it will be resolved.

Several months ago, a new policy was distributed along with a cover letter that we had to sign that we had read it (that, fortunately, does not mean that we agree with it), which contained multiple pages of direction that we were not to make anyone feel uncomfortable with their chosen lifestyle and what gender they chose to be, etc., etc. Shortly thereafter, we began to notice the influx of transgender "its" into one of our facilities. They asked to be housed together, but at least that request was ignored. Then at least two men (that is what they are by biology) made it known that they were no longer men, so they were granted the opportunity to be transferred to the women's prison up north. Several women there are now expecting! Then one day my supervisor printed out the roster and at the very top was a name of someone having been sent to our hospital with a female name. My supervisor took it down the hall to the sergeant and asked, "Can this be?" It was confirmed.

Then one morning I had a visit with an inmate that showed up, and at first I didn't notice a whole lot except that the hair was more than shoulder length. "It" sat down and I introduced myself and when "it" spoke, I almost startled; the voice was definitely female. Not being allowed to ask, I simply began to ask about the past life and "it" was thirty-three years old and had served four years in the army. I asked about the home life, parents, etc., and "it" said that the home life was fairly normal until "it" "came out." I did not explore that expression, but when "it" finally left the room, I did not have a clue as to "its" gender.

The reason I told you that was that you would pray for us. I have always been forthright with all of God's truth in teaching the men, even in the areas of lifestyle and God's wrath upon alternate ones. I can almost anticipate some of these "its" asking to join the classes and then…! The one I spoke with probably won't as "it" said "it" was a Wiccan and before that an agnostic. Will you pray the protection of the Blood upon this situation?

In our chaplain prayer time, we were all with equal disgust and alarm taking note of such and the other part-time chaplain said, "Just how much longer do we have before we cannot keep a clear conscience here?" I said, "Perhaps until the time spoken of in Scripture wherein 'the night cometh when no man can work.'" He said, "I never interpreted that Scripture that way, but you may have it right!" "Brethren, pray for us!"

Saturday the 18th of June, I received a text message from that chaplain that he had fallen and fractured his femur where his artificial hip attaches. Just when we are feeling so keenly the increase in our load, this happened. Well, God knows all about it and so I will just continue to obey Him and leave all of these uprising issues in His hands.

Oh I must tell you something that our supervisor told us the other day that made all of us rather bug our eyes. He said that however many years ago he and his wife had their wedding day all planned, and the day before it he developed a serious blood clot. He ended up in ICU for treatment and when the nurses found that his wedding was planned for the next day, they said, "Well, that's no problem; you can get married here!" They quickly obtained an arch and flowers and managed to get a white shirt and tie on his upper body and the marriage knot was tied in ICU! I guess it proves that "Many waters cannot quench love, neither can the floods drown it:" —nor anything else that might come along either!

Many changes have taken effect in the last month, and they are still ongoing; some good and some not. On July 17th we plan to resume Sunday night services after two and one-half years. The men are really looking forward to it and we hope to see a good turnout right from the start. I finished enrolling the names who have been in services and Bible studies and we have about one hundred and eighty to start off with. The services will be at 5:30 in all three facilities, so it will take three chaplains or two chaplains and a volunteer to hold them. The other part-time chaplain is supposed to come on July sixth.

We are also inheriting another Islamic Imam from the prison that closed up and sent the inmates here. He does not teach the same as the one we have had for years, and so there is some tension and concern in the air about it. I guess there are more than one brand of Islam just as of any other religion.

Two of the men in prison are soon to get out. One of them said, "I have been in prison for thirty years from the age of eighteen. Before coming to prison I had no contact with church at all. My parents were Catholics, but I had little or no thought of God or church. All the church I have ever known is church in prison, and of all the groups that have come into whatever prison I have been in, your group has been the only people I have ever seen and met who I would believe have the real thing."

The other man was released on parole a few years ago and is now back on a parole violation for a short time. When he came back, he immediately wanted to talk with me. He said, "Chaplain, when I left a few years ago, you strongly warned me not to go back to my old neighborhood up north, but to stay where I could go to a good church. I walked out of prison and walked away from God. I am so sorry now. All I want is to get fully right with God. I will not go back up north this time, but do as you say and make it the business of my life to be right entirely with God. I don't care about anything else anymore; money or job or family, if they are going to pull me to the world. I just want to know that God is pleased with me."

So, do you see why souls like these pull our hearts out to have a place to shelter and nurture them into real saints? Our church body is almost desperate to see this happen. Too many already have, I would fear, slipped through our fingers and away from us who might have made it for God had they had help.

We sometimes have several former inmates in our Sunday services now, but we don't want to lose any that God entrusts to us. When God first opened this door and led us into this ministry, my mother said to me, "Son, if God wants to fill this church with former inmates, let Him do it!" She has now been in glory for fifteen years, but I believe some of her prayers are lingering on.

Now I also mentioned that I would alert the prison administration as to our involvement in helping men when they get out of prison, simply because it is far easier to ask before than explain afterwards. It is easier to get permission than to ask forgiveness. So, I wrote a letter to the administrator of the prison and sent it to her. Months or even a year or so before, I had sat down with the associate administrator and the superintendent over the chaplains and told them everything we were doing with inmates who choose to come to our church. You see, the prison officials constantly warn us, and that very strongly, of forming personal relationships with the inmates. (Pause for an insertion here: I have often told the inmates that they and I are both aware that we are not to be forming personal relationships in the prison between inmates and staff, but that I have been hired by the State of New Jersey to preach the gospel to them. If I do that properly, and they respond to that and give their hearts to God until He accepts them as His sons, then we are blood brothers! So there for personal relationships!)

So after I had covered all that we were doing with inmates coming to our church, the two men looked at each other and then at me and said, "Chaplain, we have no problem at all with what you are doing; how could you do otherwise. If anything further develops, just inform the administrator." So that's exactly what I did.

A day or so later she called me and said, "Did you send that letter to anyone besides myself?" I said, "No." She said, "That's all I wanted to know," and I've heard no more, and will ask no more. Just please pray for us that in all of this God will cover us with the all-sufficient Blood!

Thank you for all you do,

William Cawman

August, 2022

I WOULD LIKE TO introduce you to a man that has my heart rather excited. He is the dentist who works in the prison here, and he is a Messianic Jew. Even though he has been taught the Baptist doctrines, his heart is definitely reaching for the higher life and a closer walk with Jesus. We have had several opportunities to visit about it as we once in a while take lunch together. One morning both of us were held up in the lobby because of some movement inside the prison which had the compound closed. He really began to open his heart to me and I testified to him of how deeply Jesus was satisfying my own heart by His indwelling Spirit. When the compound finally opened, he said, "There was a reason for the compound being closed today. You have really given me some things to think about and I really want to get closer to God." Please do pray for him. When a Jewish person really comes alive with the life of Jesus in their heart, all the Old Testament feasts and sacrifices and holy days become thrilling to them.

Several years ago, perhaps four or five, a fairly young man who had been in many of my Bible studies and services was preparing to leave on parole. I sat down with him and tried to prep him by warning him that he was not safe to go back out without being filled with the Spirit. It seemed that everything I told him had no penetration; he was absolutely filled with self-confidence and self-sufficiency. Everything I tried to tell him brought the response: "Oh yes, of course!" As I sat and looked at him and he felt so sure that he would be all right, I could hardly contain the desire to scream at him, "No! No! You won't be all right!"

Yesterday I was enrolling new requests for the Christian services, and all of the sudden I took a double look. He is back! Now this is not a typical low-life street person who seems to be at home in and out of prison. He has a family (not as in wife and children) and a job, and it would seem a person would be willing to do anything other than come back into prison having already tasted of it. But here he is. Perhaps we make prison life too comfortable! And yet when I think of how I would feel locked up in prison with every liberty taken away and all friends absent, I cannot imagine taking chances that would bring me back. Maybe I am missing something in the equation; but to be very honest, I am not looking for the missing link!

I told you last month that we were planning to start up Sunday services again. Well, the letters DOC were designated to mean "Department of Corrections," but we often wonder if it does not more accurately mean, "Department of Confusion," or "Department of Change." I had sent up a new module to the man in Trenton who is over us all and he approved it and sent it to the department that sets up the modules. As soon as I received it back, I spent several hours removing all the names from the weekday services and entering them in the Sunday night module. No sooner had I done this than the man came down from Trenton and told my supervisor that he could not come in on Sundays. That makes complications that I will not enumerate here, but now I will likely have to go move all the names again back into weeknight modules.

Do you see why those three letters might need to mean something other than they were intended to mean?

I will be very honest with you, my dear praying friends: things like this often bring me to the brink of thinking that maybe the time has come to retire from this ministry. Then I look into the faces of men that I love and am watching grow in grace, and I have to swallow hard and look up and say, "Lord, You opened this door; You have kept it open so far; You will have to be the One who tells me that my work is finished; not me or any other circumstance or inconvenience or difficulty." He has not told me that as yet.

The moving of prisoners throughout the state prisons is still going on. We hear rumors of what is happening, but only know the facts after we see them happen. The nearest prison to ours has now emptied out into ours, but still we have vacancies. If you remember, a couple of years ago one of our housing units caught fire due to a dirty lint duct from a dryer igniting. Soon after that, they closed down that whole facility (one third of the entire prison) and we didn't know what the future of that would be. Now they have redone that housing unit and reopened the other unit in that facility and pretty well filled it with incoming inmates from the prison that closed. Just the other day I noticed some requests coming in for services from the housing unit that had the fire. I enquired, and sure enough they are now putting inmates in that one. The rumor is that they are getting ready to close up another prison further north.

Whatever and however soon all this will settle down, who knows? But meanwhile we are scrambling like Mother Hubbard to keep track of all our children. Nearly every week I have to update the rosters for service attendance due to so much moving around. I must say, however, that with the opening up of facility one and all of the new inmates there, I am finding a revived spirit of interest in the Bible studies and a real eagerness to start more services. At least that is encouraging.

God alone knows how much more time we have to labor before the "night cometh when no man can work." And when I think of that, it only drives me closer to Jesus, that I might by all means help a few more find their way to Him. I can see that God has His hand in an area of protection here in the state prison, and I am not only thankful for it, but because of it, I know I can trust Him with other things that will inevitably come out of this recent hellish tidal wave of rebellion against God and His laws. Just a few months before the policy was issued that we were not allowed to make anyone uncomfortable with their choice of gender or any related issues, a policy was issued which forbid any chaplain to perform a marriage within the prison or that involved an inmate on parole. Very shortly after, we began to see an influx of transgenders and other mix ups which could easily have been used by Satan to target us into trouble with the agenda of this demonic blast straight from the pit of hell.

But, mark you, Satan is not finished! Sodom and Gomorrah cannot hold a feather of weight compared to what is coming against us now. However, Jesus gave us clear warning as to our response to all of this. Listen to His words from Luke 21: "Men's hearts failing them for fear, and for looking after those things which are coming on the earth: for the powers of heaven shall be shaken. And then shall they see the Son of man coming in a cloud with power and great glory. And when these things begin to come to pass, then look up, and lift up your heads; for your redemption draweth nigh."

Permit me to make a few comments on these verses as it may very soon, if not already, apply directly to our ministry here in the prison, a State institution.

First of all, Jesus warned us that we are not to become victims of fear. Satan always works through fear. Have you noticed that the majority voice of right in our country is fast backing down in fear before the demonic aggressiveness of the minority wrong? If you dare to even begin to express your views to someone you don't know, they immediately shrink back from agreeing, even though they do? Supposing Daniel had done this; or the three Hebrew boys? The evil power behind this hellish agenda is fast closing the mouths of those who are right. Shall we back down along with them, or shall we stand like Daniel and the three Hebrews? We have brothers and sisters in Muslim and Oriental countries who are willing to give their blood and their heads for God and right. Shall we bow to this evil agenda just to save ourselves from persecution? God help us!

But Jesus also instructed us that when we see these things (the very things we are seeing) come to pass, we are to "Look up!" He doesn't want us glued to the latest lies from the news media, nor does He want us taking on wrong attitudes and picking up carnal weapons. He said to "Look up!" Our martyrdom may come in a different cloak than slit throats or bullets or fire. My heart cries out, Lord, whatever the cost or consequences, I will be true to that Good Old Book! Say, do you know what that Book says? It says: "the triumphing of the wicked is short!" We are seeing such an accelerated tsunami of moral corruption that it cannot last long without total self-annihilation.

And then "As I live, saith the Lord, every knee shall bow to me, and every tongue shall confess to God." When that time comes, and it may, that you do not hear from me because I have stood by the Word of God, let me meet you with a shout of triumph in that soon coming moment when He shall stand as complete Conqueror over all His enemies. What will this old earth and all its trials matter then? We have sung with deep emotions for years in our missionary services the words, "…with eternity's values in view…" Do we mean that?

"Chaplain," you ask, "are you afraid you are about to go down before this incoming upsurge of hell's demons?" No, I am not! I am only wanting you to know that if I do get in trouble with the devil, I will do so with both feet planted firmly on the never-failing Word of God. If the very things I am writing to you right here fall into the wrong hands, I can be branded as the author of hate language. I deny it not! I hate the devil; I hate sin; Ps 26:5 "I have hated the congregation of evil doers; and will not sit with the wicked." Ps 119:128 "Therefore I esteem all thy precepts concerning all things to be right; and I hate every false way." And while so hating all of that, I feel an upsurge of sweet peace and love for all mankind swelling up within me.

But now, Chaplain, this letter is not about you but about

the ministry in the prison. All right, but "What I have written I have written." Please pray for us!

Now I would like to make a request in all earnestness. In every camp meeting I have been in this summer so far, and in every one I have heard anything about, God has been moving in definite power. What all He is preparing us for, I do not know and I do not need to know. Now I would like to ask you to help me pray that the same purpose for which God is moving in our camps, will spread also into the prison services. With all of the eruptions and interruptions we have been through ever since Covid came to plague us, we have never gotten back to the way services and Bible studies were before it all. I am not asking God to simply restore what used to be, but to move in upon us with such power from on High that His great purpose can be accomplished inside the prison as well as outside. As of this writing, He has seen fit to keep the door open for ministry in the prison, and therefore He must still have a purpose in us being there. I am expressly happy in whatever His will is and however He leads in getting it accomplished, but that does not mean that I am just laid back about it! I feel a fresh sense of urgency for the need of the hour. I have felt it on my heart several times recently to preach from the text: "But ye are a chosen generation..." and that we are. Whatever God desires and designs to be done in the closing hours of time, He has chosen you and I to do it. My heart, with Isaiah's says: "Here am I; send me!"

Thank you again so very much for all your prayers for us,
William Cawman

September, 2022

I HAVE ALWAYS BEEN reluctant to call any attention to the chaplain, as these letters are for prayer support for the inmates, but I do have something I want to share with you (I have with a few of you already) of God's wonderful micro-management recently. It was not only while our Blessed Jesus was here in a human body, but every so often even yet, our response is: "And were beyond measure astonished, saying, He hath done all things well" (Mark 7:37).

On August 12, my wife and I flew from Philadelphia to Rapid City, SD, and then the other evangelist picked us up and we drove on out to Ridge, MT (Population count there is 3). God was helping us in a very precious way in a most rustic wilderness camp in Ridge, MT. Service after service, God's manifest presence was powerfully real. After preaching on Tuesday evening, I went to bed and soon became conscious of mild pain/pressure around my heart. I got up and took a couple Tylenol and around midnight finally dropped off to sleep. When I got up Wednesday morning, I still did not feel normal, although the pain was pretty much gone. I went to the early morning prayer and asked the brethren to pray for me. They gathered around the altar and prayed and I know that God was hearing the prayer. After breakfast, one of the brethren came and asked how I was feeling. I told him I still did not feel normal and he suggested that we drive into Spearfish about an hour away and have me checked rather than risk an emergency, two hours from a hospital.

I agreed and so we left and went to the urgent care unit in Spearfish. They said that they did not have means to really check me as was needed and so sent me by ambulance to Rapid City. There a very able cardiac team did blood work and thought it best to keep me overnight and have an ultrasound and stress test the next morning. My wife was able to stay overnight with a church family right across the street from the hospital and we both had good night's sleep.

The next morning, after the said tests, they concluded that it may have been nothing more than an altitude change as they found no blockage or restrictions. My son, meanwhile did some research himself and found that symptoms like that were noted in people after having Covid. Whatever it was, we then returned to the camp.

But now—up in northeast Montana there was a dear old-fashioned saint who had been isolated up there for eight years teaching school on a reservation. She had not been in a camp meeting for all of those eight years and yet had held true to God and her testimony in spite of very little outside spiritual help. She had been told that there was a camp two and a half hours south of her and she really wanted to be able to get to it, but had very little information about it. She finally was able to get a few contacts but was about to give up due to not getting any answers. You see, no one's phones work at this camp as it is so far from towers and in the mountains.

Finally, just as she was about to give up, she decided to call the last number on her list, and when she did, the pastor who had taken us, being then in Rapid City, got the call. He gave her directions and then we headed back to camp. She arrived on Saturday morning in time for the Bible study. God's presence was again so deep and real as a spirit of worship went up from the group. Suddenly she got to her feet and almost exploded with thanksgiving as she told the story of how she got there after almost giving up. She then testified to the keeping power of God even though she was living all alone out there in the wilderness.

When she finished, the pastor came to the front and said, "If Bro. Cawman had not had that heart episode, this woman would never have been here! Truly the steps of a good man are ordered by the Lord." Even if the symptoms had been a few hours before or after, we would have missed her final effort to call. With that I just placed myself anew in the hands of God and told Him that my physical heart as well as my spiritual heart was all His, and that He could just flip it around to any purpose He has for it.

But that is not all I have to tell you about this trip. On Monday after camp, we flew from Rapid City to Chicago and found that we had a five-hour layover which would get us to Philadelphia after midnight. I lifted my heart to God and asked if it would please Him to allow us to get an earlier flight. We were certainly not looking forward to five hours in the Chicago airport followed by such a late home arrival. I then went to check and found that there was an earlier flight but that it was already overbooked. The agent said we might try it, but our baggage would still have to come on the later plane which would not help us much. So—again it was mine to simply say, "Yes, Lord!" And let me testify that I did not find my heart saying, "But... Lord!"

When we got on the plane, my wife was at the window, I in the middle, and a tall black man sat down next to me. My wife (bless her heart) never lets anyone off without a slice of her sweetness. She asked the man if he lives in Philadelphia and he said he does, near Fairmount Park. She asked if he likes it there and he said it is getting worse with crime and they are thinking of moving across the river into NJ. She then asked what brought him to Chicago. He dropped his head for a minute and then looked at us and poured out his bleeding heart. He is a medical doctor and so is his wife. They have been married for fourteen years. Three years ago, her baby sister died, a friend committed suicide, and her father died, all in short order. She turned for help to a cult in Texas and she has been gone for three years. He had been to see her and to find out about it. He said he was stunned that she couldn't wake up. They have re-written the Bible to direct all praise and worship to the cult leader and his brother. One of them died and the other one continues to minister to them from his prison cell where he dwells because of child molestation charges. The doctor has been praying and fasting for her to wake up. I laid my hand on his shoulder and said, "Sir, I want you to know, we care about this," and asked if he would like us to pray with him. As I prayed with him for a while, he was just wiping away the tears. He thanked us over and over and said, "To think, that I had to get on this plane to find someone to talk with like this!" I gave him my card and invited him to call and talk more and that we would be helping him pray for her. He said he was going to keep in touch with us. He also told us that he has gotten rid of his television as it was taking important time that he needed far worse than anything on it.

All right, Lord, so much for our comfort level when there is a bleeding heart that needs help! Will you pray for him? I have been asking the men in prison to pray for him also.

When I returned, the new part-time chaplain told me the men were really wanting me to return to them. And, thank the Lord, I sensed no jealousy coming from him over it. Then I stopped to greet two of the men in one of the Bible studies. When I did, I heard something that I have not heard before in all of my seventy-nine years. So now of course you want to know what it was, don't you? Well, I have been making an effort at using my voice in song for almost the whole of those seventy-nine years, and have never been congratulated or even commended for its quality. I have not been invited to become a soloist, nor have I have ever craved that reputation, because I can hear myself, and I absolutely detest the quality of sound coming from my vocal cords. The only time I can enjoy my own singing at all, is when it is nearly drowned out by a noisy engine or by others singing around me. But one of the men said, "Chaplain, when are you coming back to our services? We really miss you and I really miss the singing. The others don't have us sing and I really miss it." The other chimed in, "Yes, Chaplain Cawman can really sing!" Now I told you that only for your amusement, not for your agreement, for I want you to retain the spirit of truthfulness in all things.

The man I have written about who is so addicted to K2, and struggles fiercely between the call of God and the power of the addiction, came in to visit and let me know that God just will not leave him alone. He feels the pull of the call of God and really wants to come clean and enter into a relationship where he knows God's full smile. Please pray for him. I encouraged him to stand up and resist the devil in everything he knows to be from him, and plead with God for a new birth with power to live above all sin. The struggle has been fierce and long, but how can I give him up when I remember my own prolonged struggle, an addiction to spiritual failure rather than to K2? He is a most naturally winsome young man, and I would love to see what God would use him for if he really gets completely delivered and filled with the Spirit.

The property that for a while looked so hopeful as a retreat for men wanting to get established in a new life seems at least for now to have closed. We are still looking to God for direction, and knowing how intricately and effectively He accomplishes His will as noted at the beginning of this letter, we know we can trust Him to supply this need, perhaps in a way we have not yet dreamed of. There does seem to be at least a temporary provision for a man who will be released this fall, and who has expressed strongly his desire to just get away from all his past and seek to know God in His fullness. Please pray for him also.

We continue to have many new cases of Covid among inmates as well as staff, but thankfully we are not doing anything about it except for a five-day quarantine after a positive test. On the Monday before leaving on Friday for the meeting I talked about above, I took my usual weekly test. On Wednesday morning at the breakfast table, I received a phone call from the Vineland health department informing me that my Monday test was positive. They then proceeded to outline my lifestyle for the next five days. I was to isolate myself from my wife (believe me—had I done so she would not have isolated herself from me!) I was to have no contact with her except while wearing a mask (have you tried a kiss through a mask yet?), etc., etc. I listened with no patience to spare until they were finished and then went immediately to the Urgent Care and asked to be tested. It was negative. I went from there directly to the prison and when I walked into HR, the secretary said without a moment of other greeting, "Chaplain Cawman, is there anything we can do for you before you leave?" I said, "Yes, there is; you can receive this negative test result from me." She took a look at it and said, "Go on back to work."

We still need prayer for the situation I have described to

you several times over the poor attendance at our religious services. We tried to just wait it out as we knew there were many moves being made, not only of inmates as they filled the prison back up, but of new officers coming in to replace the many retirements this year. But now that things are calming down a bit, it is only getting worse. The few inmates that show up complain that they haven't been there for weeks because the officers will not call the services out nor unlock their doors. This is coming from every quarter until we know it is the truth. It happens for anything related to the Christian or Catholic services, but not to the Islamic prayer time.

I am planning to write this situation up in detail and ask the other chaplains to sign their names to it and send it in, asking for a resolution. Please, please, pray that it will be heard with understanding and favor, and that we can again have all the men who want to come, be able to do so.

Meanwhile I keep telling the men that we are just experiencing what might well be the beginning of persecution for anything naming the name of Jesus Christ. They understand and are being patient, but it is not right and needs to be addressed.

Thank you so much for all of your prayers for us! I mean it!
—with Christian love,
William Cawman

8
God's Hand is Still Upon Us

October, 2022

Well, the DOC aka "Department of Change" continues to live up to its reputation. We now have a pretty sure hope that we can start up Sunday evening services again. The men have been begging for them ever since they were stopped. Until we are able to get a volunteer cleared to come in, we plan to have Sunday evenings at 5:30 for facilities one and three, then facility two as soon as we get enough help. I just sent in the October religious service schedule and calendars for approval, and provided they are cleared, we will start.

Along with it, we have had to comply with orders from Trenton to start allowing services for all other groups each week also. I can never remember having to do this except for the Jewish inmates and the Jehovah's Witnesses. Historically, we have always had a rabbi and a volunteer for the JW's so that we did not have to provide coverage for them, but we cannot get a rabbi to come in because no rabbi will agree to be vaccinated. I can't disagree with them, by the way.

Now, I am glad that I can report to you an answer to your prayers. I have written numbers of times about the difficulty we are having ever since Covid shut us down for a while, in getting the officers to call out the services and unlock the cell doors so that the men can come to our services. I also told you some months ago that I had sent a letter to the administrator regarding the involvement our church is having with ex-inmates, in order to be in the clear with it all. I asked for prayer for both.

Both were answered in one visit. For a while I thought that perhaps the administrator didn't think the involvement of our church significant, and all I heard was a phone call from her asking if I had sent the letter to anyone besides her; which I had not. After weeks went by, several inmates told me that the special investigations unit had interviewed them, asking what I was teaching and whether I was recruiting people for our church on the outside. Each of the inmates told me they had never known me to be recruiting for my church in any way. A couple of weeks later, I was summoned into the special investigations department and was set before a camera and recorder while they asked me questions regarding it. When they finished, they told me they were completely satisfied that there was nothing out of order and that the administrator would get back to me.

So next a meeting was set up with my supervisor, the superintendent over chaplaincy, myself and the administrator. They asked why I had sent the letter to the administrator instead of to my supervisor. I explained that I had done that for two reasons. Several years before I had talked about the issue with the assistant administrator and the superintendent, and they told me that they had absolutely no problem with what our church was doing, and that if anything developed further, I should simply tell the administrator. So I said I was just following those instructions. As to not telling my supervisor, I told them that it was not anything to do with chaplaincy or even with myself as a chaplain, but that the letter was from our church and I just happened to be the secretary who wrote it.

With that they told me that they saw nothing whatsoever out of order with the prison rules nor with my position as a chaplain.

The administrator then said that if there was anything else they could do to help us, they were behind us. So, with that open door, we presented the difficulty we were having with officers not calling out our services nor opening doors for the men to get out. Immediately the administrator and superintendent together said that they wanted us to give them a chance to straighten it out without it going up to Trenton. We knew that they knew that if it went to Trenton, it would not look good on their resumés. We agreed, and within a week our prayers were answered. The services were called out and the doors unlocked and our numbers multiplied wonderfully. It even affected the morale of the men to see that they were finally able to get out and come. After a couple of weeks like that, I wrote a note of thanks to the administrator and superintendent. Please help us pray now that this will continue.

Now for something better than politics, I want to thank you for your prayers for the man I have been writing about who is in such a struggle between the call of God and his addiction to K-2. Some have asked how the drug K-2 gets into the prison. It is possible to send a piece of paper the size of a postage stamp through the mail with enough of the drug on it to be very effective, and it seems there is nothing that will detect its presence. Anyway, the last visit I had with this dear man was encouraging beyond any yet. He seemed desperate to be really filled with God. If all he was feeling was a desire to get free from an addiction, I would not, I am sure, be feeling such a pull toward him, but he clearly and strongly manifests a real hunger to get completely right with God.

He told me that someone told him that if he would fast completely from food and water for three days, he would receive the Holy Spirit. He had done it and asked me if that was right. I told him that fasting, for him, was a very good thing just to regain control of his appetites, but that it would not give him the Holy Spirit. I told him that only by trusting completely in the Blood of Jesus, not in any works of his own, could he be filled with God. I then prayed with him and asked him to pray, and afterward he just hugged me with all his might and told me how much he really loved me. Now I want to see him love Jesus like that! Please keep praying for him.

Certainly, it is not God's will nor plan that a person struggles to come into rightness with Him, but if there has to be a struggle, let's pray that it will end in victory. Someone aptly said that it was not to Jacob's credit that he wrestled all night, but that he surrendered in the morning. In reading the life of Adam Clarke, it is painful to follow his intense and lengthy struggle to find peace with God. Years later, in reflecting back on this prolonged struggle, he commented that he was enabled because of it to help many other struggling souls. If that is the case, here is a man who, once he comes through to victory, would never give up on anyone else for sure!

God has been especially near lately in the Bible studies and services—especially the Bible studies. We are studying the Life of Christ, and we seldom get farther in one study than one incident in His life. What a pattern He is for us! The men get so excited and are so full of questions and comments that it is a thrill to teach them. And, guess what? The thrill is not coming from getting them to endorse some favorite platform or belief of mine, but it comes directly from pointing to the Lamb of God, who taketh away the sin of the world. The truth as it is in Jesus needs no explanation for it to make sense; it just does!

One man in particular, often sits looking at me with wonderment and an element of surprise, and then asks some question revealing former teachings of the doctrines of devils. As soon as we just simply allow the Bible to answer itself, his cloudy expression gives way to a smile of satisfaction. Oh my, I am getting blessed just thinking about him and others who are drinking in the truth. Actually, I would love to invite John

Calvin himself to come to our class and let the men point him to something so much better than the favorite doctrine of the father of lies!

We are still experiencing a lot of movement of men, and I don't know when or if it will settle down. This means that every week I have to pull up the rosters of men enrolled in services and move them to whatever facility they have gone to. This past week I had just finished this and gotten a number moved and then printed out the activity reports, when I went over to facility one and noticed a line of men with their belongings in their bags ready to go somewhere else. I guess it could be called "job security" for me at least.

And I can see this will continue at least for a while, because one whole tier which has been for several years a special needs unit is now empty waiting for new inmates from somewhere. All of the special needs inmates were sent to a prison further north, which meant that several people working with them as well as several inmates working there were put out of a job. One of the inmates who has worked with these men for years is really feeling the loss, not because it was a job, but because he really loved the men he was helping. He could be seen at all hours of the day, transporting wheel chair inmates, or helping them with other bodily needs, and he really loved these needy men.

He also has an evening assignment in the prison hospital, providing hospice care for the ones who need it. Let me tell you about one of them. I love to visit with this man. He is a paraplegic and is dying of cancer as well. Yet, when I just walk up beside him, I can feel a radiance coming from him. The last time I visited him, he was trying his best to hold in his deformed and mostly paralyzed hands, a plastic dish with what looked like boiled chicken chunks in it, and which I confess that I would have to have been almost starved to not want to throw them in the trash can. He looked up and started expressing such thanks for his food. Most of the men in that hospital have nothing good to say about it or about the care they get or don't get there, but not this man; never a word of complaint comes from him, but only praise to God. I immediately sense the Holy Spirit witnessing that he is my brother, and as I hold his deformed hand and pray with him, I love him without an effort. I sometimes wonder who will stand beside him on the great day of judgment! His smile on that day would quench just about any false claim or excuse for less than perfect love to God.

At the other end of the hallway, I find just the opposite oneness with another man. He declares with authority that these man-made viruses have gotten him where he is; then he tells me not to worry about the death of Queen Elizabeth, because she will rise up from the dead and carry on her work. He cannot hear what I say back to him, and so if I try to interrupt him (there is not a chance to say anything without interrupting) and pray for him, he doesn't even seem to hear it and just keeps on sharing his wisdom, happy for the chance and ear to do so.

So you might want to ask if the life of a chaplain is boring or same old, same old? Judge for yourself!

Please help us pray, now that we have more men able to come to our services, that God will descend with real revival power among us. As long as He tarries, there is still one more to harvest.

In love, William Cawman

November, 2022

IN ALL OF GOD'S wonderful ways of dealing with the children of men, He never runs out of methods to get through to them, does He? Let me tell you of one that is rather amusing. A man who left the prison on parole almost five years ago has kept in touch with us and comes to our church whenever it works for him to catch a ride for the two and one-half hour trip. He is a very interesting man who is capable of entertaining whoever cares to listen. Last month he made arrangements with his parole officer to go down to Kentucky for our fall convention. Everyone enjoyed having him there and he enjoyed himself immensely.

Just yesterday, he called and talked to our pastor and told him the following story: He said he really enjoyed being at the convention, but when he got home one of his rings was missing. He had no idea where it went, but right after that his other ring broke. Then he said that the bracelet on his arm fell off, and that it wasn't broken so there was no reason for it to fall off. When it did, he looked up and said, "All right, Lord, if You don't want me to wear those things I won't!" It reminded me of the song I heard as a teenager, the name of which was "The Hornet Song." One verse said, "He didn't make the people to go 'gainst their will; He just made them willing to go!"

Isn't it always best to leave souls in God's hands? He told us to be fishers of men. Too often, perhaps, we have been guilty of sitting in the comfort of our sanctuary and singing, "Bring them in; bring them in; bring them in from the fields of sin…" And then as soon as God does bring a soul in, we set in to clean the fish. God is expecting us to bring them in and let Him do the cleaning. This brother cannot blame anyone in the church for speaking to him, but he was willing to listen when God did.

I want to thank you again for praying for the situation we had a few weeks ago of the officers not letting the men out for our services. The administrator effectively changed the situation until now they are calling them out and we are having record numbers.

The other day we gathered for Bible study, but we never got to the study. God had something else for us that day, and what He has is always so much higher and richer than what we can provide. One of the men got up and said that he just needed to give a testimony. He began to thank God for the men being able to come together again, and then he began to just thank some of the brothers and tell them how much he loved them. As soon as he sat down, another got up and agreed with him in thanking God and the brothers for such a beautiful thing that they could once again come together like that to worship and fellowship.

It wasn't any time at all until God's presence was rich and deep, and I interspersed the testimonies with a few words of exhortation and encouragement wherever I felt the prompting to do so. The hour went by just like they do when you are in the presence of God. It was the best service I have been in in the prison for a long time.

The following week we did open the subject from the life of Christ: the subject being His discourse to Nicodemus on the new birth. We got no further than to open the subject when God settled down again and so anointed the subject of what it really means to be born again. There were questions and more questions, and the atmosphere became alive with the reality of salvation from sin.

Isn't it wonderful that if we let the Bible teach its own theology, we need not defend it or explain it? Every effort to reinvent or reinterpret the Words spoken by God ends in a dismal quagmire of contradiction to that very Word. But when the same Holy Spirit who inspired its writing is allowed to interpret it, it penetrates and seals itself to the inner consciousness of the whole of man's real need.

And without the Spirit of God dwelling within the heart, men become so warped in their spiritual thinking that it borders on the ridiculous. Let me give you a graphic example of it from just the other day. It was my turn to sit in for the Jews and Buddhists to have their weekly service. With shortage of staff, we just allow both groups into the chapel and let one group meet at one end and the other at the other end.

First came down a few Jews (or at least that is what they say they are) and I had taken their weekly allowance of grape juice and matza bread. Then came one man for the Buddhist service. He looked a bit bewildered and without any sense of direction as to what he was there for. He was the only one who responded to the call and he didn't seem to have a clue what to do. In a moment or two the Jewish inmates, thinking him to be another Jew, called to him to join with them, telling him they were all in this together. I watched as he sat down at the end of the row of them and began to munch on the matza bread and sip grape juice, and I gathered he did not have any idea of what it was all about. After a few minutes in which he had munched down a matza cracker and sipped some grape juice, a second man came down who has been practicing Buddhism for some time and spoke to him. He got up and deposited the rest of his cracker and juice in the waste can and went with the second man down to the other end of the chapel. Do you remember Jesus speaking of the blind leading the blind and both falling into the ditch? What a poor exchange for "…the path of the just is as the shining light, that shineth more and more unto the perfect day."

The man I have told you about from time to time who has had such a terrific struggle between conviction for sin and the chains of his drug habit has been much brighter the last couple times I have encountered him. I need to sit down with him again as soon as possible and give him some more encouragement to really seek a genuine deliverance from all sin and a genuine birth into the power to live above it. Please pray for him whenever he crosses your mind. He has known nothing whatsoever in his brief life except the dregs of back-alley sin and the pseudo cure of charismatic prophets.

Before you receive another letter, a man who has long embraced the doctrine of heart holiness will be released after thirty years in prison. He entered at the age of eighteen, never having been to church at all except perhaps a few Catholic ones, and so all he has known of church is what has been offered him in prison. He told me the other day that for a long time he has realized that the people who have come in from the holiness churches are the only ones he has any interest in following. I told him of another man who I had watched for over twenty years grow in grace and holiness, but that when he got out and started attending a holiness church, had experienced a growth spurt that was conspicuous and glorious. I told him that all he had known of church was prison church, and that he had always been surrounded by many who had no relationship with God at all, and that when he comes out and enters a church with a strong brotherhood of saints who unitedly love and obey God, he would feel much like he had entered heaven itself. He glowed and said he could not wait. Please pray that he will not listen to any other voice but will completely avail himself of the opportunity to become rooted and grounded in God.

I asked him where he would say he is in his spiritual walk. He smiled profusely and said, "I know I love God and just want more of Him!" I tried to warn him of the many who felt they had it settled to go with God until they met the hurricane cross winds of temptation to take a lesser way. He says he is aware of that and doesn't want to fail.

We have started Sunday evening services again in two of the three facilities and God has been blessing it. The Sunday services are all held at five-thirty, so that allows me to get back to our own church for the Sunday night service. We hope to have the other facility started by the first of December, but since the services are all at five-thirty, we need three chaplains or volunteers all at once. One volunteer is being allowed back in, so that should help, but please help us pray that starting these services again on Sundays will bring a revival down all through the prison. I would really love to be able to bring back the volunteers from our own church, but so far, all volunteers that come in must be fully vaccinated and have the latest boosters. Could you pray that this restriction or requirement would be lifted? The state is recognizing exemptions for staff, but not for volunteers.

On Wednesdays from eleven thirty to twelve thirty the chaplains meet for prayer and Bible study up in the second floor of the administration building. The two Muslim chaplains (we inherited another one from a prison that was closed) do not attend, but the Catholic chaplain and the supervisor and the three part time chaplains are usually always there. The other day the subject came up as to how to handle those who hate us. Of course, we looked at Jesus' example and instructions, and then the Catholic chaplain asked this question: "If there is someone in your life who is honestly just simply obnoxious and argumentative to the point where you really don't even want to be around them, is that hatred?"

He looked directly at me, and so I responded: "In Ephesians chapter four, we are instructed to be angry and sin not. The way we sin through the emotion of anger is when we allow Satan to move through that emotion instead of God. The same situation probably applies here; we cannot help it if a person is thusly obnoxious to the point we don't want to be around them, but we dare not allow Satan to use our distaste and dislike and disgust to generate a festering of ill-will toward that person." He seemed satisfied with that, and such is a sample of some of the things we reflect on during those times together. We have agreed that we will avoid theological arguments because we know we do not all agree on everything, but to be honest, the times together have been a very effective bonding as to a team effort to bring men to salvation.

Occasionally another staff member or two will come join us, but most of the time it is just the chaplains. We do not allow it to become a forum to discuss institutional issues or problems, but we try to keep it to spiritual matters. Occasionally also, one chaplain will just unburden something from his own inner struggles and we will pray for him.

I mentioned in another letter that one of the dentists who works in the prison is a Christian Jew. I have had several opportunities to take lunch with him, and he always opens up his hunger for more of God. I try my best to point him away from a stumbling Christian life to the better way, and I never find either resistance or unwillingness to listen. I would love to see him enter into the glorious life of holiness, so please help pray that he will seek until he is filled with the Spirit.

Please pray that whatever it takes, a fresh awakening to sin can sweep through the prison. The plague of the present generation is that none of them are sinners. The "doctrines of devils" (so named in God's Word) that have infiltrated the thinking of today's minds, have persuaded masses of totally unregenerate souls that they are Christians and that they are going to be just fine at the end of life. It is rare indeed to find anyone who admits to being a sinner. They will readily admit that they sin, but they have been persuaded that their continuing in sin does not render them a sinner. And all of this believing of a rank lie out of hell is so diametrically opposite to the teaching of God's own Word that will judge them on that great day. The Scripture clearly states, 1 John 3:8, "He that committeth sin is of the devil; for the devil sinneth from the beginning." How today's religious teachers can defiantly declare that they sin and remain Christians is very difficult to fathom, but it is being done so effectively that no one feels any longer that they will be lost. We need to pray, not only for those in prison, but for the world all about us, that we see a sweeping wave of old-fashioned conviction for sin. Thank you for your continued prayers!

With love for all, William Cawman

December, 2022

THE VERY FIRST DAY of this month started off with a heart-warming and unusual contact. The men had been asking for pocket New Testaments and so I went to our supply and took out several handfuls and took them to the chapel area before going to my office. When I entered the chapel, I noticed a Jewish man sitting there alone with his books spread out studying. I said "Good Morning" to him and proceeded to put the Bibles on the shelves.

He asked me, "Are you having a religious service here?"

I said, "No, I am just bringing some Bibles for distribution."
He said, "Are you a Christian?"
"I am."
"Have you ever read these words: 'We are troubled on every side, yet not distressed; we are perplexed, but not in despair; Persecuted, but not forsaken; cast down, but not destroyed?'"
"Yes, I have."
"Were they written by Paul?"
"Yes, they were."
"Was Paul a good man?"
"Indeed, he was a very good man."
"Did Paul actually write those words, or did someone say he said them?"
"No, he wrote those words himself."

He then proceeded to ask more questions regarding the authenticity of the Bible, and detecting a reaching man, I just sat down and began to listen to him. He then took his Yarmelke (Jewish skull cap) off and said, "I am a Christian; I believe in Jesus Christ." With that he began to open his heart and said to me, "This meeting was ordained of God."

I said, "Yes, I'm sure it was, and I can see that you are really wanting to know more about Him, aren't you?"

"Oh, I am; can I ask you some more questions?"

He is sixty-five years old, serving a life sentence for three murders thirty-three years ago. His father's family had Jewish roots; his mother was an Italian. He apparently knew nothing of religious substance until he began searching for truth in the prison system. He had just been moved to our prison from a northern one. He then closed his books and we talked for a while and he gave me some court documents pertaining to his case. I told him that I would not leave him alone in his search, but that I would put him on the appointment sheet very soon and we would talk and pray some more. He seemed very delighted with that prospect and then we had prayer together. Please pray for him as we will meet again soon.

When I mentioned this visit to my supervisor, he asked, "What was his name?" When I told him, he warned me to be careful as he said he has been a manipulator for many years. At first I thought, "Well, maybe I'd better not be too anxious to visit more with him." Then with more reflection I thought, "No, he needs God and truth no matter what his track record has been."

Another day I had a written request from a man who said he wanted to talk with a chaplain. When he came in, he told me that he was Jewish, but that he had not realized when he answered to classification that he should have told them that. His parents and grandparents were German Jews and he had been brought up in that, although he had not seriously practiced it. He said this was his first time in prison and that his mother was very anxious that he practice his Jewish faith and so he wanted to be enrolled in the Jewish services. But he had been told that he could only enroll in one faith and that he really wanted to learn more about Christianity. I told him that as of the last two years, the state allowed inmates to sign up for more than one faith, so I could enroll him in both. Even though he was Jewish, he had fathered two girls by a Methodist woman, and because of the difference in their beliefs they had never married.

After he was incarcerated in the county jail five years ago, the mother of his girls moved on and married someone else, so they never talk at all. But he does have contact with his daughters and since they are Methodists, he wants to know more about the New Testament so that he can help them. As I encouraged him to really seek God and truth instead of a belief system, he seemed very open and said he wanted to do that. I told him that sometimes God allows just such a blockade to come into a person's life to bring them to face truth and not lose their soul in hell. He agreed that he believed such was his case. I gave him a Bible and would ask you to pray for him as I continue to visit with him and trust God to open his heart.

We have brought back one volunteer couple who I have

met numbers of times before when they would come in before Covid. Because of that, we plan to open up Sunday services again in Facility Two also, making three services all at five thirty on Sunday nights. That, of course, will take three chaplains or volunteers. Would you please help pray that God will move the state to lift the vaccine mandates for volunteers until I can bring back some from our church?

Due to the fact that we have received a huge number of new inmates over the past few months, some of the classes are needing to start with the foundations of Bible teaching again. I asked a class that is mostly comprised of new inmates this question: "Do Christians continue to sin?" As nearly as I could tell, over half of the class responded readily that they do indeed. There is coming an awful day of reckoning for all the false prophets in our present age that are teaching such blasphemous contradictions to the clearly stated Word of God. One could wonder what they do with such Scriptures as 1 John 3:8,9: "He that committeth sin is of the devil; for the devil sinneth from the beginning. For this purpose the Son of God was manifested, that he might destroy the works of the devil. Whosoever is born of God doth not commit sin; for his seed remaineth in him: and he cannot sin, because he is born of God." But just as Satan distorted God's commandment into a lie to Adam and Eve, so he continues to contradict God's clearest statements down to this day.

We are still receiving influxes of new inmates as they close down other facilities in the State. It continues to add more men to our services which is good. However, as we are continuing a study of the life of Christ, those just coming in have missed all the discussions previously, so they have to try to pick up as best they can on what we are presently studying.

If you look in the back of a Thompson Chain Reference Bible, you will find a harmony of the Gospels which takes about four pages. That is the guide we are using, and we very seldom get to more than one number, or one event in the Life of Christ as there are so many lessons to learn from it. The men are really enjoying the discussions and are profiting from them.

In our prison hospital there is a sad case; a man who has been in prison for forty-some years and is dying of multiple diseases. He seems to be what would be labeled a "psychopath" in that he just takes it all without any show of emotion or concern. He just tells the chaplains that he is lying there waiting to die, but seems no more concerned about it than anything. It is hard to imagine facing eternity with no concern whatsoever. One certainly wonders what choices have been made back through life to bring one to such a state as that. What a shock it will be to pass directly from such a stupor to stand before the Great White Throne!

A man who was released two weeks ago plans to come to our church this coming Sunday night. His parents are being very protective of him, which is really not a bad thing at all, but they are not keeping him from church, and we are hoping they will come sooner or later too. Please pray for him and them.

Another one gets out in two more weeks and he also is very desirous to come. One of the men in the church has offered to give him a place to start out so that he can come. Please pray for him also. We have learned with a great degree of pain at times, how important it is for these men to get their feet down in God immediately after getting released. Satan stands at the door with a vengeance when a soul he thought he had shows signs of escaping his clutches.

My supervisor and I are planning, since Christmas is on Sunday this year, to have a service in each facility on Christmas Eve. We will each take a service at 8:30 Saturday morning on December 24, and then another one at 9:30. So between the two of us we can have a service in each area. I so much wish we could again bring visitors in for these services as we used to do and give the men a very nice Christmas; but vaccine restrictions are still preventing such from happening.

One of our officers suddenly died of a heart attack, which

for a short while made an impact on the other officers. But—do you remember how we used to hear so much about the Vampire Bats, which would fan their victims gently with their wings to lull them back to sleep if they detected any stir or awakening in them? What a description of Satan's deadliest weapon—complacency. I have experienced it in the physical many times. I have been driving and suddenly realized that I was drifting off to sleep. Rousing myself I would resolve that I had to guard against that at any cost, only to find the same thing happening again. Such is a very dangerous state physically, but how much more so spiritually!

None of you would envy our piano renditions for our services just now. I may be the only chaplain who even tries to have the men sing in the services, but we do have—thank God—some very good hymnals with many good songs that are very profitable for the men to learn. But our pianos!!! You see, when I first started holding services in the prison, they had provided us with three brand new, ebony, upright acoustic pianos. They were wonderful for a while, but after about four years they were getting very much out of tune. When they bought them, they immediately drilled holes down through the beautiful ebony finish and inserted large screws which they then covered with silicone caulking to prevent the inmates from getting at the strings, which they could use as weapons. So now, four years later, what do we do? To get a piano tuner in would take much red tape, so I sent a request up front saying that we would like to trade them out for digital pianos. They agreed, as long as I would get three bids on the digitals.

Well, as you can imagine, every piano dealer that I contacted was delighted to trade out the acoustic pianos for digital ones, so we ended up with three lovely pianos. At that time, we could also bring in volunteers to play them, and for many years this was a real asset to the worship services.

But that was twenty years ago, and by now two of the three pianos have a certain key that when struck goes off with thrice the volume of all the rest, which is very disconcerting to say the least. Besides that, we cannot use them unless there is an inmate who knows how to play. We did have one elderly man who played very well and very worshipfully, but he is now in our hospital awaiting his end. In one facility we have another who says he can play, but he needs to know ahead of time so that he can go over the songs, and even then it is painfully pathetic.

L. L. Hamline (Methodist bishop) tells of a service he was in where the pianist played very Biblically: they did not let their right hand know what their left hand was doing. Such is our present state of musical accompaniment, and I thought it not amiss to appraise you all of it so that you could send any sympathies you deem appropriate along to us.

I am pleased to tell you that with the retirement of many officers this past year, we have seen a remarkable change in attitude toward religious services. Whoever was spreading such negativity about us seems to have passed on, and custody has been very cooperative and friendly to our work among the men. I know some of you prayed about this, and so I want to report that God has answered those prayers. Thank you!

With love, William Cawman

9
NEW INMATES—SAME OLD PROBLEMS

January, 2023

A NOTHER YEAR? ALREADY? It hardly seems possible that time can be flying by so rapidly; but then we are getting closer to our great eternal Home. That is certainly a wonderful hope since this old world is not our home!

In the last letter I told you how that in facility three I am encountering a backwash of Calvinistic teachings among men who have just arrived in this prison. I have noticed for a long time, that whenever a person adopts this "doctrine of the devil," they soon become extremely unteachable. Such is not the nature of Christ at all. So, I asked our church to cover me with prayer and went back into the class. I told them that I was going to make some rules for our study. I said that we were not in this to argue theological differences. I told them about a very popular TV evangelist a few years ago who declared that he was so certain of his eternal reward that he would not be afraid to be found dead in the arms of a prostitute. I said, "Now if what he said is true, then let's just throw this Bible in the trash can and be done with it. What he said is a flat blasphemously contradiction to the written Word of God, for the Word declares: 'Know ye not that the unrighteous shall not inherit the kingdom of God? Be not deceived: neither fornicators, nor idolaters, nor adulterers, nor effeminate, nor abusers of themselves with mankind, Nor thieves, nor covetous, nor drunkards, nor revilers, nor extortioners, shall inherit the kingdom of God.'"

So I continued to say that between his statement and the truth of God's Word, there were many false teachings and errant theologies and that we were not in a forum to pit theology against theology, but that we were taking this class to get ready for heaven. I told them that if many people would search as diligently to find the grace to stop sinning as they do to find loopholes to continue in sin, they would be much better off. And then I told them that any doctrine that makes any allowance to continue in sin cannot be of God.

With that, we went on in our study of the Life of Christ with a much clearer atmosphere; so thank you to everyone who helped us pray about it. David said in Ps 119:128: "Therefore I esteem all thy precepts concerning all things to be right; and I hate every false way." I freely confess, I do too! I hate the doctrine of the devil. One of the favorite arguments they bring up is the fact that the Scripture says we "…are sealed unto the day of redemption." They have been taught that this means we can never be lost once we are saved. But did you notice the three dots in front of that statement? It would be best to read what the three dots replaced; the whole verse says: "And grieve not the holy Spirit of God, whereby ye are sealed unto the day of redemption." Instead of teaching that we cannot break the seal, the verse is warning us not to do it by grieving the Holy Spirit. Can't the devil twist and warp to his own advantage?

In the meantime, the Bible study in facility two is growing very refreshingly. The men are vibrantly taking in the truth and then I hear that they take it back and enjoy it among themselves on the tiers. I come away so refreshed by the eagerness with which they accept the truth and respond to it. I wish you could all sit in for a class or two and experience it with me. I don't know whether I or they enjoy it the most. What a difference between battling with Satan's false teachings and feeding hungry souls! I believe I understand at least a little bit of what Jesus said in His High Priestly Prayer; "For I have given unto them the words which thou gavest me; and they have received them…" When the one giving God's truth can feel it being received, that Word becomes rich beyond all description.

In our class Wednesday afternoon, December 21, our study was about the four men who brought the paralytic and let him down through the roof to Jesus. We never got half-way through all that is taught in that incident in Jesus' life. The subject of what kind of faith God recognizes took the time away and we were all ever so reluctant to close the class time when it was up. If there was any disharmony among the men, it was so overshadowed by those in accord with truth that it was not felt at all. Thank God! And thank you for praying for us.

But now I want to tell you about one of the men in facility three in particular. As he was vocally asking questions, he apologized and said, "I am not trying to argue, but I just want to know that I'm saved!" That struck a chord in my heart, and so after the class I said to him, "I am going to schedule a one-on-one visit with you about what you said in regards to knowing that you are saved." He said he really wanted that, so in a few days I put him on the visit list with plenty of time to work with him.

When he came in I asked him to tell me about his background. He seemed all too ready for that, and what a story he told me. His grandmother was a full-blood Lenape Indian, but at that time such a lineage carried a stigma that was uncomfortable, so he was actually raised by his aunt, though he did not find that out until he was grown. At a very young age he began to have serious thoughts about God, and though he was brought up a Catholic, he began to attend a Baptist church and gave his heart to the Lord at the age of thirteen.

Even though he often thought about God, and even though his life was spared many times by the hand of God, yet he wandered away, and because of false professions in "Christians," he finally turned his back on God and actually blasphemed publicly his anger toward Him. He then got into taking and selling drugs and drinking at a great rate. He stole cars and ran all over the eastern part of the country dealing with drugs and never once was stopped or caught.

He met a woman and lived with her for twenty-one years, but she finally had to put him out because of his life style. His aunt got him a hotel room and dumped him. He looked out his door and saw a beautiful girl standing outside looking very distressed. He opened the door and asked her if she needed help. She said she desperately needed some heroin. He had every other kind of drug, but not that, so he agreed to take her to where she could get it.

With that, they began living together and one and a half days later, he overdosed and passed out cold. The girl immediately took his gun, his drugs and sixteen thousand dollars from his pockets and then called for help and fled the scene. When he came to, his gun, his drugs, his money, his car, and hotel keys were gone as well as the girl. Then he received a text message from her telling him that she had it all and for him to come get her. He did and then told her he would like to marry her. They never did, but soon there was a child on the way, and he became very concerned over the safety of the child with all the drugs and alcohol she was taking. He tried to get them both to rehabs to get cleaned up, but when she got out, he found her with someone doing drugs like never before.

He yelled at her and began to fight with the one helping her. Then he ran out the door and when he went to go back in, he got the wrong door and walked in on another couple. That cost him his freedom and he is now paying the consequences. He said that the baby was born and is completely healthy and beautiful.

"Now," he said, "how can I help but give my life to God for saving me from all that could have happened?"

I listened quietly as he told his story and then I said to him, "There is no question but that God has spared you over and over for a reason, and now I want to address that statement you made in class that you wanted to know that you are saved. You are not going to know that by studying theology, but by obeying God and opening your heart to let Him come in and cast out all that sin. Then you will know by the witness He gives."

He said, "I appreciate that, but I don't agree that we can lose our salvation because the Bible says that we are sealed unto the day of redemption." With that I felt the familiar barrier rise up against hearing further truth.

I find more and more that the spirit that accompanies the endorsement of Calvinism is unteachable and resistant to all truth. Way back in the mid-fifteen hundreds, a young man by the name of Servetus wrote a book of his own theology, which itself was flawed with non-Scriptural errors, and to which all the reformers objected. When Calvin became acquainted with it, and Servetus desired to come to Geneva, Calvin said, "If ever he enters the city, he shall not leave it living, if I can prevent it." Servetus, aware of the danger, did come to Geneva, and on Oct. 27, 1553, Calvin had him burned at the stake. It would appear that such a spirit of intolerance of an enemy still inhabits those fully given over to this devilish doctrine.

Because of the futility of mere argument ever winning over those thus indoctrinated, I choose to simply present the truth and let it fall where it may. And so, after about an hour of visiting with this man, he thanked me for pointing him away from theology to a living relationship with Jesus Christ, but during the next class time, I could see he was feeling very contentious. At the close of the class, he came up and said, "I would like to talk with you again, but I will not be coming back to the class." The week before, when he hadn't come, there was a marked difference in the atmosphere, but when he returned, the evil spirit in the room came back with him. Pray for him; that's all we can do now.

There is another answer to your prayers that I want to tell you about. For quite a period of time, actually several years, we were encountering a growing animosity among the officers to our religious services. It became more and more conspicuous and I asked you to pray about it.

With all the retirements that took place during this year, we received a whole new influx of officers as well as two new captains, who replaced the ones we had. Before long there was a very obvious upswing in the morale and cooperation of nearly all custody. We are not struggling now with getting the classes and men called out, and the officers are totally cooperative with all we do.

On Wednesday, December 21, the administration put on a special food spread in the visit hall and invited the whole staff to come and eat. After our Chaplain prayer time, we went in to partake and both of the captains were standing there watching. I got my plate and sat down and then motioned to one of them to come over. He did so, and I said, "Could I just give you a bit of raw-boned truth?"

"Sure, lay it on me."

I said, "Ever since you captains have taken the helm of this prison, the morale of everyone has taken a definite turn for the better. I have worked here for twenty-five years, and I know what I'm talking about."

He said, "Well, thank you, I appreciate that. But I must tell you that both of us are short-term and we both retire in a few weeks. But we will do our best to leave a legacy behind."

I said, "I surely hope you do so, for it has been so refreshing." So, again, thank you all for praying this to pass, and please help us pray that whoever follows will have the same outlook.

On Saturday morning, December 24, my supervisor and I each took two facilities, one at 8:30 am and the next at 9:30, and held a Christmas Eve service for the men. We had a good turnout and I preached to them on the question, "What will you do with your Christmas Present?" I took it from the words of Pilate: "What shall I do then with Jesus, which is called Christ?" I pointed out to them that every soul that comes into the world will at some point in life be faced with the same question, even if they have never heard His name, for "That was the true Light, which lighteth every man that cometh into the world." (Jn. 1:9) I begged them to make the right choice and open their heart's door to let Him come in and take complete possession of them, and they would have the best Christmas they had ever known.

And so, another year with its victories, its rewards, as well as its many disappointments has now slipped into history, never to be changed. We look forward, trusting alone in the faithful Holy Spirit.

In Him, William Cawman

February, 2023

NEW YEAR'S SUNDAY WAS a very precious service in the facility of the prison where I was assigned. Two men, in turn, got up and simply poured their hearts out in fervent desire that the future would not be as the past. The first one is the man I have written about for some time, who has fought—and often lost—a fierce battle with drug addiction while still expressing a strong desire to know that he is truly born again. As he spoke, I could nearly have cried, for my heart just bled for him, still suffering under the binding chains of his captor. I honestly believe that a good number of the men present felt the heart cry just as intensely as I did.

Such are those whom the Great Physician came to heal! Years ago, God spoke those very words to my heart. I had gone to a homeless shelter in Philadelphia to ask if they would be interested in my bringing a youth group into their home to sing and speak to the women and children sheltered there. I looked around on the broken and shattered countenances made hard and old-looking, through sin's relentless wages. After receiving a very warm welcome to do so, I went out and opened the door of my truck and climbed behind the steering wheel. I looked up and asked, "Jesus, do You really want us to come in here to these hardened, broken lives?" I had no chance to go further before His sweet Voice said so clearly to me, "They that are whole need not a physician; but they that are sick." His Voice brought instant tears to my eyes.

Another scene I remember so well was an altar service in Guatemala. A twenty-some-year-old boy was kneeling behind the piano with a puddle of tears beneath him while his body was trembling with conviction. My heart was drawn over to him and while I leaned over the piano, the prayer that came out was "Oh Savior of the sin-sick soul, get at him!"

I tell you there is something sweetly precious about a seeking soul and a seeking Savior coming together. I so much want to see this young man let Jesus come into his heart with sin-stopping power. Please pray for him.

Let me share with you some of what a chaplain learns without enrolling for the education. On Thursday mornings at 9:00 –10:30, it falls my lot to sit in the room with the Odinists. I have nothing to do with it except to be ears in case something out of order is discussed. So this past week, they began a study of creation. They had a large full-color book with illustrations and the account. They passed the book around and each took a turn at reading. This is what I learned by what came through to me even while I was trying to read a book of my own. Way back in the beginning of all things, a huge white cow emerged from an iceberg in a sitting position and then gave birth to all of the Nordic gods. They grew rapidly by drinking of her milk, but then one of them died, so they took his eyeballs out and flung them into the heavens and they became stars. Another of them suffered frostbite in a big toe, so they cut the toe off and tossed it also into the sky making another star. Then the gods went to a huge Ash tree beside which was growing a huge Elm tree, and they transformed the Ash into a man and the Elm into a woman.

I went back to my supervisor and asked him if this was not labeled a correctional facility. He said it was so called. I then related that I had witnessed ten men, each with a brain in his head, studying such nonsense and wondered just how it might provide some correction to their former dysfunctions and crimes. He said, "It takes more faith to believe that than it does to believe the truth!"

Oh the insanity of the carnal mind. I could not believe that these men with any intelligence at all, could be acting so seriously as though they were learning the truth. Could I identify myself with the Psalmist when he said, "I hate every false way!?"

Thank you for praying for the troublesome class in facility three. The last few have been much better and the discord seems to have quieted down. Two of the troublemakers have quit coming and the one who just moved over there from my supervisor's Bible study in which he was also a troublemaker, came for the first time but was very cooperative, notwithstanding the track record he has developed. Whether he is just trying to get his feet down or not I do not know but will find out soon, I am sure. If he begins to present the same troublesome spirit, I will ask him to drop out. If he does not, I will remove him. The devil has no invitation to our services!

There is another man who has been coming for some time, who I have not fully figured out. He carries an air of criticism and a disgruntled countenance to a very conspicuous degree. He came into class this week and before we had hardly started, he said, "Chaplain, I've got to say something! I'm just plain angry! They don't even give me time to get a shower before it's time to come down here and I just don't like the way things are going around here."

With that I cut him short and began to exhort as to what a Christian's response to trials should be, but it didn't bring one bit of change to his disgusted countenance. Yet this same man can get up and sing a song and have the entire congregation clapping and exonerating him with loud amens! I've looked on and said, "Lord, I will not get my directions from congregational feedback, nor will I seek after it." Exuberant congregational feedback does not necessarily always indicate divine anointing.

Wednesday afternoon at 2:30, January 18, was a very special day for the Bible study in Facility Two. We were looking at the superiority of the Great Sacrifice over all that went before it and yet how it went back into all history and perfected those who had died in faith. God just came down among us and saturated the atmosphere with a spirit of worship and praise. I felt lifted out of myself and so did the twenty-seven men with me; at least it certainly seemed they were all in one accord. It was one of the most precious services I can ever remember in twenty-five years of prison ministry.

It was an up-to-date manifestation of Jesus' words: "And I, if I be lifted up from the earth, will draw all men unto me." Nothing in all the realm of the human can even begin to be compared to the Power that still flows from the riven side of Christ!

That morning, I had called down a man for a second visit, and this time he really opened his heart to me. He is very versed in Biblical truth and believes it too. He has been married for thirteen years and has six children, and it seemed a good marriage, but in spite of it, he repeatedly cheated on his wife. Finally, she began to step out on him, and now that he is in prison, she has invited the other man to live with her. He is so broken hearted that he has been seeing a psychiatrist to try to help with his deep depression. On top of his depression, he has been diagnosed after coming to prison with two leaking valves in his heart that are depriving him of sufficient oxygen, and the prison is offering no help with it.

As I began to listen and feel for his situation, I tried to divert his focus away from his sorrows and direct him to fling himself on Jesus for a complete change of heart. He seemed very earnest in wanting that, and promised he would seek first to be right with God, and then trust Him for his domestic disappointments. He told me that he has read his Bible over and over, and that he can see throughout it that God hates divorce, and that he has no intentions of disobeying God and going to hell.

I told him I would gather up some good reading material for him and then visit him again next week. He seemed ever so grateful for that. Oh the tangles that Satan can get a person into and then blind them to the only One who can untangle them. Please pray for him if he comes to your mind.

On Thursday, January 19, the main water line coming into the prison broke, causing a complete shutdown of all water for the whole prison. The following day it was still not repaired and so notice went out to all staff to only come in for a brief time to do what had to be done, but can you imagine the situation of 3500 inmates as well as officers trying to operate with no water?

On that same day, when I came out of the prison, the whole front of the prison was lined with white Suburbans with state tags on them. I enquired as to what was going on and was told that the detention center has become so corrupted with K2 that the nurses are refusing to even go there because of the polluted atmosphere; so they were getting ready to transport the guilty offenders somewhere else. Where they will take them is a good question when they are already in detention. Such are some of the problems of sinners trying to control sinners!

I am so happy to report that the week following the wonderful service in Facility Two Bible study, the aroma of the week before so lingered among the men that it just immediately resumed the same sacred atmosphere. I said to the men, "If you are wondering why God so honored us last week with His presence, it is because we were simply lifting up Jesus. Sometimes it is necessary to preach and teach on every subject covered by the Word of God, but when we focus on lifting up Jesus, heaven comes down to meet us." That's all it took! They began to lift up praise to Him again, and we had another sacred time together.

Well, now I have the answer to the paragraph before that one. I found out that indeed they had nowhere to take the rotten eggs, so they just put a bunch of dogs in there for the day to clean house, and then I found out that they are so overloaded with men that need to be in detention that they have set apart one tier of a housing unit where they will be locked into their cells also.

I think I have told you, but on Wednesdays from 11:30 to 12:30 we meet together as chaplains and pray for the institution and each other. The Muslim chaplains don't attend, but the Catholic one does and seems to be in wonderful harmony with the effort. This week one of the sergeants from custody came in after we had started and wanted to join us. Not knowing whether he would be called out at any time as he was on active duty, our supervisor asked me to pray for him. When I finished, he sat there for a moment and then shook himself and let out a "whew!" and then grabbed my arm and shook it. He said he really felt the prayer and that he is coming back next week and recruiting a few others to come. Please pray that God will be able to awaken numbers of the officers to their need.

I know I mentioned this in the last letter, but there has been a definite and conspicuously felt upward morale in the officers by and large. While a year ago, there was such a negativity among them toward us, now many of them greet us in passing with very favorable comments.

Do you remember the parable of the Sower as told by Jesus? Might I remind you that not one word ever spoken by Jesus was insignificant? The very first reason for seed not bearing fruit was that birds of prey came down and snatched the seed away. I have lost count of how many times my hopes for certain inmates have been soundly disappointed, not because of the old chains of sin and the allurements of the world, but because shallow churches with an attractive program have captivated them due to their undeveloped discernment. I believe I could say that only those who have left prison completely sanctified have stayed with the way of truth. Please help us pray!

William Cawman

┼┼┼

March, 2023

THANK YOU SO MUCH for your continuing prayers for us. God has been so near and precious in the Bible studies in Facility two. Last Wednesday our event in the life of Christ was His healing of the man with the withered hand, but I must tell you that we thoroughly enjoyed the hour of meditation and discussion about Jesus' teaching on His beautiful gift to us of the Sabbath, but never got the withered hand healed. We will have to have another session with the poor fellow next week. Aren't you so glad that Jesus is better at what He does than we are?

Notwithstanding our feeble attempts to portray the Almighty Power of Christ, He honors it with an overwhelming sense of His nearness and Presence. It seemed in that class that the thirty-some men were all in such harmony with the teaching that it makes it an absolute delight to be with them.

I would love to see the same level of accord take over in the Bible study in Facility three, but so far I would have to report that just as conspicuous as is the harmony of one study, the disharmony of the other is equally felt. It is largely the work of one man, who in the last letter I told you had moved from my supervisor's class into mine. On the first class, he was very vocal, but very cooperative; but I had a feeling deep inside that he was merely setting me up. When he is in the class there is a dark and oppressive atmosphere that surrounds him. His arguments are all in favor of his right to sin and still be a Christian. He is a perfect fit with the Pharisees and Sadducees who laid wait for Jesus to entangle Him in His words. He then goes back to the tier and sows discord among the inmates. There is an effervescence of demonic arrogance that repels my spirit just like the devil does. Please pray that God will intervene and either convict him of his wickedness or remove him from our study.

On a brighter note, I have now had about three visits with a man who seems to be really growing in the Lord. When I first met him, he was very distressed and yet very open about Bible truth. I gave him some booklets on holiness and he has been reading them and opening up to them. He told me that ever since we started visiting a peace has come into his heart that he did not have before. He feels his sins forgiven and he has a voracious appetite for the Word of God. He told me that along with the booklets I gave him, he picked one up in the chapel by James Gills, a man who floods the prison with his new age books. He said that he would read back and forth and that the one by Gills was so incoherent and confusing and the one from the holiness writer was so clear that he threw the Gills book into the trash so that it wouldn't confuse anyone else.

Then he asked me for more of the writings of John Wesley, which I will be most glad to give him. And yet with all of that, he says that he can only read anything other than the Bible without wanting to get back to it. I told him I saw no problem with that at all, and then told him about the old grandma living away out on the prairie by herself. Some travelers through the area just happened on to her and discovered how much she loved her Bible. They told someone else about her and so they too went for a visit. After several others stopped in and found themselves so refreshed by grandma's love of God and His Word, they got together and bought her a big set of commentaries, so that she could enjoy her study all the more. After some time, again someone was passing through and stopped to visit grandma. They asked her how she liked the commentaries. "Oh, children," she exclaimed, "they are wonderful! I have been really enjoying reading them. The only thing is, I find a lot of things in them that I can't understand; but when that happens, I just go to the Bible and it straightens them right out!" He liked that story. Please pray that he will soon find the fullness of the Spirit, as he is definitely wanting all God has for him.

Now a week later I need to tell you with joy that we got the withered hand healed! At first it seemed we would not even get there this week, as the preliminary scenes to it were bringing up so much discussion. But after a while we felt the way clear to get back to the dear fellow with the withered arm. We observed the fact that when Jesus told the man to stretch out his hand, he could have looked Jesus right in the eye and said with all honesty, "I can't." The fact of the matter was, he couldn't; he never had. But instead, he stretched it out! We then attacked the modern philosophy that says "there is nothing we have to do to be saved; Jesus did it all." This man, in the very face of "I can't," did it. He willed to obey and the healing power of God accompanied his willful act. We compared it with several other cases in the Scripture where faith was given when obedience was complete. I gave them my own testimony as to how many years I struggled to sanctify myself, but how, when I simply and lovingly obeyed God, He fulfilled His promise.

Again, God really visited His truth with His conscious presence, and the time was up all too soon again.

This past Sunday night I had largely this same group for the worship service. I preached to them from Proverbs about six things, yes seven, that God hates. I named out and described a number of the traits of the carnal nature, letting them know that it was far below the heritage Jesus purchased for us to allow them to continue to disturb us all our days. I do believe God is speaking to this group of men clearly and that they are listening. Please continue to pray for them.

Let me relate something outside of the prison to illustrate

something else I want to tell you. Several years ago, I was scheduled to hold two revival meetings in two different churches, back-to-back. One of the churches would have seating capacity for probably four hundred and fifty, the other one two hundred and fifty. Both of them had about twenty-five people and in one of them the sparse congregation all occupied the very back seats of the church. In that one, the Sunday School superintendent only appeared on Sunday morning; for no other service. After all, I guess he wasn't needed except for his one-day-in-seven function.

In both of these meetings, which by the way were both labeled "revivals," the atmosphere was so stifling and dead that there was nothing to revive. There must, of necessity, be some remnant of life if there is any hope of reviving it. I remember calling home to my own pastor and asking him to pray for me as I felt the smothering atmosphere even affecting my own prayer closet.

I went directly from these two meetings to a mission field in Guatemala. A group of pastors gathered in and before even one message had been preached, a dear national with arms waving started up the center aisle just running over with glowing victory. He had just been through a deep dark valley with the loss of his precious wife, and on top of that had actually been attacked on the streets by a gang who knocked him completely down, but he was manifesting that which Jesus promised He had come to give—life, and life more abundantly.

In that same meeting one morning there was such a weight of Divine worship that all heaven came down around the Mercy Seat. It was so precious that I was just standing to one side reveling in it, when the Spirit gently whispered, "All right, son, just soak this up and then go back up north and be faithful!"

This describes exactly the difference in the present Bible study on Wednesday mornings from the one on Thursday mornings. I am quite sure it has nothing to do with the day of the week! It is the difference between hungry obedient hearts and dull ears. I could deliver the same message in both places and experience two totally opposite atmospheres and acceptance. But then, Jesus found the same thing as He went from place to place also.

For three weeks in a row, I have filled in for my supervisor's Bible study as he has been on vacation. That group is different yet. A lot of them have been moved here from other prisons that have shut down, and as they listen to me teach them, I can sense that they are hearing truths that are new to them, and consequently there is a difference in their responses from either of the other two.

But now a question arises. Is every single heart in the Wednesday study fully right with God and in perfect harmony with His Word? Absolutely not. Is every single heart in the Thursday study dull and non-receptive to the voice of God? Absolutely not. So it goes to show what an influence goes out from each of us; affecting those around us far more than we are aware of. Even a few hearts aflame with hunger for God can claim the atmosphere for Him, and just a few who are at enmity with God and truth can spread a fire-extinguisher over a whole service. In fact, the Bible actually says, "…one sinner destroyeth much good." A dear old sister years ago had nowhere to attend church except a very cold and formal one. Someone asked her how she kept alive spiritually in such a church and she told them that she would go to her pew and get down on her knees and pray a warm circle all around her, and then get up and sit down right in the middle of it and worship the Lord.

The Department of Corrections is finally taking steps to restore some normality after all of the Covid restrictions, and I am hoping and praying that they will soon lift the vaccine requirement for volunteers to come in. Many Sunday nights one or more of the facilities cannot have their worship service because of not enough chaplains or volunteers to cover them. Please help us in prayer for this need.

Just a little side note about the prison. In March of 2011, I had an all-day layover in Paris, France, and so I made a tour of several buildings there. I spent a couple of hours admiring and walking through Notre Dame, a fabulous piece of architecture which took two hundred years to build from 1100 to 1300. They had no electricity, no steam power, no dynamite, or anything else except hammers and chisels and it was just as sound in 2011 as in 1300. The prison I labor in was finished in 1998, the same year I started working in it, and it is falling apart everywhere. The door frames are rusting away, the pre-cast concrete walls are leaning and separating in the corners, the ceilings are sagging, the roof leaks and the sound systems are nearly all broken. Please understand, I'm not complaining; just explaining!

One of our Bible Colleges (let me remind you again that I am not allowed to give any names in these letters as per the state of NJ rules) gave me a box full of good holiness books to give to men wanting them in the prison with the promise of more as we can use them. What a blessing it will be for sure, as most everything sent in by publisher overruns, etc., is new age garbage. I honestly cannot even begin to understand what would inspire a person to write so many books on nonsense such as how to save yourself. It is just as far off base as is the bizarre trash I hear taught in the Odinist services. Christianity without Christ is more worthless than anything else in the world, I do believe.

We will soon be coming up to one of the brightest seasons of our Christian year, the Resurrection Day of Christ. We generally have special services on Good Friday, but also now that we are having services on Sunday evenings, I am looking forward to a visitation from God. Please pray that it will prove a season where the Blood that was shed for our sins, and for the cleansing of our hearts, and then the Resurrection Power that Peter felt after his long dark night will be felt by many. "Blessed be the God and Father of our Lord Jesus Christ, which according to his abundant mercy hath begotten us again unto a lively hope by the resurrection of Jesus Christ from the dead, To an inheritance incorruptible, and undefiled, and that fadeth not away, reserved in heaven for you…" Please give it again, Lord!

William Cawman

10
"How Forceful are Right Words"

April, 2023

First of all, in this letter I want to share part of a letter I just received from a man that I have written to you about from years past. If you can remember back around November of 2015, I wrote of a Colombian man who was awakened to his need, prayed through to a wonderful case of salvation, and then six weeks later discovered a deeper need and sought and found a full cleansing in the Blood of Jesus. He then enrolled in classes from one of our Bible colleges and finished a four-year course in two years. After that he was sent to a prison farther north in the state, and every once in a while, he sends me a letter of updated victory in Jesus.

This letter is dated March 4, and I will share a good portion of it with you:

> May the blessing of the Lord increase on your ministry and life. I see them everywhere; an apple here, a smile there, a new soul longing for deeper closeness to God, a man going under the water, my job teaching others, listening to the Word as it teaches me. I no longer feel the weight of decades of imprisonment because "If the Son therefore shall make you free, ye shall be free

indeed." Many people, dearest Reverend, and you know this well working in a carceral setting, live in compounded prisons of their own making. The fence and razor wire are the most innocuous of the barriers that imprison people. Deep in the heart, sin shackles people with more chains than they can handle. Ah! If there was someone who could break them?

It's been over seven years since the Lord broke my chains, and every day I marvel at the grace that was willing to reach me while I was yet a sinner and at active war against God. While my interior life tells a story, my public life in ministry and in the church has a different one. When the Lord said, "In the world ye shall have tribulation..." I never expected it to come from within the Body. I may have shared with you years ago that the first time I brought a message, on Numbers 21: 16-18 where the princes of Israel obey God and dig a well in the middle of the desert, with the idea of teaching about the need to have the well full of clean water before anyone could drink. What did I say? From that day, brothers I thought were brothers turned against me with a viciousness I have only seen in the world. Since that day, I have fended attack upon attack, but by God's grace I remain unmoved. I have learned firsthand how the evil one opposes the biblical message from within the church just as he does from without.

It breaks my heart, rather than getting angry, I realize that when Paul spoke that "the natural man receiveth not the things of the Spirit of God... because they are spiritually discerned," he was not solely speaking about the natural man in the world, but addressing also the natural man within the church. Going to church does not mean a person can discern the things of the Spirit. The only solution I can foresee to this problem of spiritual dullness is to practice knee-ology. Only God can do the work and He encourages us to ask Him for what we need.

...I get a sense that the holiness movement is a lone voice, a little flame struggling against the wind. Thank God that the flame of the Spirit is something the evil one cannot quench. We can quench it, but he can't.

I am well, strong in the Spirit, and I have been busy with ministry and study. On study, rather than reporting on accomplishments, all I have to say is that I have yet to find a Bible College that actually preaches what the Bible teaches about the Baptism with the Holy Spirit. Instead of discovering good Bible interpreters, I discovered that Satan was the first to attempt Bible interpretation: "Hath God said?" (Gen 3:1) Although I have earned a few degrees, my learning has come from the Bible itself. Now I understand why some ministers are dying by degrees.

(Note: he is definitely referring to any Bible colleges he is finding where he is, rather than the one he completed a course from.)

I still have close to three years before I am sent back to Colombia. I see the end of this road, but at the same time I only plan for what I have here and now. The needs of this church behind the walls are too great. This week we received close to 100 people from Southwoods and Northern State, many with gang affiliations. Thank God for sending them here. I have already organized fishing expeditions in the mess-hall to invite them to church. While here and there I still have the privilege of preaching, I have found that one-to-one relationships have more effect on many people. I learned that through your own effort to disciple me through personal interaction. While I can sadly affirm that the church here is far away from the standards of the Word, there are people in the church giving testimony with their life of the sanctifying power of the Spirit. We have a brother form Korea who is a delight in testimony. Nothing can take away his joy, and when asked he immediately points to the Spirit as sanctifier. A man from Uganda is an example of a man of prayer. He too, points to the Spirit as the Ultimate solution to sin. I rely a lot on his faithfulness to prayer to encourage my own. Then we have an almost invisible group—to the eyes of many—of very simple people who live a life in the Spirit with great humility. I see God doing wonderful things in them, but many dismiss them as that, simple people. "But God hath chosen the foolish things of the world [myself included] to confound the wise."

I have been called to greater responsibilities in the church and I intend to serve with honor and faithfulness to God. I do foresee problems because people do not like hearing about sin, but by God's grace, I will rely on His wisdom to be able to teach to hostile ears.

…Please extend my love to the holiness church and know that I have not stopped praying for the Malawi mission. Profoundly grateful for the love you extended and extend to me, and because of Him.

It is rather heart-warming to think that we have, through your prayers and the grace of God, not only men scattered here and there who are holding faithful to the God they have found, but we also have a few missionaries to other parts of the world. Several years ago, there was a man from Sierra Leone in the prison, and he really got saved and was walking in the light. He was a very quiet man, yet there was a glow about him that was unmistakable. After some time, I called him in for a visit. I began to enquire as to just where he was with the Lord and I asked him if he knew from experience what we were teaching about a sinful nature that remains in us after we are saved. He immediately said, "Oh yes, I know that." I then asked him if he ever felt any of those uprisings of sin now, and he said very definitely that he did not. Shortly thereafter, he was released and deported back to Sierra Leone. We had talked about it before he left and he was looking forward to being with his family again and telling them about the Lord. After he arrived there, he tried several times to call me on the phone, but each time we got no further than our greeting and the call cut off. I don't know what the problem was, but I had no number to call him back. I trust he is still living for Jesus there and being a missionary to those around him.

Now, I have a very wonderful answer to your prayers to tell you about. You have been praying that the vaccine mandate would be lifted so that we could get our volunteers back into the prison to help with the services. When I returned from a meeting on March 28 and went into the prison, I got as far as the check station in facility two and was told that the administration area where my supervisor's office is was closed as a crime scene. They said I could go on to my office and that my supervisor was there also. I went down and he was glad to see me and so we sat down to talk. He said, "Well, do you want the good news or the bad news first?" I told him to just bring it on, so he told me that the good news is that they have lifted the vaccine mandate for volunteers and so for me to get him a list of those I wanted from our church.

Then he told me the bad news that while I was gone there was much interference with the religious services to the point the man from the capital had to come down to look into it. Please pray that this will get straightened out. As to the crime scene, a 300+ pound Muslim man had attacked a female officer in the medical area and they had to send her out to the hospital. Then the officers attacked the inmate and he had to be sent to a specialized hospital as he was so beaten up. So prison life goes on!

Thank you for all your prayers,

William Cawman

May, 2023

THANK YOU EACH ONE again for your faithful prayers for us. God has been helping us and we are so thankful for it. We had both Good Friday and Easter services in each of the facilities and they were blessed of God. For Good Friday I traced the sacrificial lamb from the first Passover through to the Lamb of God, and it was precious. Then on Easter Sunday I preached from the thought that God keeps His appointments. I started with the appointment Jesus made with His disciples in which He told them that after He was risen from the dead, He would meet them in Galilee. Even though His death lay between the promise and its fulfillment, He kept the appointment. I then reminded them that He has made an appointment with each one of them: "There I will meet with thee, and I will commune with thee…" Then I spoke of the final appointment He has made that He is coming again. There was such an enthusiastic response from them through it all.

I don't want to sound discouraged by what I need to relate to you, but a situation has grown astronomically worse in the last little while. When I first started ministering here in the prison twenty-five years ago, it was relatively infrequent to find drugs among the prison population. A few days ago, the assistant administrator was in my supervisor's office with him and myself, and really vented his frustrations over what they are going through. The most common drug now flooding the prison is K2, which is very difficult, almost impossible, to detect. It can be sent in or brought in, in significant quantity to give a person a high, on just a sheet of paper, and is almost impossible to discern. They have largely started making copies of any incoming mail so that what is sent in that way will not reach the inmates, but no matter how they try, we are saturated with it. The detention center (hole) is so filled with the smoke that no civilians want to go over there.

The superintendent said that they bring in teams of dogs to sniff it out and clean it up and five days later the place is full of it again. It is sad but known that officers can make good money by acting as the go-between to get it to the inmates. So, while it used to be only occasionally that they had to deal with someone using it, now it is simply out of control.

An inmate that I have tried to work with for maybe two years or more is one of the victims. In previous letters I have even requested prayer for him. He pulls my heart out with his battle between his hunger to really get right with God and his addiction to this awful drug, The other day I had put him on the schedule for a visit, and when he came in, he was obviously bombed out. I asked him how he was doing, and he said, "Chaplain, I just came down to tell you ... " then he just sat there for a long while. I finally asked, "What is it that you need to tell me?"

"Chaplain, I think it's over with. I'm hopeless. I think it's just downhill from now."

I asked him if he was using K2 and he said, "I just took it before I came down here." I asked him how often he took it and he said that he takes it all day, every day. I said, "Do you want me to give up on you?"

"Oh no, please don't give up on me." I said, "God won't give up on you either, but you are going to have to do your part and say no to this even if you think you will die. Eternity is coming up very soon, and you don't want to spend it in hell, do you?"

"Oh, no, I don't, and I know I will if I overdose on this stuff."

I had no choice but to report it to the sergeant, who asked me to write it up as a report. I did so, and not long after the visit, they called him down and did a urine test and searched his cell and found nothing. That is how difficult this deadly drug is to stop.

My heart aches for this dear man. He is like a son to me for the feelings I have to see him set free and happy in God, but I can't save him, no matter how I would love to. He loves me too, and wants me to keep visiting him.

That same day I visited with a man that mental health requested me to see. He sat before me with tears, telling how empty and upset his life is. He had been on mental health drugs for some time, but thought he could rid himself of them and so quit. Now, four months later, he is almost suicidal, and he said that no one wants to listen to him and get him back on the drug again. Then his grandmother just died, leaving even more of a hole in his life,

I asked him if he had any faith in God, and he said he did. I urged him to really open his heart and pray to God and ask Him to come in and bring a peace that no person or drug could give him. He seemed to understand that such is what he should do, but then would again lapse back into his need for medication. I told him I would see him again in a day or two and urged him to really pray believingly to God.

Then the same day I had another visit with the man I have written about who really seemed to understand the Scriptural teaching on holiness and was seeking it. He came in, obviously discouraged and distracted by the things his wife is doing, perhaps to spite him for what he has done. I listened to him unload all of his frustrations and then I faced him with the fact that Satan was winning the battle in his life to get him so caught up in attitudes and problems at home that he has gotten his eyes off of what really matters most-his complete conformity to Jesus Christ. He admitted it, and I hope and pray that he will turn back again to really seeking the Lord.

I told him that if he turns away from seeking and finding heart holiness, none of the other issues in his life will come out right either, but that if he will really seek first to be fully God's, that would unlock God's arm to move in behalf of all the rest of life's complexities. Please pray for him too.

I am so thankful that not every day seems as discouraging as that one did.

Please also continue to pray with us that the volunteers from our church will be reinstated quickly. We really need help with the Sunday services in particular.

We have a number more of the officers who will be retiring this summer, and the State has not made recruiting new officers attractive enough to nearly replace them, so it is soon going to be a real shortage of custody, which in turn affects our religious services. One bright spot, however, is that the administrator has really clamped down on the officers who do not call out the services or unlock the doors for the men to attend. Thank God and your prayers for that!

The Bible study in Facility Two continues to be such an inspiration as we are now studying the Sermon on the Mount. No sermon past or present can begin to compare with that one. The men are getting much good instruction from it.

We have seen God working even among the staff who are not part of chaplaincy. One mental health worker has never seemed friendly at all toward us, and even appeared deliberately to ignore us. The other day she came to my supervisor's office while I was talking to him and told us that there was a young man in the hallway that wanted a chaplain to pray with him. My supervisor told her to send him down to the room I had been using and that I would be right down to pray with him. He had lost a family member and was deeply struggling with his emotions. I talked and prayed with him and then my supervisor did the same. I plan to follow up the visit tomorrow. The woman who told us has seemed very friendly ever since.

And then a woman who is the supervisor of social services is really changing too. She has claimed to be an atheist, but her grandfather who raised her was dying. She asked one of the other chaplains if we still meet together for prayer and he assured her that we do and that we would be doing so in just a few minutes. She asked that we pray for him. We did, and later she came down to the office and thanked us. In a few days we got word that he passed away at the age of ninety-four. I met her and gave my condolences which she really seemed to appreciate and we assured her we would continue to pray for her. She thanked us for it.

We cannot always see what God is doing behind obvious exteriors to soften hearts toward Him, but every once in a while it is reassuring to see that He is not leaving a single soul untouched. We have been in revival services in our church, and one night the evangelist preached a wonderful message on "Prevenient Grace;" that Light that shines into every heart even before the grace of salvation is given. Certainly, here are two examples of that very thing. Thank God for it!

On my way into prison Thursday morning, April 27, an officer that I have known and worked with for years was on his way out to be retired. I wondered for a moment what all the commotion around him was about until I noticed that his officer uniform shirt was torn to shreds and hanging out. As he passed me he shook my hand and thanked me and told me to keep up the good work. I thanked him as well and wished him a new retirement shirt!

We have now had enough requests that we are having to start up a service each week in all three facilities for both the Jehovah Witnesses and the Christian Science. Fortunately, there is a volunteer for each group who is willing to come in to teach them, so I had to figure out an evening slot for each service, but we won't have to do anything other than that. I cannot begin to grasp what attracts people to any other religion than the true one. And someday soon, everything except being completely right with Jesus Christ will meet with severe disappointment.

In case you might well wonder, I do not bow or bend, or even try to dodge the issues that are such hot topics in today's circles of all this WOKE philosophy, or whatever it might be called. I clearly preach the teachings of God's Word without any apology, and thus far I have had nothing except appreciation from the men in my classes.

I know that many of you are praying for us, and I would like to renew the request that we could see a genuine revival of conviction for sin and some definite new births. Anything other than that will fail to keep my heart going back, after twenty-five years of this. I believe God still has work that He wants to accomplish and it will only be done in answer to prayer.

With love and appreciation,

William Cawman

June, 2023

IT IS ONLY MID-May, but there are so many things happening that I don't want to forget to tell you if I wait until the end of the month, that I will start now while they are fresh on my mind. I may as well start by telling you what I told the other chaplains during our latest weekly prayer time. Our supervisor had suggested that after many weeks of praying for others, we just go around the circle and pray for ourselves. The Catholic chaplain started with a few requests, one of which was that his sixty-five-year-old brother-in-law had just dropped dead of a heart attack. The supervisor asked me to pray for him. I was on the other end of the circle from where we started and after one of the other part-time chaplains had announced that he would probably be leaving us in September, I told them that my time in the prison wasn't up to me. I hadn't started this and it was not up to me to end it, but I was just leaving it in God's hands. My supervisor immediately said, "Good," and one of the chaplains said he would like to pray for me, but my supervisor said, "No, I want to pray for him." The following day he really thanked me for not planning to leave them yet. It was a very heart-warming time of praying for each other so I will just tell you as well as them that I am not in charge of when my days in prison will be over.

In the last letter I told you of a man that a mental health worker had asked us to pray for. I have visited with him three times now, and will definitely continue to do so. Yesterday, he began to tell me of all the things that are troubling him as to family, his sentence, his cell block atmosphere simply soaked with drug smoke, etc. He is forty years old, served in the military and while in Germany, married a woman and had a son. She divorced him when he returned home and he married again and had another son who is now about five years old. After listening to all he had to say, I said, "Now, let's look at this through some other door than through your torn-apart emotions. Would I be right to assume that had you not come to prison, you would have gone right on in your efforts to live for your own desires and end up in hell for all eternity?"

He immediately answered, "I'd without a doubt have been dead, the way I was going."

"Then," I said, "Why don't you start thanking God for the rough hand of mercy that stopped you and gave you a chance to turn around and get this life and the next in order?" He readily agreed and admitted it all to be true. I told him I would not leave him alone, but would be praying for him and seeing him and expecting a miracle of inward transformation. Please help me pray for him. He is right in mid-life and the last half can be so different than Satan had in mind for him.

And then I told you in the last letter about the man I have worked with for years who came down to see me all stoved up with drugs and that I reported it to the sergeant. They found nothing in his urine and sent him back to his cell. Yesterday I had put him on the list for another visit and he came. He was alert and friendly, but told me that he had been tested for drugs. He said that someone had told on him that he was using. I said, "Really?" Then he said, "Why did you turn me in?" I said, "Were you drugged up when you visited me last?"

"Chaplain, I was trashed!"

I said, "Don't you know that I am required to report things like that?"

"Oh, really?"

"Yes, and now let me ask you, 'Have you taken it since?'"

"No!"

"Well then, see it helped you; now stay away from it. Listen, I love you just like a son and I loved my son enough to give him a few whippings."

With a big smile he said, "I don't need any more of them."

Now do you see how difficult it is to control this awful drug? Three hours after taking it, no trace of it was evident. It is no wonder that the prison is just saturated with it. I talked to the sergeant next to my office and he said that it is almost impossible to know what all they are smoking: bug spray, hair spray, K2 and now K3, marijuana, and all kinds of things.

That same day I had another visit with the man I have been so eager to see really seek a pure heart, as he does understand what it is all about. But again, Satan has been distracting him from the goal by making things even more tumultuous with his wife at home. I did my best, I hope, to try to alarm him as to what Satan was doing to him, and how it would make the difference for all eternity if he continues to let Satan distract him. Please pray for him.

God has been helping us in the Bible studies, but there is a Scripture that is being played out in living drama. It is this: Ec. 9:18 "Wisdom is better than weapons of war: but one sinner destroyeth much good." I have mentioned before the man who is actually possessed with a demon of Calvinism. After I took him off of the Bible study list because of the dissension he was causing, he would not even look at me when he came to a Sunday night service. My supervisor said he did the same to him. When he was in my supervisor's Bible study, he created such a disturbing atmosphere that my supervisor was relieved to see him moved. But—he ended up in mine! After he left my supervisor's Bible study, the numbers grew by leaps and bounds, until now he needs a larger room. Since he was in mine and is still in that facility, my Bible study has lost nearly a third of those who were attending. He is definitely accomplishing Satan's agenda— "…one sinner destroyeth much good." Please pray for us that such hindrances as this can be either removed or brought under conviction and changed. Perhaps this is simply a repeat of what Paul faced when he said: "Alexander the coppersmith did me much evil: the Lord reward him according to his works: Of whom be thou ware also; for he hath greatly withstood our words."

The next time I had the Sunday service in that facility, I was looking over the list after the officer checks the names off as they enter, and his name was checked off, but he was not in the service. I would strongly suspicion that after his name was checked and he came in the door and saw me there, he turned and went back out. He at least is saving me from the curse that Jesus spoke of: "Woe unto you, when all men shall speak well of you!" My wife says that her grandfather said that no one is good for nothing. Some people are good examples of a poor example.

But getting back to the Bibles studies, the other one of my Bible studies is a delight to teach, as the men are so eager and in harmony with the truth.

I had another visit with the man I mentioned above who while in the military married a German girl and then she divorced him when the army sent him back here. I have seen a remarkable change in this man in the last three or four visits. It was a mental health worker who asked that I pray with him, and I found him distressed to tears and almost suicidal with grief over how his life had gone and all of the troubles it was bringing him. But last Wednesday he told me with a bright and gleaming countenance that he was finding such help as he never had by his visits with me. He knows enough of Scripture to follow the admonitions I give him as to the real cure for all that is wrong in his life. I am not sure if he is yet genuinely born again, but he is definitely changed, and I long to see him go all the way with God into a pure heart.

And then there has been a second man that mental health referred to us and I am also seeing a drastic change in him. He is physically a rather alarming sight to look at because his face and arms are tattooed with all kinds of symbols of his previous life. I have not asked him what they all mean, but it is certainly nothing good. He told me that God is really helping him in prayer and in reading the Bible, and that he really wants to leave all of the old life of sin behind. But he says that people naturally shun him because of his symbolic tattoos and he wishes he didn't have them. I told him to go to Jesus and ask Him to fill his heart with His love and peace and joy and then

Jesus would shine right out through them. He seemed very relieved over that prospect.

Let me give you a comparison that might describe my feelings toward men like this. Across the country I have seen several billboards picturing a military veteran whose face is horribly disfigured and his limbs missing. When I see that billboard, it almost makes me cry. I would really love to find that veteran and put my arms around him and thank him for all he has suffered for my freedom. I really would love to do that. This is the way my heart feels toward a man that Satan has marred and marked like this man.

And so I said to this man, "Just seek for a deep and real relationship with Jesus, and then whenever Satan tries to taunt you over those tattoos, just tell him that it is his fault you have them, so just be gone because you no longer belong to him." How his face brightened with this!

But that same day, I believe it was, I learned that one of the brightest Christians in the prison had been sent to another one. You would have read about this man back across a number of years. He is one of the ones that took the four-year course in Holiness Theology that the president of one of our Bible Schools came in and taught. He did well in it and has lived a shining example of true holiness for years. He is now just a couple of years short of completing his sentence and they moved him up north to a program that is designed to help men reenter society more effectively.

At first I was surprised, then somewhat disappointed, and then I realized that God might have needed him in another prison to bear witness to the holy life. It is the same prison that the inmate from Colombia was sent to that I have written much about also, and that inmate has written me several times about the universal opposition to the message of holiness in that place. Thank God, he has not compromised, but just tried to pray and bear witness to whoever might receive it. Now I will write to him and tell him to look up this brother just arrived, and I know he will be delighted.

They were both in the Theology course and both graduated with good marks. Please pray that whatever God has in mind for him, it will be accomplished.

It is always a disappointing thing to see a good and exemplary holy life moved away, as much as we need those kinds of witnesses, but God has a right to send His own wherever He needs them.

Thank you for your prayers for us; we need and appreciate them.

William Cawman

11
THE HEART OF KINGS IS STILL IN HIS HAND

July 1, 2023

THIS MIGHT BE STRANGE, but in this letter, dated July 1, I need to tell you about May 31. You see, I mailed out the June letters on May 31, before this that I am about to tell you, took place.

When I walked into my supervisor's office that morning, sitting in front of his desk was his supervisor, the man from Trenton who works for the commissioner and is in charge of all chaplains, state wide. He saw me come in and immediately asked me to take a chair. He had come down for an unannounced visit and was doing just that. We visited for a while over personal matters and then over needs and concerns we have presently in the prison. After an hour and a half, my supervisor told him it was time for our weekly prayer, and invited him to come up with us. He readily assented and we spent an hour together with all chaplains except for the Muslims.

He spoke of the elements from the left wing he is contending with and I spoke up. I said, "Dr. ———, I have been here the longest of any of the chaplains and so I am not a stranger to the atmospheres that come down to us from Trenton. I want to thank you for being a buffer between the radical left-wing agenda and us, and for keeping the door open for us to labor here." My supervisor immediately responded, "I second all that, and I want to thank you too." The supervisor said, "Men, I want to be very clear: I do not want any of you to compromise your sincerely held religious beliefs to policies coming out of Trenton." We all thanked him again.

Then we each prayed around the circle—six of us—and then the supervisor sat back and said, "Gentlemen, I want to thank you for what I have found here today. I came in unannounced, so you had no chance to plan something, but this has been the very best chaplain meeting I have ever been in. I wish I could take what is here and plant it in every prison in the State."

I said, "Dr. ——, what would happen if you set aside a day and call all chaplains in the state to prayer?" He said, "That is a very good idea, and I am going to implement it right away." I said, "It will be far more important than all the training sessions you could have." He said, "That is exactly right."

Then he told us that a few years back, before he had any position except that of a state chaplain, he was sent down to our prison to get him away from some that didn't get along with him. He told us that he was to be a chaplain in the ECU, the prison hospital. He said that was the last thing he wanted to do, but he went. A man was there with a big hole in his stomach and a foul odor about him, and he really didn't want to be there. He walked down the hallway and called out, "Chaplain in hallway; does anyone want prayer?" The obnoxious man called out, "No, get out of here!" The next day he did the same thing and the man responded the same except that the man in the cell next to him said he wanted prayer. So he said he went in and prayed just as loud as he could that God would save everyone on that floor. The next day when he went over, he found the man who told him to get out, down on his knees. The following day, the man was gone and they told him that they found him dead on his knees.

All in all, it was a very encouraging morning for all of us. But now—strange as this may sound, it is the rock-bottom truth. This supervisor needs a work of grace that will start by severely editing and purging his vocabulary! He is pastor of his own church, and in charge of all chaplaincy in the State, but it is unnerving to listen to the extremely ungodly language that comes out of his mouth. All of this I leave now without further comment, and leave you to pray as you feel led.

Have you ever sensed that a preacher was hard up for illustrative material? I wasn't today. The topic for the day was Jesus' teaching in the Sermon on the Mount, Mat. 5:38-42 which begins with: "Ye have heard that it hath been said, An eye for an eye, and a tooth for a tooth…" A man came in with a good-sized fresh shiner on his right eye. After we had prayed and sung a couple of choruses, I announced the topic and then asked the brother to come up and stand beside me. I asked him if he could read without his glasses and he said he could. I then asked him to remove them and told the class to take a good look. Then I asked him to read: "Ye have heard that it hath been said, An eye for an eye, and a tooth for a tooth: But I say unto you, That ye resist not evil: but whosoever shall smite thee on thy right cheek, turn to him the other also." He did so in very good nature, and then I dared to ask him how the Scripture had worked for him. He said that he did turn the other cheek outwardly, but inside he didn't. So I made it clear to the class that he still needed a further cleansing, and he readily agreed. It was just too good an illustration to pass over!

As I took what many would term a "bunny trail" over the issue of the inner response to receiving a blow to one cheek, I reminded them that we sing before each class, "To Be Like Jesus." I took them to the cross where the soldier picked up a nail and hammer and took a vicious blow to drive in the nail. I asked them if the soldier had missed the nail and hit his own hand, shattering the bones, and ripping off the skin, if they thought Jesus would have found pleasure in that. They immediately agreed that He would not have. I then suggested that He would have reached out the other hand and healed the mangled hand of the soldier. I pointed to what He had done to the High Priest's servant's ear. "Now, I said, do you really mean what we sing: 'To Be Like Jesus?'" Then I went on to tell them that such responses do not come from practice or learning, but from the complete indwelling of Jesus' Holy Spirit moving in and replacing the responses of the old nature. You see, I so deeply love the work of holiness that I cannot pass an opportunity of exalting the crowning work of Calvary.

As I did so, several of the men were all smiles as they believed and accepted it; others bore on their faces a very clear Nicodemus response: "How can these things be?" Many times it seems more difficult than teaching the truth of heart holiness, to un-teach the false sinning religious notions they have been taught. Could I just be very blunt? I agree with David, "I hate every false way."

You might find it interesting, if not disgusting, if I tell you recent developments among the Odinists and Wiccans. You see, we now have over seventy of them and a group of about twelve were coming together weekly in the facility where I am assigned to monitor them. In that group there is a particular inmate who is serving a life sentence and who has made trouble in nearly every prison in the state. He has law suits pending against chaplains and other staff, but he is pretty widely known by now for what he is, so it isn't taken very seriously.

He was definitely the leader of the group I was monitoring, and was continually making demands for more and more literature and such things as animal crackers and apple juice, etc., in order to perform his religious rituals. A few weeks ago he stopped coming to the gatherings and the number dropped about in half.

Then the date of June 22 came up and that date is a high

day for both Odinists and Wiccans as the Summer Solstice. They get to congregate from all the facilities for a morning session and then receive a special meal at noon. I was assigned to put the names on the appointment sheet for the day and all was set. I had an appointment that was going to make me a half hour late the morning of their feast, so my supervisor went in to cover until I got there. Was I ever glad it worked that way! When the troublesome man who hadn't been coming to the regular gatherings came in, he immediately noticed another inmate who he labeled as "gay," and he spoke to several others and they got up and walked out. My supervisor stopped him and said, "Where are you going?" He would not tell my supervisor, even though by that time he knew why. The supervisor said to him, "I am ordering you to tell me why you are leaving." He said, "Good luck with that," and walked out.

About that time I walked into the situation and was glad I hadn't been there. My supervisor left it with me and went to report the man's behavior all the way up to the Trenton office. Just what action they can impose upon him for such is rather sketchy as he is in for life anyway, so has nothing to lose.

Now—I spent too much time and paper telling you that just so that you could look up to heaven just now and thank God for having been taught the way of truth! There is nothing whatsoever of the likeness of Christ in false religions, and yet people are attracted to it because of the blindness and perversion of their sinful hearts. Furthermore, our national leaders are so anti-Christ in their sinful hearts that they go to no limit to be sure these perverted religions are provided for and made available to the inmate population. If such fervor were only put forth to promote and provide for the only true and living way, where would we be?

In last month's letter I told you about two men who were referred to me by the mental health department and who have been responding so well. I have had several visits with them both and it just pulls my heart out to see them really getting something from God. The man who had been in the military and has a son in Germany from his time there is changing so remarkably from where I first found him. He is studying the Bible diligently and praying, and God is helping him to find a whole new outlook on life through a relationship with Him.

The other man, who I told you is so deplorably tattooed up, is also finding a real contact with God in prayer. I wouldn't be at all surprised if he has not already found a new birth. He told me that ever since he has been coming to see me, he is completely different, and doesn't ever want to go back to the old life again. He has a tattoo on his forehead, among many others, which he told me is a symbol to kill all snitches. (A snitch is someone in the prison system who tells on others) He told me that he hates every one of his tattoos and is determined when he can to have them removed. Such a process is very painful, but I believe he so hates them that he would be willing for anything to get rid of them.

I told him that I had heard of one case, where a man went down into the baptismal water and came up completely rid of his tattoos. He immediately wished such could happen to him. I told him the best thing he could do now is to go to God in earnest prayer and say, "Jesus, I got these tattoos while I was serving the devil. I don't want them and wish I had not gotten them. I am going to surrender them to You and let You do whatever You see best about them. If you can use me just as I am and shine through them, I leave myself entirely in Your hands." He really appreciated that and said he was going to do just what I had told him. Actually, the Spirit that is now shining through him does not at all match the looks that accompany the tattoos, so I don't know just what God will do with him. They certainly are not dampening the love that has developed between us. Please pray for him, that he will not stop short of a fully sanctified heart.

The inmate that I told you about who had come to me all stuffed up with K2 or something similar, had an episode with custody and is now in lockup. He has only a couple of months until he is released and so will probably remain there until he goes home. I have been to see him and he was rejoicing that he has not touched drugs since being there. It is not that he couldn't get them there as the place is full of them, so I am encouraged for him. I will try to visit with him there every so often, and trust the Lord to really save him.

This past week in our Bible studies, we have come in the life of Christ to the Lord's Prayer. If you want to know how precious it is, just turn to it and pray it with a real focus; you will find more than you ever dreamed in that precious prayer! Thank you again for all your prayers for us!

In Him, William Cawman

August, 2023

WHERE SHALL I START? There are so many needs, and as well there are evidences that you, our dear Christian family, are praying. So I will just start in and see how many of these I can squeeze into this letter.

First, I will follow up with the inmate who I told you about in a recent letter, who after many visits over several years, came into my office all bombed out on K2, or something similar. I told you how I had to report this to the custody who then went and tested him and found him negative. He later admitted that he was as high as could be—so much for the accuracy of drug testing!

The first visit that I had with him after that, and had faced him with how serious it was to go on that way, I was praying for him and out of the corner of my eye I saw him trying to steal a pen from a pen holder on the desk. He saw me looking at him and put it back. Of course, this did not lend much inspiration to the prayer I was trying to pray for him.

Shortly after that he was sent to lockup for stealing the cord from a TV. What he wanted it for, I don't know, but after some time in the detention center, I went over to visit with him. He seemed in good spirits and told me he had been free from all drugs for three weeks and was reading his Bible. He was hoping that he could just stay there until his go-home date which is coming up very soon. However, after I had been away in two camp meetings and come back, I found him in facility three requesting a visit. I put him on the list and when he came in, he looked and acted much better than he had for a long time. He told me he was still free from drugs and was looking forward to being released.

I talked very seriously to him, telling him that he had one more fighting chance to change his course and prepare for heaven. He agreed. I cautioned him about opening the door even a little crack to anything he knew to be wrong. I told him to run like Joseph did from Potiphar's wife and not linger around temptation of any kind. He listened and agreed with what I was telling him and said he really did want to live as God wanted him to. He felt so bad about the way he had acted lately, trying to steal the pen, etc., and admitted that the drugs he was on had him out of control.

He said he would write to me as soon as he could after being released and I promised to help him all I could. Please pray for him. I have spent many hours with this young man, trying to pull him out of the chains of sin that had him bound so tightly. I would love to see him really turned around and living for God.

Then I had another visit with the man with all the alarming tattoos. He says he is really finding a connection with God in prayer and that things are so different from a short while ago. These captives of Satan are not going to find him let them go easily, so please help me pray for them that they will really go through with God.

And do you remember the one whose wife and son live in NY and who had spent a number of years in the military in Germany and has a son over there which came before his marriage? He said he is also definitely finding a peace with God and growing spiritually. I asked him about his wife and he said he talks to her on the phone. She had told him she would like to come down and visit him. He said that he told her not to do that as it is so far that he didn't want her to make that sacrifice. I said to him, "You call her back and invite her to come! She needs to see you and you her. No matter the sacrifice, it is a vital part of your marriage to be with her in person." He beamed and said, "I will do that right away."

The other day I walked into my supervisor's office and with a wry grin on his face he handed me two legal size papers from a pad, hand-written on both sides, from one of our over three thousand inmates. When I had a little time, I read his opening statement, directing us to read and reread the valuable information he had inscribed therein. He used much Scripture and thereby showed that the "man of sin" spoken of in Scripture was George Washington, the Free Mason. He belabored on and on over it and then turned to the statue of the liberty lady on top of the capitol building. He observed that she is facing east and is therefore welcoming in this flood-tide of evil and that no statue in Washington D.C. is allowed to be taller than she is.

I returned it to my supervisor, thanking him for the enlightenment and saying I would never be the same again. He turned and went down the hall laughing. You see, we have some very thrilling moments when our men do what is right; we have some very dark and discouraging moments when some turn back to their old ways again, and then we have other moments...

We've been having a lot of disturbance among the Odinist inmates and today after reporting three of the worst of them, they were put on a bus for another prison. Church pastors, please do not follow our example in your church!

We have had a really good time this week, still in the Sermon on the Mount, discussing Jesus' words in Matthew 6:22 & 23. Taking the whole of Jesus' teaching about light and darkness, I believe many of the men saw things in a different light than ever before. One of them said on the way out, "That was really a good class!" Another said something similar and I could tell it was new and welcome light to them.

We have an inmate who is Jewish by birth, and even though he comes down every morning to pray with his phylacteries, he says he is really a Christian. He is serving a life sentence after multiple murders in his early life, and as you can imagine, is not very popular with anyone in the prison system. However, he stops me at times with questions and down inside I know he is thinking deeply about his spiritual condition. Today, he stopped me and asked, "Chaplain, just really what is grace?" He said he had been thinking a lot about it and wanted to know more. He told me, which I already knew from his record, that he was an exceedingly bad man, and he really struggles to understand how or why God would want to forgive him. Not being set up for a formal visit I didn't have time to really explain as fully as I would have wanted to, so I plan to have a real visit with him soon. Please pray for us! He asked if he could attend my Bible study and I told him I would gladly put him on the list.

And then there is another lifer who is now thirty-four years into his life sentence. He has been with us for years and has been in my classes and services off and on, and we have visited a few times but not recently. I felt a nudge to set him up for a visit and he readily came down. He said, "Chaplain, I have been wishing so badly that I could talk to a chaplain, and I was so relieved when I saw my name on the list for today." He then told me how in the last little while a number of men he has been with for years are now going home and he has no hope of it. Along with that, loved ones are slipping away and he has been sensing such a loneliness and depression.

My heart went out to him and I began to tell him that sometimes God in His love and mercy, takes away from us the things we were finding comfort in, so that we might draw closer to Him. He immediately told me that he had been thinking that too and had been spending much more time alone with God. I urged him to just throw himself into the arms of a loving

God and ask to be completely filled with His Spirit. I also told him that I would try to visit with him regularly to try to help and encourage him. He seemed so very thankful and then told me the next day in class how much the visit meant to him. We certainly never know what lies painfully behind a countenance that would never give it away, but I want God to help me to sense these needy souls and be there for them.

Another younger man came to me and asked me to remove him from both Islam and Odin services (what a strange mixture that is to begin with!) and put him in the Christian services. I did so, and today he came for the first time. As he greeted me, I wondered if everything was all right with him, and I soon found I was not mistaken. He fell asleep for almost the entire class. I am quite sure he was drugged up with something. I may have to call him aside and probe into his condition a bit further.

I think I told you several months ago that I had requested new digital pianos for our three chapels, as the old ones were starting to break down and sound terrible. I turned in the request and it was sent back to me with proper signatures on it and then several months went by. I called the business office and enquired about it and they told me they had sent the order to the piano company. I called the piano company and they said they hadn't received it, so the business office sent it again and now they are scheduled to be delivered early next month. Thank the Lord!

Speaking of pianos, please help us pray that my wife can soon be reinstated as a volunteer to play those pianos!

The part-time bilingual chaplain who has been with us for years is planning to retire in about six weeks, and indeed his replaced hips are so bad that he is really struggling to get around the prison. We have been working friends for many years even though we do not at all agree theologically, but we still are not sure who will be able to replace him to minister to the Spanish services.

Actually, the whole chaplaincy department is by now composed of senior citizens. My supervisor is past retirement age and needs to wear a heart monitor for the next couple of days. The other part time chaplain who is not bilingual is also past retirement age and struggles to stay abreast of several bouts with cancer. The Muslim chaplain is past seventy and is showing it. Only the other Muslim and the Catholic chaplain are under sixty, so as you can imagine we give and take plenty of teasing regarding those things that stacked up years bring on. I provide the distinction of the eldest among them, but sometimes I think I am physically better than the rest. Thank You, Dear Lord!

Two more men from my classes are being released very shortly and both have said that they really want to find a good church and would like to come visit us. Please pray for them. Thank God for the few who have stayed and become a part of our church family, but so many have come and then fallen back or else been captivated by the glamourous offers of churches who are so far from Biblical living and yet so dynamically emotionally appealing. Men coming out of years in prison, with very little discernment and very little church background, are so vulnerable to the offers of these false churches.

Do you recall the exhortation of Paul to Timothy thus: "Now the end of the commandment is charity out of a pure heart, and of a good conscience, and of faith unfeigned: From which some having swerved have turned aside unto vain jangling; Desiring to be teachers of the law; understanding neither what they say, nor whereof they affirm." Well, we have one such in one of our best Bible studies. He always sits on the front corner to my right, and at times seems to be in harmony, but then all of the sudden, his well tutored graceless brain pops up and he feels the need to bring the teaching back into alignment with his impeccably developed theology.

The other day we were having the most delightful study on the entrance of Light dispelling the sinful darkness and how the moment Jesus comes in, sin must depart. All of the sudden he sprang to the soapbox (and this is always done with an air of absolute authority) and quoted the Scripture about the Grace of God teaching us. He said that God always starts with our understanding and then as our mind is renewed, it flows down through the rest of us, and this takes a lot of time.

We returned to our glorious topic and left him on his throne by the wayside. Gazing upon Truth is too precious to take time out to argue with carnal ego.

Thank you again for your prayers for us,

William Cawman

September, 2023

FIRST OF ALL, LET me get something straightened out that I told you at the end of the first page of last month's letter. The man who I said was Jewish from birth, was thought that by maybe everyone around him as he always came down to pray the Tefillin and was classified as Jewish. The next time I had a scheduled visit with him, he told me that some of his European ancestors were Jewish, but he said, "Chaplain, I'm no more Jewish than you are Italian!" Now perhaps that was but step one in getting his life straightened out, for today I visited with him again and probed a bit deeper.

You see, he is a fairly high-profile criminal who is charged with three murders. He has shown me a pile of court charges as well as legal efforts to get whatever so-called justice he can. I had given him some good books to read, but then I faced him squarely with these words: "Now if you really want to get right with God and prepare to spend eternity in heaven, the very first step is to face the absolute truth about all of your past and acknowledge it to God and to all that were affected by it. There is no way to obtain God's favor and indwelling until you have confessed to all that has ever been wrong in your life."

He looked perplexed and said, "How can I ever confess all

the sins I have committed?" I told him that he must be willing to come completely clear and then God would show him what he needed to confess to get right with Him and everyone else. He said that the whole case in the courts was confusing and muddled up. I told him that he knew full well what he had done that was sinful and wrong and that is where he needs to start—by being completely truthful with everyone about them.

There had been a code which cut our visit short, but perhaps before this letter gets mailed out, I will have another visit with him and find out how he responds to that. Please pray for him and for me. There is no question but that God is giving him a wake-up call.

And then the man with the alarming tattoos came down right after him. He immediately confessed that he had yielded to temptation and gotten high again, but that he felt disgusted with himself and so dirty for doing it. I told him that was good that he felt that way and that he could thank God that He is a God of second chances. I told him to ask God to forgive him and then seek and ask Him to really come into his heart, because He promised that to those who receive Him, He will give power to become the sons of God.

The same forgiving and patient God who bore long with the chaplain until he finally laid hold on the Power to quit the sinning business—a different type of sin, but just as addictive—can also help this man to grasp the same Power and come forth to new life! My heart longs to see him do it!

The last two weeks in Facility Two have been precious times in the Bible study. The men are so lively and responsive that if there is any discord in the room, it is completely unfelt. I come away refreshed and blessed in my own heart. Last week the lesson was on Jesus' teaching in the Sermon on the Mount regarding Judging (Mt 7:1-5). This week it was on the next verses about asking, seeking, and knocking. I believe Jesus is present with us as we study His words just as much as He was present when He gave them. I think sometimes that I might know a little bit of what Jesus felt when he looked up to His Father and said, "I have given unto them the words which Thou gavest me; and they have received them..." No words can describe the joy of seeing hearts receive God's Word.

My supervisor has been on vacation this week, so I had to cover his Bible studies as well. That also was a very vibrant group that I was with Sunday night and again on Tuesday afternoon. I spoke to them on Sunday night from the words, "Blessed are the pure in heart...", and Tuesday afternoon I contrasted the story of Abraham not withholding his son with the story of Annanias who held back part of the price. Again, I could feel the truth taking hold on many of them, and it is a relatively large group too.

Well, I did have another visit with the formerly thought Jewish man. He had been reading the material I gave him and had a lot of questions. Perhaps his name should have been Nicodemus? I tried as quickly as I could to answer his questions but kept pointing him to the reality of a new birth. I told him the story of the hungry hearted man who came to D. L. Moody and said that he would really like to be a Christian, but that he had a lot of questions he needed to ask. He had them all written down on a sheet of paper. Moody took him into the inquiry room as they called it then and suggested that they start with prayer. The man's hungry heart prayed clear through and he jumped up and danced about the room for a spell and finally settled down. Then Mr. Moody told him they could look at his questions and he looked with wide eyes and said, "Mr. Moody, I don't have any questions!" He liked that story, but as yet I can't feel that he is at the point of forsaking the broken cisterns for the Living Water, but I will stay with him.

The same day I had scheduled another visit with the former military man who had spent several years in Germany in the service. He came in and sat down and immediately said, "Chaplain, I'm about to give up! Every time I try to do what is right I get attacked from every angle and I'm just so tired of it all I want to just quit. I signed up for a job in food production in the I-Building just to get away from everybody and my own thoughts and that is the only place I find any relief. My wife and I are just arguing now all the time and I just don't even want to try anymore."

I said to him, "That is exactly what Satan wants you to do and by it he will rob you of every good thing God has in store for you and finally drop you into hell. You don't want that, do you?" He shook his head in the negative. I then tried to tell him that it is inevitable that Satan will try everything in his power to draw him back into his net, but that if he will just set his will and plead the Blood of Jesus that was shed for him, he could soon find something worth living for here below and heaven hereafter. He seemed to revive somewhat with that and promised he would seek the Lord.

I told him that despair may not be the worst sin in most people's thinking, but that it sends more people to hell than any other. I begged him to rise up and reject the devil's tactic he is using on him.

I believe I told you in a previous letter about the man who is one of the most obviously miserable men I have ever met. He seems angry and disgusted with everyone around him as well as the prison conditions, and he shows it all over him. Some time back, in spite of all that, he got up in a service, came to the front, and sang a typical contemporary song (if it can be called that) with all of the motions and rhythm, and had the men almost beside themselves with delight. I have not allowed him to do it since.

Anyway, I called him down for a visit because he requested it, saying that he just had to talk to me. He never came for the visit because he said later that they did not let him out of his cell for it. The next week I put him on again and a stand-up code drill went off and cancelled that visit. The next class time before we got started, he got up and said in his miserable way, "Chaplain, I've just got to say something." He started acting out as he blew up in front of everyone, saying, "I just can't wait to get out of here and get back to a good church where we just praise the Lord and dance and shout and have a wonderful time. I just can't find that in here."

I simply said before the class, "I'm glad you can't for that is not of God at all." Then I went on with the class and ignored him. So a few days later we finally got together for a visit. When he came in I said to him, "K——, if I am going to be able to help you, you are going to have to let me be bluntly honest with you; will you let me?" He nodded a "yes." I said, "It is obvious that you have been immersed in very charismatic forms of worship that is not of God at all, but is led by demon spirits. Jesus did not come to give us powerful emotions but to save us from sin."

He said, "Chaplain, let me tell you something. Whenever I try to pray, I hear terrible voices trying to stop me."

I said, "That is all the more evidence that you have been under the influence of Satan, not the true worship of God. You need to turn your back on all of that and humbly seek for God's forgiveness and a new birth that will assure you that you are right with God."

He said, "When I try to do that, these terrible voices will not leave me alone. It is only when I try to pray that I hear them."

I said, "Then you need to rebuke them in the name of Jesus and cry to Him to deliver you from them. We are just about ready to go to Bible study. Would you want me to call you up front and ask the men to come up and lay their hands on you and ask God to deliver you?"

He said he would, and then he said, "And Chaplain, there is something else too. I have books and pictures in my locker that I need to get rid of. I have pornographic pictures on the inside of my locker doors, and I know I need to get rid of them."

I assured him that God would never hear him or deliver him until he got rid of everything he knew was not pleasing to God in his life. It is such a serious atmosphere when you know full well that God is giving such a person one fighting chance to get right, and if they do not take it, they will be worse than ever. Oh the struggling sin-sick souls that are so near the Living Well and yet go on hugging their sins to their bosoms.

But, on a brighter note, the man serving a life sentence who has just recently been through a long spell of depression and is now responding wonderfully to all the light he receives, is gaining ground from week to week. I recently gave him some good holiness books and he told me today that he really believes that is what God is doing in him right now—purifying his heart from all that sinful nature within. He mentioned again that he doesn't know why he hit such a low spot in his life at the turn of this year. I told him it was nothing short of the mercy and love of God, calling him into a deeper walk with God. He said that he really believes that and that he will not stop until the work is done. He thanked me for calling him down right at this critical time in his life. Please pray that he will go all the way through with God. He has been there long enough to have seen others find what he is seeking for. He mentioned particularly the Colombian man I wrote about several years ago who after forty-five years of a very wicked and hateful life in which he killed one person and wanted to kill two more, surrendered to God and was gloriously saved, then a bit later recognized his need of a deeper work and prayed through to that also. He said that he had lived either close to or with that man both before and after God changed his heart and he was amazed at the difference in him.

Thank you for praying that my wife would be cleared again to go in with me at times. Any volunteers had to start all over after the Covid nonsense shut them out. Now she will be getting a notice from central office in Trenton and have to go through the training again and she can go back. Thank you again for praying for this. I am looking forward to her help again as the men just loved her teaching them choruses. We are not opening the door to the smorgasbord of volunteers that were there before as many of them were not helping the men at all. Thank God for a supervisor that wants to raise the standard! Thank you for all of your prayers for us.

With love and gratitude,

William Cawman

12
IS A CHAPLAIN'S LIFE BORING? NEVER!

October, 2023

W E NEVER CAN PREDICT what will happen next in the Department of Corrections. All of the sudden we started having a rush of requests from the Detention Center for Jewish meals. You see, the detention unit is sort of the prison within the prison. It is where inmates are sent for punishment and correction who violate the rules of the prison at large. This past month we started receiving multiple requests to be reclassified as Jewish from the inmates over there. Obviously, someone was agitating it, but my supervisor said we were having a Jewish revival! By the way, all the requests were denied.

Let me tell you something that, if I am not mistaken, demonstrates pretty effectively what is happening in America. Every year since 9/11, we have had a remembrance of it in front of the prison under the flags. We would have some reflections given by a chaplain, a prayer offered, and then often I would play the national anthem on my trumpet while my wife accompanies on the keyboard. Then they would have the honor guard of six officers in full regalia lower the flag to half-mast while I played "Taps" on the trumpet. After that one of us chaplains would go to the command center and they would turn off all radios and open the intercom to all areas of the prison while we offered a prayer at the exact time of the two twin tower attacks. Usually, we would have perhaps fifty or so from administration as well as other departments who would gather around the flag pole for the event.

This year, we put out notices of it, put about the same program together, and gathered at the flag pole and went through the ceremony as usual. No one came! I said to my supervisor, "The American spirit is dead!" Everyone is afraid to be identified with anything. I can't help but believe that is the primary reason for it. People walked by going and coming from the prison, but no one stopped to listen. Jesus said that in the end times men's hearts would fail them from fear. We are witnessing that in living drama. Everyone is afraid to be identified with might be unpopular with the radical loud minority. Would God we could see a today's version of Patrick Henry and our Founding Fathers!

I have had several very encouraging visits with the elderly black man who is serving a life sentence. I have had him in services and classes for a number of years, then it seemed he dropped into the background. I put him on the schedule for a visit, and he thanked me over and over for it. He had been watching other men he had known for years getting released, with no hope of that for him, and he had gone into a slump both spiritually and emotionally. The visit really perked him up and he has been brighter and gaining ground ever since.

I gave him some good holiness books which he has been reading, and in our last couple of visits, I have sensed him getting ever closer to God. He has such a contentment in his face that it makes him actually handsome. I was questioning him the other day as to how his heart reacts to God and to circumstances around him, and I would wonder if he has not already entered into heart purity. He is influencing men about not recognize. Hopefully they are new recruits as we certainly do need them. The state is paying an unbelievable amount of money each day in overtime because we are so short of officers. And I hear that another group of them are about to retire as well, which will hardly make up for the new ones coming in. It leaves us very conscious of a low morale among the custody, which in turn affects everything else we try to do, such as getting the men out to services on time, etc. Please pray for this situation if it comes to your minds because it so much determines how much time we get for our services and studies.

My wife has one more class to attend and then she will officially be a volunteer to go in with me, especially on Sunday nights, to help with the piano playing. She and I are both looking forward to her being back in with me, and the men are too.

Please help us pray also that our pastor will soon be cleared to come back in, as we certainly do need him on Sunday nights. Our Sunday night services are from 5:30 to 6:30, which then gives us time to get back to our church for the night service at 7:30.

Thank you again for all you do.

William Cawman

November, 2023

I AM STARTING THIS letter early in October because there are things I want to tell you before I forget to do so. I have mentioned in letters before that one of the very first boys I ever visited in prison comes at times on Sunday mornings now to our church and sits beside me. The other day I noticed on the roster that one of the other ones has now been moved to our prison, so I put him on the list for a visit. At first he didn't remember me, but as I reminded him of a few things when we first met, all of the sudden he threw up his hands and said, "Yes! Now I remember you!" After a quick update I began to inquire as to his spiritual state. He told me that he well remembered that night on the cell floor when he poured out his heart to God and a peace came into him that he had never known before. I asked him if he still had contact with that same God and he assured me that he prays to Him every day and reads his Bible. But he told me that he is worshipping somewhat differently now; he has for some time been worshipping like the American Indians. I was disappointed in more than one way. I immediately realized how sadly the so-called Christianity he has known has let him down and sent him searching for some other medium of communion. I can only hope that God hears his heart cry beyond the mistaken outward, for the Native American religion is totally demonic. Please pray for him. I will no doubt meet with him again, and he did seem to appreciate my praying with him.

A few years ago, the State of New Jersey passed legislation that changed some of the older sentences given to young offenders. He and the other one still in prison had been given sixty years without parole, but that has been changed to a minimum of thirty years with the possibility of life. He served thirty years and then was given a hit of three years and is halfway through that. Then he can be reviewed again for parole.

I had a phone call from the inmate I have written about off and on for over twenty years. He is the one who was a third generation Mormon. After serving twenty years in NJ he was deported to Michigan to serve another twenty, but recent reviews of his sentence may soon make him eligible for parole. He was wonderfully sanctified while still here in NJ and has kept up a precious walk with God and been a real witness to all around him. It is so precious to watch the genuine work of heart holiness keep a person year after year and see the spiritual maturity develop that brings glory to our Father in heaven.

For several years now he has been privileged to train seeing eye dogs right in prison with him for blind people who cannot afford to pay for one. He told me, and I am very eager to see it, that he is writing a book which relates all the commands they teach to seeing eye dogs to commands we need to learn as Christians. He is not only closely walking with God, but has a brilliant mind as well, so I am sure the book will be superbly helpful.

After a Sunday night service in facility one, a young man asked for a visit with me. He began at once to tell me that about two months ago, he made a definite choice to take God's way, and that ever since then a peace has come into him he never had before. It sounded a whole lot like good old-time salvation to me! I am encouraged for him and will not wait long to visit with him again. I have some good books laid out to give him.

Now, I have probably encountered a number of people in my lifetime who would be identical to the one I am going to tell you about, but this is the first time I ever had someone openly confess it. My supervisor handed me a request from an inmate in which his declaration of faith was: "Myself." "I pray to myself but obey Jesus." When he handed it to me I said, "So you are giving this to me?"

"Yes!" Now, how can a person obey Jesus and pray to himself???? Pray for me as you would feel best.

Every once in a while, I pull up the religion report to see where we are in numbers. Perhaps you would be interested, so here it is:

Muslim: 615; Protestant 462; Catholic: 260; No religious preference: 160; Odinist & Wiccan: 84; Jewish: 52; Buddhist: 27; Native American: 9; Religion profile blank: 1569.

The Protestant category includes Jehovah Witness and Christian Science and Seventh Day Adventist, and those three account for 57 out of the Protestant community.

So the total population of just this prison is presently 3240 and our maximum capacity is around 3500.

Today I was starkly reminded again of how many serious needs are buried behind smiling faces. Last night I stood before fifty-four men, and as I preached to them, most of their faces were lit up in response to the truth preached. Today, Monday, I put several of them on the appointment sheet for a one-on-one visit. You see, in facility one, my supervisor has the Bible study, so most of the inmates in that third of the prison I only see on Sunday nights when my turn to rotate there comes up. Most of the men I put on the list were ones who had just come to the prison in the last year or two and were new to me except for seeing their faces on Sundays.

At least three of the men I visited with, even though they were pleasant looking and responsive in the Sunday night service, simply broke down in tears as they unburdened their heavy-hearted inner selves. At the same time that I felt such a compassion for them, I realized how great is the need to sit down with more of them and hear their heart cries. Bible studies and church services are good, but it is when they can sit down and feel safe to unload that their inner self comes out in torrents.

One man, full of energy and hyper-activity and approaching his senior years, always seems very upbeat and helpful to others when in church services. As soon as he sat down with me, he began to unload a deeply troubled heart. He had been dumped into a Catholic group home by his parents when only a few years old. He said he got along all right with that until he turned eight; then the older ones in the home began to abuse him and molest him. It made him so angry that he picked up a large stick and beat one of them severely. He tried to tell the caregivers and even the priest, but they paid no attention to him. To this very day, he has horrible dreams at night that he is being molested, and screams out until his cellmate wakens him and tells him he is screaming. He is literally tormented by it.

Then, about two years ago, his wife called him and told him she wanted to tell him something. He said, "Are you telling me that you want a divorce?"

"No, I want to come see you." Then he heard nothing more and so he called the house and a man answered. He became very agitated and asked the man what he was doing there. The man asked him if he was sitting down. He said he was not; there was no place to sit by the phone in the prison. The man told him he needed to be sitting down, so he went to the dayroom and got a chair. The man asked again if he was sitting down and he began to get angry. He cursed the man and said, "Why don't you just tell me what it is?" The man then told him that his wife had suddenly passed away with a heart attack. That made him mad again and he began to curse God.

Now, here he is sitting in front of me asking how he can get rid of all this pent-up anger in his heart.

I told him that he would never get rid of it until he got down to the core of the onion layers and confessed all of his sin and anger to God and asked Him to come into his heart. I told him that the Bible promises that through the Blood of Jesus we can be made a "new creature." With that he said, "Chaplain, you're only the second man I've ever known that has made me cry, but these are good tears; I needed them."

I talked some more to him and had prayer with him and told him I would follow up with another visit, but that he should not let up for a moment in asking God to come into his heart and change him completely. Then, as a child of God he could ask God to heal the horrible dreams that were plaguing him. He left in a much different attitude and said he would certainly do just that.

Another man also just broke down and sobbed out his heart, but I did feel confident that he is already finding a healing in the Blood of Jesus. I explained to him about the necessity of going right on after he knows he is forgiven and asking God to cleanse him from all the remains of inward sin. He seemed to comprehend that and expressed a real hunger to know that he was completely pure within.

Then the last one I visited barely sat down until he was in tears. "Chaplain, this was God-ordered. Just today my wife gave me notice that she wants to get a divorce. You couldn't have known that in order to call me down, but I really needed to talk to you. I'm just going to be open and confess to you why I'm here. I can't be comfortable to do this with anyone, but I feel I can trust you to listen to me and not throw me away like the church I was attending did." I assured him that I had no right to throw a person away for any sin committed, as I myself had committed the greatest sin in God's sight, which was the breaking of the greatest commandment.

He told me that from the very time the internet became available he had discovered pornography on it and went into a thirty-year addiction to it. All that while he was going to church and even helping in ministry. One day his son discovered a porn site on his phone and told his girlfriend. Her mother was a detective for such things and immediately reported him. The law came in and searched his home and computer and it put him in prison. His wife was devastated by all that he had hidden from her for all those years, and now wants rid of him.

Tears were flowing as he told me he had repented to God and asked God to cleanse him of it and that now for two-and-one-half years he has been totally clean of it and will not even look the second time at anything tempting on TV.

With that I began with examples from church history of prominent men who never went on to be cleansed from the carnal mind and consequently fell into errors that have plagued the church ever since. I told him that it was a wonderful thing that he feels forgiven of God, but that he needs to ask God to fill him completely with His Spirit, until nothing ever comes back again. I went to the Scripture where Jesus talked about the man from whom the unclean spirit had been cleansed, but that by not keeping the inner fire of love for God burning hot, he went back to the house where he came from. He listened with tears and told me he hates his past and does not ever want any part of it again. He knows the Scripture full well that if his wife does leave him, he must remain that way for life, and he accepts it.

Now I must tell you that even though there are times when this ministry could discourage, needs such as I encountered today, just draw my heart to commit afresh to God to labor on as long as He wants me to. A broken heart God will not despise, and I cannot despise it either; it pulls my heart out of me.

I know many of you are praying, and I thank you; will you pray for some more definite miracles of God's transforming love and grace among these men?

Thank you.

William Cawman

December, 2023

WE SHOULD NEVER UNDERESTIMATE what God is doing with His Word! A twenty-eight-year-old man has been in my classes for at least two years, as nearly as I can recall. He seems very quiet and unexpressive, but faithfully attends. On Wednesday, November 8, I noticed as soon as we had finished praying before the class, his eyes were wet with tears. As we went on with the class, he suddenly just burst into more tears. He wiped his eyes and before long burst into tears again. I could sense that he was deeply moved by something, and after a bit I asked him if there was something he would want to say to us. He shook his head negatively, and so we went on. At the close of the class I asked him if he needed me to call him down for a visit. He nodded his head that he did.

The next day I sent for him and when he came into the room, he was smiling grandly. I asked him how he was, and he responded: "I'm fine." I then asked him what was causing the tears in class the day before, and asked him if something was troubling him. He said, "Oh no! I'm just so happy that I'm right where God wants me to be with Him. He just won't let up on me! He keeps right on following me!" By that time he was crying again.

"Then," I said, "so are you telling me that those are tears of joy?"

"Yes, they are!"

We visited a while and I asked him a bit more about his former life. He has never married or fathered children, but had become involved in drugs and had committed a robbery. I asked him if he was confident that God was so filling him that the old habits were gone, and he very positively answered that they were and that he wants never to go back to that again. He wants me to continue to visit with him.

So you see, we never know how God is working within those we meet every day; but we do know He is being just as faithful to every soul as to this one. Oh that more would respond to His tender drawings.

The next Sunday night I detained him after the service and gave him some good books to read. He welcomed them in his typical way. The next week in class he wanted to ask me something after the class time. He stayed behind until all the others were gone and then asked, "If I give you some money, can you put it in your church for me?" I thanked him for having that desire in his heart, but explained that we are not allowed to receive money from inmates. He understood and said he would have his family put it in for him, but he would rather not have his family know he did it.

That day in class, being Thanksgiving week, I asked the men to name out something they were thankful for. He looked up with a charming smile and said, "Salvation!" Isn't it precious to see the real jewel of grace work, when so many around have only a head knowledge of such?

We now have, at long last, a Jewish rabbi. He is presently volunteering, but hopefully will come on as another part-time chaplain. He seems very pleasant and eager to work with us, and it will save all the rest of us from having to answer the many needs that the Jewish inmates come up with.

If you remember, a while back I wrote about a man who practices all the Jewish rites and ceremonies, and who approached me and began to ask questions about the Bible and said he believed in it. As I visited with him at his request, he admitted that he was not Jewish, but practiced it for the politics involved, whatever that meant. I have had a number of visits with him at his request, but have not yet found much if any real hunger for God's transforming grace. He is quite a notorious trouble-maker who is serving a life sentence. The new rabbi, in referring to some of the inmates he has already discerned to be other than what they profess, brought his name to the foreground as one of them. I looked at him and said, "And what would make his name come to the top of the list?" He laughed.

I trust I had the mind of the Lord in this, but sensing him to be more of a manipulator than a hungry soul, I gave him the studies we had done a couple years ago on the disease and the cure. I told him to read them over very carefully and let me know how it affected him. I then asked the Lord whether I should continue to visit with him if there was no obvious light dawning on him through them. After asking him what he got out of them, I felt as though I was up against an impenetrable mud wall, so I felt I needed to spend less time with him and move on to others who were responding more conspicuously. Certainly, I would still like to see him have a break-through, but for now, I may just let him soak.

It reminded me of some advice I gave to the young people who were ministering with us on the Boardwalk several years ago. One evening a little wizard looking man stopped one of our young men and argued theology with him for an hour. The next night he came again for a second blessing. The next morning I told the young people that Jesus said He would make us fishers of men. I told them about a time when I was fishing along a pier with my daughters and there was a string of people fishing from the same pier. All of the sudden a man at the end of the line caught something and it began furiously swimming back and forth, causing everyone else to pull their lines in to get out of his way. After a time it surfaced and he detected it to be a stingray, a junk fish. He cut the line and let it go. I told them that as fishers of men we needed to discern when it was time to politely cut the line, because all the time that man had occupied our missionary, hundreds of people passed by that were deprived of receiving a tract.

So if God brings that inmate to your mind, pray that this soaking time will get his attention and make him think seriously about where he is headed.

I guess it is part of human nature, but if others see you do something once, they simply let you do it from there on. A few years ago I needed to set up some classes which can only be done by filling out a template and sending it up to Trenton for them to put it in the computer program we use to schedule and track what the men do. From there on, all the other chaplains simply say, "Can you send up a module for me?" Near the end of each year, we have to add any new ones that any chaplain wants to teach as well as renew the expiration dates for ones we want to continue. So just the other day I finally got together all the requests from the Muslim chaplains, the Catholic one, the Jewish one, and all the Protestant ones, and then as well all the other religious groups that meet. They are now sent up to Trenton and what a relief to have that done for another year!

Then as well, I fell heir to the development of the religious schedule calendars for each facility each month. Any religious holiday or event is to be listed on it, so it is not a repetitious production. Due to the fact that ever since around the early 2000s we have not been provided a secretary, all of the clerical work that chaplaincy involves has to be divided among us. We all realize how much time it takes away from what we would rather be doing, but it is what it is.

I would say that our supervisor is very sensitive to not overburdening any of us and knows that we would rather be putting our full time into ministering. He has been a very good supervisor and expresses his thankfulness to us often for all that we do. I sometimes wonder how he gets everything done that falls his lot as supervisor. His desk is piled with things not yet done; the floor around his desk has about three stacks (that is, if they were stacked!) of finished papers, and his whole office is full of boxes and periodicals. Once or twice while he was on vacation, I went in and straightened it all up. When he returned he never said a word, but soon had it returned to his comfort level. I love him!

The other day I was working in a spare office that we use down the hall from the supervisor's office. He came to the door with a big grin and handed me an inmate request. He said, "I'm not sure what to do with this one; I need your help." On the slip it read something similar to this: "Hi, I am a presbeterian and I need a kosher tray for my meals because I do presbeteria." My total expertise in the area was to laugh with him.

We are planning a special Christmas service in each of the three facilities, but since our church is the only one doing it, we will do it for three successive Sundays, Dec. 10, 17, & 24. Hopefully my wife and I and our pastor his wife and some of their daughters will be going in for it. Please pray that it will be a special visitation from God that will touch many of their hearts with the true Christmas message.

Looking forward into the coming year, could I ask you to pray that my pastor can be quickly reinstated as a volunteer? We so often need another minister on Sunday evenings, and because of not having anyone, we have to cancel one of the services. During Covid all of the volunteers' passes expired and have to be renewed again. Then after the background check is completed satisfactorily, they have to take two sessions of training again. The training is mostly what salvation and common sense would dictate anyway, but it is required of everyone.

Recently, since I had been gone the week before, I went in on a Monday even though it was a holiday. I was going to get ahead on the appointment sheets for the week so that I would have more time for visitation. When I opened my computer to start my work, I found a whole list of training classes that I was required to accomplish by opening them up on the computer. I thought, "Well, I may as well get this over with," so I launched into it. I found it difficult to stay awake during much of it as it was sort of like retraining an English teacher the alphabet, but I endured it and soon the day was over with nothing else accomplished, except that such was behind me. A few days later, my taking the courses having been acknowledged uptown (as we call Trenton), I received another list of required training sessions to be taken. Such is the futility of legislated righteousness, I suppose. PS. Please don't report my comments to Trenton!

Our church is scheduled to be in revival services December 5 through 10. I received a call yesterday from a former inmate. He has been teaching Bible studies on holiness to a few people near him and about two and a half hours from our church. He had asked me to send him the books we had covered in classes while he was in the prison, and that is what he is using in the Bible studies. He told me that he and three of the men he is teaching want to come down for the Sunday while we are in revival. Please pray that God will speak to them just what they need. One of the men he is teaching was also an inmate in the prison for several years.

This is the man I believe I told you about a while back who went to report to his parole officer and the officer told him that they had sent out spies to check on him and found him on the street corner passing out tracts and witnessing to people. The parole officer told him he need not come back, but he reports to him anyway. You see, if one is doing right, there is no need or desire to hide, for it is a pleasure to live out in the clear with everyone.

And now as another year is closing out, the future is more uncertain than I have ever known it to be in my short lifetime. But that very uncertainty has a central core of certainty! The prophecies of God's Word are unfolding in living drama before our eyes. Will there be yet another year to work in this vineyard, or for that matter in any sector of God's great harvest field? Such uncertainty surrounding a definite certainty, calls to us loudly that we must be about our Father's business while the day lasts. So, we face the future, whether long or short, not with fear, but with a fresh challenge to live for Jesus and Him alone. Pray for us!

William Cawman

13
ENCOURAGING SIGNALS

January, 2024

GOD HAS SO WISELY and deliberately withheld from us the knowledge of that split second, soon to come, when the last year, the last month, the last day, the last hour, the very last second, abruptly and unexpectedly, ends forever this earthly time, and eternity begins. He has, however, shown us sufficient in His Word, to know that it is rapidly drawing near. If Jesus should tarry another year, what would I most want to spend that year doing?

I have recently been with some who are passionate about fulfilling some earthly dream this coming year. I have been with some whose lives are planned in such fashion that I cannot place any other label on it except that which the Scripture itself places on it—"Lovers of pleasure more than lovers of God."

I will honestly and frankly open my inmost heart and tell you that such plans for the coming year make me ache inside. Oh that men would only use the intelligence God has given them and wake up to what will seem most important in that moment when we first stand before the Great White Throne.

I am purposed that I will not have regrets on that day. There are yet precious souls to be brought to the Savior before this microscopic window of time runs out. What else is even remotely important in light of how it will appear then?

And so, with those unvarnished but deeply honest exposures of my inmost heart, I enter another year with a passion to glorify my Lord and Savior as never before. I desire a fresh baptism of anointing to minister to the needy hearts of men in prison and out of prison. I pray that not one soul will slip through my fingers that God brings to me. My heart desires to see a genuine revival of conviction for sin break out within the prison walls; not only among the inmates but among the staff and custody as well. Every moment that I spend inside the prison, I am surrounded by approximately five thousand needy, eternity bound souls. Oh God, may this drive me to my knees!

I am glad to tell you that not only is my wife now registered again as a volunteer, but my pastor is well on his way to completing it too. How often we need another preacher on Sunday nights, and the service time is such that he can hold a service there and still make it back to the church for the evening service there. Thank God, and thank you for praying for this. All of his family who are old enough are also being reentered, but they will be put on hold except for special events until the present moratorium for volunteers is lifted.

My wife and I and the pastor's family went in on Sunday night, Dec. 10 and had a Christmas service for one facility. We planned to do the same for another facility on the 17th and 24th, but on the 17th the flu bug won the day against us going in.

Is it wrong to love to watch grace work without terminology? I am so thrilled with the young man who very obviously met the Lord in a life-changing way in class one day as I told you about last month. He is conspicuously a new creature; but I am not sure he even knows how to analyze himself. I will honestly confess that such is so refreshing after I have seen so many who knew all about it but couldn't seem to find it.

David the Psalmist said to himself: "Hope thou in God: for I shall yet praise him, who is the health of my countenance, and my God." The writer of Proverbs said: "A merry heart maketh a cheerful countenance..." Isaiah said of the wicked: "The shew of their countenance doth witness against them..." So it is Scripturally documented that what dwells within us will radiate out through our countenance. This young man's countenance is conspicuously and remarkably different for the better since that day. He literally radiates a genuine inner peace. It is a blessing just to look at him.

The other day he was sitting beside another man in class and the other man got to his feet and said he wanted to testify. He told about a time when he was out on the broad way, selling and using drugs, etc., and something happened to him. He suddenly felt like his heart was stopping and he could not get his breath. He started to climb the stairs to tell the woman he was with, but he could not make his voice sound above a whisper. As he reached the top of the stairs, he completely collapsed and did not come out of it for a while. He said that even that close to death, he did not heed the call of God. But— and then he broke— "God would not give up on me! And now He's got me!" The man I am writing about was just nodding his head in deep appreciation.

Thank God that He is a God of second chances! I owe my all to that God!

The Odinists in facility two have started coming down again to meet, so I have to sit it on them. What a blessing!!!! Now I know you want to know how to take that, don't you? Well, after they assembled and had their introductory "prayer," in which they state themselves to be all of the yesterdays and all of the tomorrows and all of their ancestors, etc., etc., they cross themselves to their multiple gods and sit down. With that they immediately launched into a list of grievances as to how many things other religions get that they are deprived of. You see, the main leader of them is a notorious trouble maker and has made law suits against any chaplain and overseer he has been under. He is a lifer and consequently has no other outlet than to be a nuisance. He suddenly turned to me and asked me when their high feast of Yule was scheduled on the December calendar. I told him it was scheduled on the 21st. He then asked if they were going to be called together for the feast or if it would be served in their cells. I told him it would be served in their cells. You see, the reason for this is that the last time we brought them together it turned into such an ugly scene as some did not want to associate with others, that we declared we would never bring them together from the other facilities again.

So when I told him that the feast would be served in their cells, he immediately responded that such was totally unacceptable. He then told the other men that all they did was take a Kosher meal and repackage it and that it was handled by Muslims and so he would instruct all the other inmates to throw it in the trash when it was given to them.

Now, you ask, Chaplain, how can you call all that a blessing? I sat there thinking, Thank You, Jesus, that you ever called me to be a Christian!!!! Oh my friends, have you thanked God recently for all that you have been saved from by the grace of our loving Lord?

The ringleader of this recently took an eight-inch diameter plastic bowl with a lid on it and then cut strips of cardboard and glued them together and then fastened it to the bowl by gluing about eight wood pencils to it. Then he pulled nylon strings from his laundry bag and wove them into four different diameters and put together the most amazing guitar or banjo. It is now kept in my supervisor's office and given to them for their "worship" service. It actually plays a tune, but very little volume. I would love to send you a picture of it, but of course no cameras are allowed.

Whoops! A few days later: the lieutenant walked into my supervisor's office and saw it and said, "What is that?" It disappeared with him. A couple days later my supervisor called me early in the morning and informed me that the inmate above described was on the bus to another prison. I said, "I am sure that makes you want to cry?"

"No," he said, "it is the season where it is more blessed to give than to receive!"

On Christmas Eve we had a special service scheduled in each of the three facilities, and my wife and I were to be in facility One. We went to the LCP to get the keys to the chapel and the officer asked what service we were there for. He was not the regular officer. I told him it was the regular Protestant worship service, but a special one since it was Christmas Eve. He turned and began to talk to the other officer in the LCP. They were not handing out the keys and I began to wonder what the problem was. Finally, he came back to the window and said that the Lieutenant would be coming out to talk to me.

When he came out he told me that they had no spare officers to run the service. I told him that the major had assured us that morning that all would be in order. He went back in and after a while another lieutenant, this time a female who I knew better, told me she didn't know what to do as they had such a shortage of officers. She said she would work on it, so I asked again for the keys and my wife and I went down to the chapel.

After a while she came down and I asked if they were going to be able to have the service. She said, "You get what you see—I'm it!" I said, "God bless you for this!" After that they called it out and seventy-six men came down and we had a wonderful Christmas service. The men were so grateful that we would come out on Christmas Eve for them, but it was mutual, for we were so happy to be with them too.

Now let me explain why the shortage of officers. Just this morning I talked with one of the Sergeants, and he told me that the prison has enough officers employed on paper, but that too many of them were taking advantage of the state provision called FMLA, and they were desperately understaffed because of it. The FMLA has been mandated by the state, and I believe it may be Federal as well, which gives an employee weeks of leave time for medical or family issues, such as a new baby or a medical need. Christmas time invites the men to take this time just to be off, whether they meet the criteria or not. So the result is that the ones left behind who are willing to work are suffering mandatory overtime and they still run short.

Wouldn't this world be a wonderful place if everyone were a Christian? Come, Millennium; come quickly!!!

For a number of years there has been a very small man from the Dominican Republic who has faithfully attended my classes and church services. He does not venture into the English language any more than he has to, but his face is always radiant. For several months now, I have noticed him visibly going downhill physically. He barely shuffles around, and is losing weight, and looks so frail. But if I ask him if he is all right, he smiles and says, "Yes." About a week and a half ago, I noticed that he was in the ECU (prison hospital). I went over to see him and he was on isolation because of Covid. I pulled his cell door open just a crack and had prayer with him and told him we would be praying for him. He seemed so grateful.

Then a few days later an inmate who does hospice work at the ECU and had him under his care told me that he was out of isolation. I went over again and tried to visit with him. I asked him if he was keeping Jesus in his heart, and he replied with a smile, "All the time." I prayed with him again and then as I looked down at him, I wondered if he would ever get out of there. I do not know if he would even come close to one hundred pounds, and is just a bone rack. I asked him if he had family and he said he does and that they are in this country, but they do not pay any attention to him.

Might I say that lying all alone in a prison hospital bed with little hope of anything but to die there, is not remotely even close to what Satan promised when he pointed to the gate leading into his pathway! The Scripture does not exaggerate when it says, "The thief cometh not, but for to steal, and to kill, and to destroy:" But thankfully Jesus goes on to say, "I am come that they might have life, and that they might have it more abundantly." Please pray for him to know that Abundant Life; here and forever!

Thank you so very much again to all who sent in Bibles in response to our need. We had such a good response that we are well-stocked for some time to come. What a blessed change from empty shelves!

With love and gratitude to all,

William Cawman

February, 2024

THERE IS A SONG which starts like this: "Isn't the love of Jesus something wonderful?..." I find it so! This year started with a trip to Guatemala, which was my twenty-ninth trip there, but the first for five years. As I stood before men and women I had known and worked with for over twenty-five years, I felt a conscious uprising of love for those dear people. Returning on a Saturday and going into prison on Sunday night, as I was shaking hands with the men coming into the chapel, I felt another conscious uprising which translated into: "Oh how I love these men!" Someday soon we shall gather around the Great White Throne of God and be reunited with the whole family of God. What a precious family it is!

The men in prison were so happy to hear of all that God is doing in Guatemala. I told them of a former gang member and how one night years ago, he knelt just in front of the pulpit and motioned me to him. I bent over and he said, "I remember one time when I got on my knees and told Satan he could have all there was of me. Tonight, I have knelt here and told Jesus He could have all there is of me." From that time until now, he has climbed steadily upward in the grace of God.

He married a fine sanctified girl from his own town. The last night of the meeting, he said to me, "I am so glad that God took out of me what would have ruined our marriage. He took the lion out of me and put a lamb in."

I told them of another former gang member who I saw struggle and struggle in and out of the gang and in and out of relationships with women. The same man (that is, in the flesh) stood and with tears soaking his happy face said, "I came to this conference to be filled with more of God. I am going home full!" What a change grace brings where all else fails. His precious wife, who he finally settled down with and married, even before God changed his heart, is also brightly bearing witness to a full heart.

To be able to bring reports like this back to men still struggling with the chains of sin, does more than all the theological teaching one can bring forth. No greater proof of God's infinite grace can be exhibited than these words: "Hear what the Lord has done for me!" After all, Jesus clearly said, "…ye shall *be* witnesses…" not "…ye shall witness." That does not exclude witnessing, but often it is as St Francis of Assisi said, "Preach everywhere you go: whenever necessary, use words."

The Sunday night after returning, I asked the men in the service how many of them wanted to see a genuine revival strike the prison this year. Many hands went up, and I told them to earnestly pray believingly for it. Will you join them?

There is a man I have met here and there over the last months, and the reason I say "here and there," is that he gets moved all around due to his preposterous inability to get along with anyone. The least provocation sends him into a physical fight, and so for a while he has been in the detention center. He asked for me to come see him, and so I did, and had prayer with him and encouraged him to really seek the Lord for a changed heart. Perhaps three weeks later he asked me to come again, so I did. He said that my first visit had really spoken to him and changed his suicidal feelings and that he was trying and doing some better. I told him I would never sell him a bill of goods, and that to be honest with him, he would never have a changed heart by trying a little harder. I urged him to turn against everything he knew would not be pleasing to God and then ask Jesus to come into his heart and make him a new man. He said he would do that and thanked me. I prayed with him and I do believe he sensed a ray of hope.

I was not in the detention center for more than about fifteen minutes, but I could not rid my senses of the smell of K2 smoke for almost two hours. Those drugs are powerful! It is a very sweet smoky smell that just lingers on and on until it finally wears away from the senses, but not the memory. The whole detention center is saturated with it in spite of fans and air purifiers, etc. I fear that custody has just given up on trying to keep it out.

At the close of Jumah prayer in facility two the other Friday, a fight suddenly broke out between a few inmates. Custody rushed in and took the chaplain to the dining room while they broke it up, but it was rather unclear as to who started it and for what reason. The Islamic chaplain is very upset and afraid because of it. He unloaded his concerns to me and then was saying that he couldn't understand why the Muslims have so many more problems with behavior than any other religious group. I was thinking to myself: "Well, chaplain, maybe it is time for you to embrace a better religion."

Pray for him.

Central office in Trenton has now come up with a new program called "Chaplaincy Challenge." They ask inmates from each prison to sign up for it, and then they come down and make a pleasant day of it by having teams compete with each other over what they have learned. It is a mixture of questions from the Bible, the Koran, the Torah, Catholicism, and other religions as well. I concluded that it is not an effort at ecumenicism, but just a test of their knowledge of religion. The inmates had a good day of it because we even had their noon meal brought to them.

While they were doing this, our main supervisor from Trenton came down and took us chaplains aside into my office and told us very plainly that he does not expect us ever to tailor our public praying away from our sincerely held religious belief for fear of offending anyone. Whatever his own religious beliefs are, I appreciated him taking that position with us. Thank God, we still have an open door for now at least.

The men are really appreciating my wife coming in and playing the piano and singing for them. I could see them visibly moved at the song "He Gave Me Something Worth Living For."

I will tell you something rather amusing. When the prison was first built, just before I started there in 1998, the head chaplain ordered three upright ebony Yamaha acoustic pianos, one for each chapel. They were beautiful instruments indeed, but custody drilled holes right down through the shiny ebony finish and installed big screws and then sealed them in with silicone caulking so that the inmates could not get at the strings. As you can guess, four years later the pianos were badly in need of tuning, but I knew what an almost impossible feat it would be to engage a piano tuner to come in and do it. I asked administration if I could trade them for digital pianos, and they said I could as long as I got three bids.

Well, twenty-two years later, the digital pianos are starting to break down and blast out on certain keys, which is very distracting. So, I sent up a request to buy three new ones and it was granted. Just as we got them, I discovered a small roof leak right over one of them, and the piano could only be placed in that location due to the security of the cord. I told the maintenance supervisor about it and he looked at it and said that he really could not call in an outside contractor for a small roof leak. So, my wife went to the fabric store and purchased a piece of canvas such as is used for Jeep tops and made a cover for it.

The Catholic chaplain asked if the three older pianos could be moved up to the small chapel where he has his services in each facility, and approval was given as long as they could be secured from the inmates. The maintenance department was notified to come up with a method of securing them, and after some time went by I knew very well that what was on the back burner would just evaporate there. After seeing what the cover did for the one piano, not only protecting but securing it, I spoke to the assistant superintendent, whom I have known and worked well with all the time I have been there. I told him what my wife had done and asked if he would permit her to do it for the other five. He said, "Sure, Chaplain, go right ahead with my approval, but don't bring too much more common sense in here. We don't know what to do with it!" Everyone who hears his comment, including the administrator himself, immediately laughingly agrees wholeheartedly.

There are two or three men in facility one who are really making spiritual progress. They want me to see them often and as I explain to them the fullness of God's redemptive work, they eagerly accept it as gospel truth. I was telling them about two men in church history, very well known, St. Augustine and John Calvin, and how because of a failure to go on into the full cleansing of their hearts as Paul taught, they went into the most damaging errors ever known in Christendom. It was news to them that Augustine, even with all the respect that is due him as a church father, was the one who led the church of his day into the grossest of errors: viz., praying to the Virgin Mary and the dead saints and infant baptism. Then I went on to say that even though Protestantism rejects such teachings as the work of Satan, he was also the first one to distort the beautiful teaching of Romans 8:28 which speaks of God's predestinated purpose that we be conformed to the image of His Son, and taught from it unconditional predestination, either to be saved or damned. This was certainly the work of Satan and the Bible labels it "doctrines of devils," and it is still doing its deadly work.

Two of the men especially drank it in and one of them with tears told me that he has been asking the Holy Spirit to fill him to overflowing, and he feels He is answering.

The other one is in prison because of an addiction to pornography. He has been clean from it now for three years and his wife says that she has forgiven him. He told me that at night he sometimes has dreams related to all that pornography he indulged in and that in the morning he feels so guilty. I tried to explain to him that we cannot commit sin in our sleep as it involves the use of our will, but that Satan never forgets where our open door was and will try one way or another to get back in. I told him that as long as it persists, not to get used to the feeling it gives him, but that the feeling was not true guilt, but abhorrence, and that he must not lose it. I encouraged him that if he keeps the door shut and pleads the Blood over it, the battle ground would begin to recede by continued victory.

The third one has a background that is already largely satisfying to him. His father is a minister and his mother, he claims, is a prayer warrior. They have an independent church which he says believes in it all— "being filled with the Spirit, slain in the Spirit, speaking in tongues, etc." It all seems so right to him that even though he agrees with everything I tell him, I'm not sure he is really getting it.

He was at a party one night and took a few too many drinks and on the way home had an accident with another car in which was a woman passenger ninety-eight years old. She was taken to the hospital and released, but three weeks later died. Her son, being a police officer, if I got the story straight, brought charges against this man saying she died as a result of the accident. A lawyer is working on his case to try to get the sentence revoked, but he doesn't know how successful it will be. He is a very bright and cheerful young man and I wish so much that he could really get in his heart what good there is in his head.

Once again it is so obvious that the closer one gets to the real work of grace, and yet misses the full cleansing of the heart, the greater the deception and the more difficult it is to see it and be delivered. I could easily draw a parallel to many in the holiness movement, but I am not supposed to be preaching here, am I?

Thank you each one again for your faithful prayers. God is answering them.

William Cawman

March, 2024

A YEAR AGO THIS month I asked a question regarding the Wednesday noon chaplain prayer time, as to whether every heart who attended was fully in tune with God. A year later I believe we have only had to cancel one of them, although I have not been at every one due to the fact that I am often gone in meetings elsewhere. I cannot help but believe, however, that God has heard some of the prayers that have gone up. I want to tell you about the prayer time on February 7, just a few days ago from my writing about it.

It promised to be a very busy day for both myself and my supervisor, due to the fact that he was leaving for two weeks on vacation and several new services had been set up and some mistakes had been made in doing so, and it was my lot to try to straighten them out. In order to have more table space to work on a project, my supervisor came down early in the morning to the chapel where my office is. He told me that on his way to the prison (he drives an hour and a half to get there) he heard a little voice suggesting to him that he had so much to do that day it might be best for him to skip the prayer time. Then he looked at me and said, "I think I recognize where that voice came from; I would rather have to stay late than miss the time of prayer." I agreed and thanked him.

When we got to the room where we have prayer, it was only himself, myself, and the other part-time chaplain. The Catholic chaplain had something come up that kept him away. We went around in turns, praying for the various requests brought up, then the supervisor just began softly humming a tune and then began to very feelingly just worship and thank the Lord. Soon tears were running down his face and he burst out with, "Oh Jesus, I love You so much!" We lingered a while almost in silence and then the other part-time chaplain began to open up his heart.

He is the only Christian in his whole family. His wife divorced him years ago and he has lived celibate for a long while. All of his children are so taken up with the worldly ways that he doesn't even want to be with them at Christmas time, for their activities and pleasures are so far from God. His oldest son joined the army, but after a time was so delinquent with drugs and loose living that he was court martialed. His father had to meet him at the plane and walk with him down the tarmac while he was made a spectacle of before his comrades. He was tried and sent to prison for some time.

After that, he continued his loose living with drugs and women, bearing at least one child out of wedlock, and plummeting downward so dramatically that his father judges him to be demon possessed. Now let me insert that his father confessed to us that his own example during his son's early years sowed the seeds for such a lifestyle, and he deeply regrets it.

But the night before he was telling us this in the prayer time, after the precious season of worship, he came home to find a package on his step. He tried to recall whether he had ordered something, and then his phone rang. His son said, "Dad, I mailed you a Bible study; can we do a Bible study together?" He told us he was almost in a state of shock. His faith was not able to grasp that it could be genuine after all he had seen his son go through, and he just sat there still trying to wrap his mind around it. Of course, he had told his son that he certainly could, but that didn't break the emotional turmoil he was having over it.

We went back to prayer. I prayed first, noting that when Jesus went into the garden the third time, there was not a far-out product of Satan's works that could ever go farther than that prayer. Then the supervisor prayed and we agreed to believe God for a desperately needed miracle. When we returned to our work rooms, my supervisor said, "Now I know for sure where that voice came from!"

That afternoon, we had a precious time in Bible study over Jesus' parable of the barren fig tree. As we stood back and looked deeply into mercy rejoicing against judgment, I could see many of the men visibly moved at the thought that mercy had prevented judgment from giving them what they deserved. While I do not know all of their backgrounds and the sins they committed, I was conscious that I myself undoubtedly fit the parable more vividly than any of them. What shame that after being planted in vineyard space with all the vineyard privileges, I failed for so long to bear fruit that it would have been only just to cut me down. Oh, thank You, Jesus, for mercy!!!

The following week in facility three, at the beginning of the class a man said, "That subject last week about the mercy of God awakened me like never before as to how good God has been to me." This man is serving a life sentence, but is walking so close to God that I would not have much doubt but what he has entered into the fullness of the blessing. He certainly believes in it and loves it.

I believe I have told you about the Odinist who is such a pain to work with. He is also a lifer and has been the rounds of both state and federal prisons and has left a trail behind him such that he is known all over the state. My supervisor has done his best to keep him pacified and has bent over backwards to provide whatever was legally allowable for him to "worship" as he desires to. He is never satisfied, and it would seem the little measure of satisfaction he does attain is derived from being such a nuisance to everyone.

For a while I was assigned to monitor the group he is in, but with my limited time my supervisor realized it was too much and he took it on. As I told you, he has, from all I can see, done all he could to keep him pacified, but in spite of it, the rascal does not like my supervisor.

I think I might know one reason he doesn't like him. A while back, in order to treat them with equal rights as the other groups, my supervisor arranged for all of the Odinists from all three facilities to come together for one of their quarterly high-feast days. When our problem child walked into the room, he saw two black transgenders from one of the other facilities and immediately raised a storm and got several others to walk out on them. My supervisor tried to stop him but he would not listen. My supervisor told him he would have to make a charge and report him. He answered, "Good luck with that!" and walked on out. Well, his actions reached the supervisor clear up in Trenton, and he called down to my supervisor and told him that he was to put the Muslim chaplain in there to monitor them. We all raised our eyebrows, but so far it seems to be working???

I sometimes try to grapple with the thought of why anyone with any degree of intelligence is attracted to such unbelievably insane nonsense as these false religions hold, but all I can come up with is that Satan, the father of lies, has them completely blinded to even the smallest grain of sensible thinking.

I am presently waiting for one more of the five inmates I had chosen to write their testimonies out to finish his, and then I plan as soon as possible to send them in book form to the publisher for printing. Please pray for this project as I believe it will be very edifying to anyone interested in reading it. It will also splendidly magnify the grace of God in its ability to bring a soul out of any background that Satan afflicted them with, into the marvelous beauty and unity of the family of God. As most of you would be aware, twenty years of these letters have been put in book form and published by Schmul Publishing Company in five volumes, but the one I am working on now is different in that it is not what I have written about them, but what they themselves have written. I plan to title this one, "Testimonies From Prison Walls." I will give a notice in a future letter when it is printed and ready.

Could I just give you a sneak preview of a statement from

one of them; a third generation Mormon; now a sanctified Christian? Here it is: "How ironic that in the beauty of the forests and mountains of my youth, cult life smothered God's beauty. But in the ugliness and stench of prison, God's light shines from every corner." Now, don't you want to read the rest of it?

I read many missionary reports from foreign and homefront missions and I often find them full of names of people to pray about. I am forbidden to give out names, so I just have to give anonymous pictures, but I would love to give you specific names of those who most need your prayers. Seeing that to be impossible, I know the Holy Spirit can bring them to your mind and heart, and they most certainly and passionately need it.

One of them that I would ask special prayer for is the young man that I told you I saw weeping in Bible study and the next day discovered that they were tears of joy. I just love to see a babe in Christ grow! And he is certainly doing so. He is starting to give some very good answers to questions raised in the Bible studies, where before I never heard a word out of him. And what he does not say with his lips, his face says it even more eloquently.

There is another, clear at the other end of the prison, who is also radiating clearly a growth in God. I love to watch his face as we sing; it is absolutely passionately opening his heart up to God with a ravenous appetite. I have noticed for years, that whenever a soul like these hears the message of holiness, it grasps the teaching with head and heart. But if the profession is of the flesh, the message of holiness is repulsed like poison. But then, we shouldn't be surprised at such an observation, for the Scripture nailed down the reason for it in the clearest language: "We are of God: he that knoweth God heareth us; he that is not of God heareth not us. Hereby know we the spirit of truth, and the spirit of error." 1 John 4:6.

There are two very common responses I often hear from men when they are faced with truth. I would not venture to give a percentage of one over the other, but the first one I will echo is given far oftener than the second. Here they are: (1) "I'm working on it." (2) "I'm asking the Lord to fill me with His Spirit." I would surmise that you, the reader, would easily guess the difference in my intake of it.

We are planning a Good Friday service in each facility and then a special service for Easter Sunday night. Please pray for these. The Christmas message of Christ's birth is wonderful, but the story of His death and resurrection is by far more powerful. Pray that God will anoint every effort with His presence. I will plan to take my wife and our pastor and some of his family in for those special services.

Let me relate an incident from years ago that demonstrates so clearly the power of the resurrection story. We had been having children's services right down in the drug alley of Vineland, NJ. I would play my trumpet and sing choruses with them, then we would have prayer and a lesson with Betty Lukens flannel graph stories. A man told us that the children of our day would not relate to those simple flannel graph lessons and he offered to work up a Power Point program for them. I felt a chill of rejection come over me. The next week was the story of the death and resurrection of Jesus. As the flannel graph story was being told, there sat a row of thirteen- and fourteen-year-old boys who had grown up watching unmonitored television with all of its horror and filth. As the story progressed, those boys quieted down and listened intently. When it was finished, they were asked how many of them would like to ask Jesus to come into their hearts. Every hand went up. The power of the simple gospel message gains nothing by technological embellishment! So may it be again this year. Thank you again for every prayer for us.

William Cawman

14
GOD'S GRACE CONTINUES TO OVERCOME

April, 2024

> *He lives! He lives! Christ Jesus lives today.*
> *He walks with me and He talks with me along life's narrow way.*
> *He lives! He lives! Salvation to impart.*
> *You ask me how I know He lives? He lives within my heart!*

ISN'T IT WONDERFUL THAT we can KNOW? How do I know that my seven-month-old granddaughter who is sitting on my lap as I write this is alive? Because she acts like it! How do I know that the young man sitting on the front row in prison church is alive? You got it!

Dear friends, the very next best thing to knowing that He lives in our heart is to know that He lives in someone else's heart. Prv. 27:19 "As in water face answereth to face, so the heart of man to man." Let's get this straight: it is not because another shares the same theological degree as myself; it is not because another shares my viewpoint on matters; it is not because another attends the same church as myself that brings a bond of kindling flame between us, it is because He lives within our hearts!

And the young man in prison did not grow into this by gradual osmosis by being in my classes; he suddenly came alive that day that I have told you about when tears kept bursting forth unbidden from his eyes and he told me the next day that they were tears of joy because he is finally right where God wants him to be. Since that day, there has been a conspicuous resurrection from the dead. How is that possible, you ask? Because of Him who said: "…because I live, ye shall live also."

On Good Friday, we had planned to have a service in each of the three facilities and I was planning on my wife and our pastor and his family helping us. It was to be an unusually long time slot from eight until ten-thirty in the morning. On Palm Sunday we were all in a convention in Pennsylvania when my supervisor called me and asked if our pastor could take a separate service so that he could be free to float around and make sure everything was going well. I told him we could work that out and he was glad.

Well, it so happened that there came into our convention an unwelcome guest—just as unwelcome as Satan was among the Sons of God—and just as un-self-conscious as he was about it. It came from the society of mutated microbes with only one positive aspect: it was no respecter of persons. People started dropping like flies with severe cold and stomach upsets. Hardly anyone escaped, and many came down with it after returning home.

Such was the case with the pastor and his family, until by Good Friday they were in poor shape to go in and start the plague among thirty-five-hundred men in prison. So my supervisor had to take one of the services after all.

My wife and I went in and seventy men came down for it in the middle facility where we were. It was a very precious service. I started in by telling them that when I entered the restroom right off of the chapel that morning, there was a spider web in the corner with a huge spider that apparently had become ensnared in his own web and died of starvation. I told them that is how the precious Blood of Jesus shed for us on the Cross found us: starved and entangled in the web of sin. But then I told them that there was not one single case of such but what the Blood that flowed from the Cross of Jesus could not restore back to life again.

We then had an opening prayer and a song. I went over the Scriptural instructions for taking communion and while they were passing out the elements, my wife taught them a chorus: "Under the Blood of Jesus; safe in His gentle fold. Under the Blood of Jesus, safe while the ages roll. Safe though the world may crumble; safe though the stars grow dim; under the Blood of Jesus, I am secure in Him." We had printed out little slips with the words and told them to take them back to their cells and put them up on the wall to look at whenever Satan came to attack them.

Then we took communion together; the first time we had done so since the start of Covid. The men deeply appreciated it too. Then my wife and I sang a duet to them and then I preached from the seven sayings of Christ on the Cross. The men were visibly moved and then at times just broke out with clapping their hands. God was definitely speaking to many of them.

During the message I said, "Men, I know full well where I am standing; in an institution owned by the State of New Jersey. But I do not belong to the State, I belong to Jesus Christ and I must be faithful to His truth." They clapped their hands. I said, "Sinful men charged Jesus with an absolutely insane accusation. They said He had declared He would tear down the temple and rebuild it in three days. Now, what court of law today, no matter how corrupt, would condemn a man to death for such a statement? But right now, we are witnessing the incoming antichrist of a one-world government charge Christians with the same degree of odious insanity. They are declaring us hateful because we will not endorse their total departure from all that God has established."

We are praying that the men will feel more deeply than ever what Jesus did for them and yield their all to Him. During the message I had pressed home to them the importance of each of the sayings of Christ on the Cross to their own spiritual needs of coming fully right with God. It seemed to reach a climax when we came to the saying: "It is finished!" I took them up to the mountain as Isaac lay on the altar with a sword just above his breast. He had submitted to his father's directions until at that point there was no remaining way to abort the death blow. It was finished! I told them that they would never know the utter joy of God's smile until it was settled beyond all opportunities to turn back that they were going to be fully God's. I trust and pray that it will be more than a passing emotion that was felt with them, but that they will get it that settled.

As the men were coming in at the beginning, an officer who I have seen many times but never had conversation with, came into the chapel and wanted to thank me for so faithfully coming in for the men. He really seemed to have a heart for their spiritual welfare, but then he began to tell me how frustrating it was becoming to try to work there with such prevalence of drugs throughout the institution. He said he was physically struggling himself because of all the drug smoke in the atmosphere. I agreed that it was so sad to see this taking place when it never was so before.

After the services, our supervisor took my wife and I and the other chaplain out for lunch together.

I wish I could give you a better update on one inmate, but the old saying is that "you can lead a horse to water, but you cannot make him drink." I have written before about a morning when I entered the chapel to get something and found a single man there studying the Hebrew writings. He asked me if I thought there was any validity to the New Testament and Jesus and Paul. I told him I certainly did and sat down and talked with him for a while. He wanted to repeat the visit, so I began to call him down every little while until one day he told me that he was no more Jewish than I was Italian. I asked him why he continued with it then and he said it was political???

I began to steer away from him to some degree until he asked for more visits. I decided it was time to come clear with him. I gave him the little booklet of Bible studies we had developed during Covid on "The Disease and The Cure." I told him I wanted him to go and study it carefully and then let me know how he felt about it. He came back with some stupid technical questions that let me know his heart was as hard as a rock. I decided to let him alone for a while and let him soak.

Then after a few weeks I was walking into the compound and met him in a wheelchair being pushed back to the hospital. He immediately accosted me and wanted to know why I hadn't come to see him. So I went. He had nearly died over severe infection in his leg that had gone to the point of giving him a heart problem. I sat down outside his door and listened to his troubles and then I asked him when he was going to get right with God and ready for eternity to which he come so close. He began to speak seriously and told me he knew it was time for him to stop playing around and get right. I assured him that was right and that for him to profess to be a Jew when he was not was nothing but a lie that God would never honor. He agreed that he would get that stopped.

Apparently, while I was gone, he sent in a request to be removed from the Jewish programs, for when I returned, I found he was not listed. A week later, after he felt better and was returned to his cell in population, my supervisor said to me, "Guess who was in the Rabbi's Torah study today?" I just shook my head. I can't make him drink. I pray that God will yet be able to get through to him, but the longer a man hardens his heart against truth, the less likely he is to ever change. Oh the absurd irrationality of the sinful heart! Here is a man in his late sixties or early seventies, nearing the end of a life sentence from which he will never be released, and still willing to miss heaven and go to hell for all eternity over whatever he meant by politics!

But back to the Good Friday services. The best part of Good Friday is that Sunday is coming! Resurrection Sunday! My wife and I went back to the same unit for the five-thirty Sunday night service. Sixty men attended the service and God met with us. It was a very uplifting time to see the men so excited about a Risen Savior. I started the service by telling them that I had an announcement to make and I wanted them to listen carefully. The room became very quiet as I announced very loudly: "He is Risen!" Then the whole room burst into applause and rejoicing.

We sang a few Easter songs together and then my wife read a story from the Sunday School paper which I could see was registering in their hearts. After that I told them that many churches put the pastor's upcoming sermon title on the sign board out front. With that I taped a sheet of paper to the front of the pulpit with large red letters: "AND." I then turned to Romans 3:26: "To declare, I say, at this time his righteousness: that he might be just, *and* the justifier of him which believeth in Jesus." I told them that for four thousand years there was no "and" between Just and Justifier, but instead an ugly "or." I then pasted that over top of the "AND," and explained the dilemma even God experienced as to being just or justifying. That all changed in one moment on the Cross as Jesus cried out "It is finished," and reached out and tore that ugly "or" away, leaving a shining "AND" whereby God can be just and at the same time justify us through Jesus' death and resurrection. Having every one of them been in a court room, they understood the dilemma and the solution!

Thank you, each of you, for your continued prayers for us; God is answering!

William Cawman

May, 2024

Sunday night, April 14, I was preaching to one of the groups from Pilate's words: "What shall I do then with Jesus which is called Christ?" My wife told me afterwards how riveted the men's attention was. One man just got on his knees while I was preaching; another came up afterwards and with tears in the background of his eyes just said, "Thank you; thank you; thank you!" It brings to my mind the words of a song:

> I know not how the Spirit moves,
>   Convincing men of sin;
> Revealing Jesus through the Word,
>   Creating faith in Him
> But I know Whom I have believed…!

Oh for a wave of conviction to settle down inside and outside of the prison.

I received a request from a man stating that he needed to talk to a chaplain about his spiritual state. I went to see him and this is what he told me. He was raised in a nominally Christian home but became somewhat disgusted with it and turned his back on it completely. He fathered two daughters by two different women and was living that type of lifestyle. He had no use for God and felt he didn't even believe in Him.

A couple of weeks before this visit with me, he told me that he received news that his oldest daughter at the age of twenty-four, had overdosed and died. It hit him hard and he was trying to recover himself and was sitting on his bunk in Indian style just suffering. Suddenly it felt like a hand pressed against his back, pushing his head down to his knees. Somehow, he knew it was the hand of God. He began to cry out to God and ask Him if He could forgive him, and he felt an overwhelming Presence all over him. He got up and looked in the mirror because he could feel a hand on his shoulder. He said he could actually see a hand, but nothing else, and it brought a calm peace and desire to be close to God. He began reading the Bible and as he did, he felt God's nearness speaking to him.

I listened to his story and then I asked him if all of that was drawing him away from the desire to sin and he said it was. So I told him it could not have been of the devil, for Satan would never change his desires that way. I left him in the room and went and printed off a copy of the Bible studies we had given to the men during Covid, "The Disease and the Cure," and told him I would call him down again in a few days. He was very thankful.

The next week I put him on the list for a visit, but when I got there, I found that he had been sent out on a trip. For what I do not know, but I will have to follow it up when he returns. Please pray for him. And while you do, why should we not be praying for all those to whom God is appearing and convicting that we never hear about. Every once in a while, we are made aware that God is working intensely in getting His bride ready for His soon coming.

The past week in one of the classes, the subject came up again as to whether we can lose our salvation. I could sense pretty strongly that the man who brought it up was not a proponent of that doctrine. I told them that we would take just a few minutes to discuss it, but we would start with this observation: Some say we can lose our salvation and some say we cannot. Both of these cannot be right; one of them of necessity has to be wrong. So instead of wasting a lot of time arguing about it; why shouldn't we live carefully enough so that we don't. A burst of applause went over the group, for which I was thankful and relieved.

I did then go on to explain that to say we cannot lose salvation makes no sense whatsoever, because if we look at what the word "salvation" means, it must mean that we are in a state of being saved from something, and in the spiritual sense it means we are in a state of being saved from sin. So if after having been saved from sinning we go back into it again, how can we say we still have salvation? Thankfully, this group of men did not offer to argue the opposite nor did they seem upset with the outcome, so we went on to our Bible study material.

We are getting multiple requests each week to join the Sunday services and Bible studies. That is certainly encouraging, but oh how much I wish the State would see fit to give us a full-time secretary again to take care of all of this clerical work. It would give us so much more time for personal ministry to the men. It would even help if they would do what they say they are going to do and give us new computers and a faster program on them. Much of the time we have to wait and wait while the thing spins and spins around its antique brain. I regret every minute I am required to sit in front of that digital screen instead of being able to talk with someone about their spiritual condition. If you would feel it on your heart to pray for this little grumbling session, I would be most grateful. I would not even discourage you from praying that the whole computer program would crash! If God would lead you that way, and then answer your prayers and let it happen, I would be most willing to deal with the outcome! And by now I am sure you can detect that I am not even remotely in love with computers, even though I am using one to write this letter on.

Our assistant superintendent who was responsible for chaplaincy just moved to another prison and another person took his position. I have known him the whole time I have been in the prison for we both started about the same time. He has always been my friend and would do his best for us, but he was not aggressively working for us. The new person so far is! We have been suffering in our Sunday night services because of the slowness of getting the evening meal over with so that we could start on time. This superintendent is moving forward to correct that. Thank the Lord, and please pray that it will get corrected. Sometimes the Sunday night services are cut so short that it is almost impossible to make it effective.

Thank you for praying about our shortage of ministers for Sunday night services. My pastor is now registered as a volunteer and can help on Sunday nights and then still make it back to our church for service. It does make a full day for him, however, as that means he preaches three times on the Sundays he is needed in prison. It is also such a blessing to the men whenever my wife goes in with me. She nearly always goes on Sunday nights, and once in a while she will come in for the Bible studies and teach the men choruses. She has started teaching them Scriptures set to music in order to fix the Scriptures in their minds. They really enjoy that too. I cannot truthfully say that we are ready to record a CD as of yet, so please do not order any.

Canadian geese really love prison life! Every year we get more of them and right now their eggs are hatching and the little goslings are growing rapidly. They are so used to being around people that they hardly bother to move over when walking past them. For all that however, I cannot find a great love for them in my heart. It becomes necessary to watch the ground all the time instead of the beautiful Spring sky and trees.

One day I was walking down the main compound and to my right was a mud puddle full of goose pruning byproducts, and in it were three half-grown geese. To my left was another along with the mother and father. As I passed between them both parents rose up to their full height and hissed menacingly at me. I looked at them and wanted to say, "If you would care to fly over the fence, there are plenty of beautiful lakes and rivers out there in the free world." Then it dawned on me that in the housing units of the same prison, we have over three thousand men who if let free would soon be right back in again.

This is definitely one factor that looms up over and over in working with men from a non-church background, let alone a complete bankruptcy of family values and structure. Unless they go all the way with God and be filled with the Spirit and stay that way, they so easily slip back into the house from which they came out, as the Scripture says, and it doesn't even seem as serious to them as it would to us who have been raised in a home and family discipline. There seems to be a powerful addiction to the familiar. When God was ready to lead Jacob into His future will for him, Rachael went and secretly stole her father's images and took them along and then lied to her father that she did not have them. What had those idols ever done for her? God was holding out before her a place in the great plan of God whereby she could become a part of His raising up a people who would bring forth His Son. But she was under a spell of insecurity to leave those false gods and launch out into the unknown future with God. So it is to those whose only security factor has been the underlife of the dregs of society. If they grow cold in their love for Jesus, they instinctively and invariably return back to the only support group they formerly knew.

I cannot leave that analysis alone to those who have the background described. How many there are who are raised in a church setting and family security but simply live the culture surrounding that lifestyle because that is all they know. One day God in mercy awakens them to their barren fig tree condition. Startled and convicted, they cry out to God and He answers them with a glorious deliverance from a form without the power. But if they do not stay completely filled with the Spirit, and allow their love for God and holiness to begin to dim, they go right back to the house they came out of and return to a headcount on the church bulletin board, but add nothing to the spiritual life of the church. In God's sight, one is just as eternally disastrous as the other.

The upcoming book of five testimonies from men who are or were behind prison walls is in its final editing stage and will soon be sent to the publisher who has committed to getting it out this summer. I will let you know when it is available and you will certainly find it a blessing, even as I did. The men have certainly done an excellent job of uplifting the redeeming power of the Blood of Jesus.

Please pray with us that even though we will be away in meetings a number of times over the next few months, the work of God can go on in the hearts of the men God is working on. Again I say that it is a blessing to have my pastor back in as a volunteer as that is one more voice for truth and holiness. The Bible studies continue to be owned of God. I have them in two of the facilities and then often my supervisor asks me to take his in the other facility. In addition to these I have a service on Tuesdays in the minimum-security camp which varies greatly in attendance. And then there are three five-thirty services on Sunday nights. We are praying for genuine revival of conviction for sin. Will you help us pray? Thank you each one again for all you are doing to uphold us in prayer.

William Cawman

June, 2024

LIFE AS A CHAPLAIN in prison does not go on and on the same. Sometimes I look back and reflect on how things were when I first started ministering here and then look at the changes that have taken place in a quarter of a century. I cannot look at those changes too long, for most of them are not good ones. The evil of our society has moved into the prison population and brought about such negative influences and practices that it could seem overwhelming at times.

The actual truth is that where a few years ago supreme efforts were being put forth to keep drugs out of prison, they are now being given in the prison and there seems to be no concern to keep them out. A sergeant who will soon retire told me privately that as soon as his time is finished, he will turn and sue the State for the damage his work environment has done to his lungs. The worst area in the prison is the lockup where men are sent for breaking the prison rules or for starting fights. I do not even go there unless it is absolutely necessary by an inmate calling to us for help, because just a few minutes in there takes at least two hours to get rid of the smell of the smoke. But there are officers who spend day after day in that atmosphere.

A few years ago, a young inmate came to me with fear in his eyes because his cell mate was using marijuana in their cell at night and he was afraid they would be found out and he would lose his date to go home in two weeks. I reported it to the sergeant in the area and he reported it to special investigations. I was called up front to write up a report on what I had heard, which was that the second shift female officer was the one bringing the marijuana in to him. They got rid of the officer. Now New Jersey has legalized marijuana, so it is no longer a sin! How many other sins are facing the same recategorization God only knows!

But, God has not released me as yet, so I am praying that God will give yet more souls for His kingdom. And He is! Bless His name! I just love to watch a man touch through to real salvation and then watch him grow in grace. That is one of the surest signs that the work of salvation has been genuine; it leaves a soul with an appetite for more. This is certainly taking place with the young man I have told you about previously who was bursting out with tears in a Bible study. He is now so attentive and interactive in the classes, and I can just feel his love and hunger for more of God.

Another answer to your prayers has come through as you prayed that my wife could go back in with me. One of the most valuable and effective witnesses I have seen over the years to men in prison is to take women in who are examples of Bible teaching. This may seem strange to you, but in all the years I have taken godly women into the prison, I have never heard one word of criticism or objection as to how they were dressed. Even though many of the men have never in their lifetime seen Biblical modesty in women, they really respect it and even comment favorably about it. May God help us to refuse to compromise and begin to take on the world in our attire. Our outward is definitely a recognizable witness to how much we love and obey God, and the world knows it very well.

Please continue to help us pray that we can see the prison schedules brought into more order so that we have more time in our worship services and Bible studies. The drug problem I mentioned above, which we never had to deal with a few years ago, causes more code 33s than I can ever remember. It seems the devil just loves to bring on a code 33 just in time for church, so that the compound is locked down and the church service is late. Now in case you are unfamiliar with a code 33, I am not! It means, "Officer needs assistance;" and then if you desire to know what the officer needs assistance for, it is called "a fight!" You see, without a change of heart which can only be brought about by the Blood of Jesus, men continue the same behavior inside of prison that brought them there, and the readily available drugs just add fuel to their fires.

Another prayer request is that for some time we have had very little attendance to the Tuesday afternoon service in the minimum camp. I asked permission to try a service on Sunday afternoons at two-thirty and we are now trying that with a greater attendance so far. We can hardly ask a volunteer to come in that early on Sundays, so it falls to one of the three Protestant chaplains to do it. However, if more men will attend, we are all willing to go in early for it. Of all areas where God is definitely needed it is there where men are getting ready to move back out into society again.

While requesting prayer for this, I will also again ask prayer for several other factors we have discovered that are impacting our service attendance and times.

One of these is, and I believe I heard it correctly today, that we are experiencing approximately one hundred and fifty code 53s a week. A code 53 is a medical emergency. By far the greatest percentage of these are drug related; something we faced very rarely only five years ago. Drugs are running rampant through the whole prison and it seems they have just given up in trying to curb it. Of course, this often takes place right at service or Bible study time, as I mentioned above, stopping movement.

Not only does it stop movement in the immediate area, but there is such a shortage of officers that they often shut down a whole area or the whole prison in order to have enough staff to attend to it. Often too, the drugs trigger fights, which then is a code 33. The only reason for this astronomical increase in prison schedule disturbance is DRUGS!

Another factor we are dealing with is that the intercom system is broken in the whole prison and they rejected the price to have it repaired. So very often and in many of the units if an officer is not particularly in harmony with a Bible study, he may just lift his voice a bit and say, "Church." Men in their cells with their fans running because of the heat do not even hear it.

Please help us pray that we can somehow see this changed until we can have the proper attendance again. I heard that on the last Sunday of May, three state prisons, including ours, went into total no movement because of shortage of officers.

Now, I don't want you to think that everything is negative, for God is still working. If there is such a thing as a normal day in prison, Tuesday, May 28, was not one of them. I arrived at my supervisor's office in the morning to find him sitting in conference with the Rabbi and a member of the Ethiopian Jewish sect. He had come from one of the other prisons and had won a law suit against the chaplain there and now he is here, trying to establish his freedom to worship. He claims that he needs a small bottle of spiced oil every day which he rubs over his entire body as he says his prayers. The former chaplain had inquired and found it to be not a requirement in any Jewish group, but then he told him that he only had enough oil for the Muslims. That did it! The inmate won the case.

Anyway, after he left, my supervisor looked at me and said,

"Can you see what I am into? Can you take my Bible study today?" I agreed and it was by then 12:10 and the Bible study was in another facility at 1:00. I closed up what I was working on and headed over, asking the Lord to direct me.

I opened up by singing a couple of songs about the Lord's return to earth. Then I went to 2 Peter, chapter 3, and focused on these words. "Seeing then that all these things shall be dissolved, what manner of persons ought ye to be in all holy conversation and godliness, looking for and hasting unto the coming of the day of God, wherein the heavens being on fire shall be dissolved, and the elements shall melt with fervent heat?"

I then told them we were going to do a study on those words. I started by asking them what manner of persons they would want to be if they knew Jesus was coming that day. Hands went up and a lively discussion followed with many good thoughts. After we had discussed that for a time, I asked them to tell me things they would not want to be doing when Jesus comes back. Again, a very lively time with many good thoughts came out. By this time, it was nearing the closing time, but I told them I wanted to ask them one more thing. I asked them if they were living just like they would want to if Jesus was their cellmate. A ripple went through the room and one man said, "Whew! I didn't expect that!" I then told them that Jesus would be coming back when they weren't expecting it too.

It was a very profitable time and I felt the Lord witnessing to it by His presence. The men were a lively bunch as they left the room.

The next day, in another facility Bible study, we were finishing with the last of seven teachings taken from Matthew chapter thirteen, Revelation three, and church history. We were of course studying the Laodicean Church. As I began to point out how and why the church slipped from what it was during the Philadelphia church to the Laodicean, I mentioned the advent of the television. I told them that all Biblically grounded and spiritual churches had rejected it from the very outset. I told them that I felt so blessed because I have now lived eighty years and never once had one in my home.

Can you imagine their responses? One man said, "How long have you been living?" I said, "Eighty years."

"And you have never had a television?"

"That's right."

"And you don't have one now?"

"No, sir, and I am so blessed. I cannot even bear to be around one." I then told them that I don't watch television on the internet or on my phone either; I leave it completely alone. I discovered that this generation is so foreign to that possibility that it wouldn't be any stranger to tell them that I have not had a drink of water for eighty years.

Then I began to point out what has happened to us in every way over the last hundred years and what the motive for it all was. Heads began to assent in agreement. So now we will return to our further study of the Life of Christ and see what else He has for us.

Isn't it just glorious to be a Christian!!!??? Thank you for your prayers,

William Cawman

15
GOD IS NOT BAFFLED BY MAN'S CHANGES

July, 2024

I WILL START WITH an observation—take it for nothing weightier than that. God does not classify sin the same as society does. If I am not mistaken, the greatest sin that could be committed would be the breaking of the Greatest Commandment. I stand guilty! For too long, with great regret, I confess that I was guilty of that sin. How can I, looking from God's viewpoint, look down on any other sinner?

Well, having made that observation I will tell you that a few days ago an inmate was sent down to our prison from another one after he had stabbed an officer. He was sent with red flags all over his name and was immediately placed in a cell within a cell in detention. He was twenty-eight years of age with a Hispanic name, and was classified as a Protestant Christian, although on his face sheet he had also been a Muslim.

Orders came from administration that he was to be visited by Protestant chaplaincy, and that they could take him only a Bible and a Daily Bread, but that no chaplain was to go alone; there must be at least two, and they were to be escorted by a Lieutenant. So my supervisor asked me to go with him and we entered the "smoke house" and spoke to the Lieutenant about it. He said that he had to leave immediately but that if we would wait, his replacement would be coming in about ten minutes. We waited for half an hour and the Lt never came. We finally left and while walking back to the office we met the assistant superintendent coming the other way down the compound. We stopped and reported that we had made the effort to see him, but that an Lt was not available. She thanked us for trying and said to try again the next day.

I then asked her what would be done with him and she said he would be shipped out of state. The following morning, I was talking to one of the Muslim imams when my supervisor and the Rabbi walked in. My supervisor motioned for me to follow him to another room and then said, "Well, I have good news and bad news. The good news is that you will not have to go visit that inmate and the bad news is that he now says he is a Muslim, so I will have to take the Imam over to see him.

Now, after that story I come back to the opening observation. We have any number of inmates under our care who have stabbed someone, but since this one stabbed one of their own, he is high-profile. So you see, we classify sin as to the degree of impact it has on us, personally. What a re-evaluation of this will appear on the Great Day of Judgment!

I would like now to make a second observation. That observation is that we humans very seldom bestow laurels where they belong. As an example, Charles G. Finney has been exonerated as a great evangelist; and I am not taking that away from him. But it is well documented that everywhere he went, a school mate of his followed him and sequestered himself in a hotel and prayed without ceasing while Finney preached.

Well, a few months ago, the powers that be in Trenton, came up with a new program called "Chaplain Challenge." A number of inmates were selected from each prison in the State and then a female chaplain from up north came in and quizzed them on their knowledge of religion. I attended the first session or two but quickly became disenchanted with it as very little of it was Christian. It was heavy on all other religions. After several winners were selected, they then competed with inmates from the other prisons until there were two winners; then those two prisons competed and ours won! Whooppeee! That last word simply reflects the excitement and publicity felt by everyone except perhaps a few—I being one of the few.

A huge trophy was sent down to our prison and the administrator then asked the chaplains to gather out front by the flag poles while he took our pictures holding the said trophy. I thought to myself, why are we holding this thing? It was two inmates inside the prison that won it; not us! In fact, I only sat in on two of the sessions.

Thankfully, when the rewards are passed out in heaven, God will make no mistake nor show a bit of favoritism as to who gets them.

Afterwards I was visiting with one of the winners of this and I find him to be very intelligently interested in completely taking God's way from here on out. He will be released before too long and will be restored to his wife and children again and he says it is settled to never fall into his old sins again. He is finding communion with God in prayer and I have urged him to press on until he knows he is "filled with the Spirit."

He told me that he had a dream, and in his dream he was standing before a large audience on the outside of prison when suddenly he made eye contact with a Muslim man who lives on his tier. He felt God speak to him and tell him to go to the Muslim and tell him that Jesus loves him. He felt a trembling and wanted to be sure that God really wanted him to, but after several days he saw him outside of his cell and felt urged to go speak to him. He went over and asked if he could talk with him a bit. "Sure," was the response. He told him about the dream he had and then told him that in his dream God spoke to him and told him to tell him that Jesus loves him. It is not the normal thing at all to choke up with tears in a prison setting, but he couldn't help it.

The man quickly turned his head away, but when he looked back at the speaker, there were tears in his eyes and he said, "Thank you; I needed to hear that!"

In a day or so, the inmate who spoke to him was sitting in his cell reading his Bible. All of the sudden he looked up and there was the Muslim he had spoken to. The Muslim looked at him with a smile and said, "I've been standing here quite a while watching you read your Bible."

I urged the inmate to stay in close touch with Jesus and follow it up. You see, this is just one instance of the many ways that Jesus is calling out to men and women as He makes a final effort to get His Bride ready for His soon coming for her. How many other scenes like this are being carried out right around us that we know nothing about?

Please pray for another man I have been very encouraged with. Since he has been here, I have watched him in services and also had visits with him, and I have seen him open his heart wide to the truth of holiness and he testifies that he is no longer having trouble with inward or outward sin. He will be paroled to his mother's home way up in the north of the State, and I do not know of a good holiness church up there to recommend him to. He says he will go with his mother to her church, but he will not give up what God has shown to him of the complete work of God. He says too that he will write to me because he does not want to end our friendship and the help he has gotten. He said he would love to come all the way down when we are having a meeting and visit our church. So please lift him to God if he comes to your mind.

I have mentioned in these letters several times before, the continuing problem we are having with getting the men called out for our services. The problem gets worse and worse. We have spoken to the ombudsman about it as well as the custody major and the assistant superintendent, but the problem goes on. We also are having the Sunday services called out later and later until we only have a part of an hour for our services over and over. After much investigation and speaking with all levels of personnel, I believe I am correct in what I am going to diagnose as the number one cause of this. Here it is:

Prior to the present national government philosophies, we considered it a highly reportable thing if we detected the presence of drugs of any kind in the prison. Now, more and more drugs are becoming legal and are so infiltrating the prison that I do not believe they are even trying to stop them. Inmate after inmate complains that he has to live with K2 or marijuana smoke in his cell around the clock. A few officers are complaining about having to work around it, but if I have heard correctly, many of them are using too.

We are, so I have been told, having an average of one hundred and fifty medical calls a month, and most of them are drug related. Then those codes in turn escalate into physical violence which calls out another code. This past Sunday night just before church time, the facility we were in had two codes back-to-back and another facility had a major one. I didn't hear about the third facility. Even though the officer allowed us to stay clear up to the call to lock in, we had but a short service.

We are actually pondering switching to mid-week services because of the shortage of custody on the weekends. Please help us in prayer that we can find a way to have effective time to minister to these needy men. I believe, to be honest, that we are simply experiencing a skirmish of the major war that is developing around us at an alarming rate, as the anti-christ moves in his agenda over our country. I try to keep the men warned not to let their spirits take on wrong attitudes because of the taking away of their rights. We may have only seen the tip of the iceberg in all of this so far.

But in spite of all this opposition, God is still moving very obviously on the hearts of many of the men. And every week I sign up more names for the Bible classes and worship services. This past Sunday I preached to the men on contending for the faith once delivered to the saints. I could see much positive reception to the message, and many of them expressed it on the way out.

Thank you again for praying,

William Cawman

August, 2024

IT IS SO COMFORTING and reassuring to know beyond all doubt that our Great Heavenly Father is still on His throne and will be forever! The song writer expressed it thus:

> *That Name still lives, and will live on forever;*
> *While kings and kingdoms will forgotten be.*
> *Through mist or rain, 'twill be beclouded never;*
> *That Name still shines, and shines eternally.*

Last month I told you that we were considering having to move our weekly worship services to midweek instead of Sundays because of the difficulties in both time allotted and interferences from codes. Well, the decision was taken out of our hands, as Trenton passed an ultimatum for the whole state that there were to be no more activities from five-thirty Friday evening until Monday morning, starting in August.

So let me tell you the pros and cons of such a change. The men are naturally disappointed that they cannot have a service on Sunday, but it had come to where we were only having thirty or forty minutes for our service time because they were not finishing the evening meal in time. Too often, besides, a medical or custody code came up and we could not have service at all.

Another factor against us is that having three services at the same time on Sunday night required either three chaplains or volunteers, and that was very often not happening. Many times one or two facilities were not able to have any service at all.

Now, here is the positive aspect of the change. We plan to have the three services on three separate days (Tuesday, Wednesday, and Thursday), and so even if all that is available is one chaplain, we could still cover them all. Furthermore, we are scheduling them to be from one o'clock in the afternoon until three-thirty. Very likely we will not get the men together until one-thirty, but we would still have a good time slot left. And even if there is a code which would delay them coming down, it would be very rare if the code would last more than twenty minutes or so. We are therefore looking forward to having an effective time once again like we used to for the services. Thank you so much for your prayers for this.

Of course, taking all the available afternoon time for these services requires us to move all Bible studies into the morning hours. This may cause a few to have to drop out because they have jobs to perform during the morning and the officers in charge of those jobs may not want to release them. Bible studies are not protected by law, but the rights of inmates to attend weekly worship services are protected by federal law, so they cannot be hindered if they desire to come to those.

By the time these new programs are all entered by the State into the computers, we will have our hands full for the last few days of July and the first few of August, moving all the names from both services and Bible studies into the new modules. The "user-unfriendly" (seriously!) programs set up for all of this do not allow a list of names to be cut and pasted into a new module, so every single name has to be removed from the old module and entered into the new one. It is very difficult to fall in love with technology when these changes demand so much time staring at a screen! I will be so happy when it is completed.

I will tell you something that is rare in the world of today. Our supervisor of chaplaincy is of such a personality that the whole department work together beautifully in times like this.

Even though these changes affect only the Protestant services, not one of the other chaplains would refuse to jump in and help enter these names to help us out. We have two full-time imams for the Muslims; we have a full-time Catholic chaplain; we have a part-time rabbi for the Jewish inmates, and we have the supervisor and two of us part-time Protestant chaplains in the department, and we all help each other whenever that is needed without a complaint from anyone.

Well, once these changes have been effected, would you help us pray that we can see a revival break out in every one of the three facilities among the inmates? With the quality time factor, we can even have some altar services whenever God moves in that way. We have long felt so hampered in having an effective service with such a short time slot in which to have it.

Now: just a day after writing the above I received a notice from my supervisor that all of what I have written has been put on hold until further notice by the State government. I thought about erasing it all, but I won't because we really need prayer that God's will be done in it all. For the present we will continue with our much-abbreviated Sunday night services, and God only knows for how long, but would you please pray with us that God will keep open a door sufficient enough for us to continue to minister to these dear men? Perhaps I will know more by the time another letter is due, but as of now, I do not even know that.

The one thing I do know, and that for certain, is that God is not finished working among these men in prison. That is being clearly evidenced by new and fresh awakenings and by His continued work in the hearts of those who have already yielded to Him. I promise God and you, our prayer partners, that I will lovingly obey God, whatever!

Think of this: what if a man in prison who Satan thought he had captured for eternity, would yet respond to the call of God and be the last soul ever to enter the kingdom and be washed in the Blood of Jesus before the rapture takes place? Someone, somewhere, will be that last sheaf garnered.

Now, look at it from another angle: what would it be like to suddenly be ushered into heaven and realize that you were the last one to make it in? Again, someone, somewhere, will be that soul. Oh God, please help us all that not one soul slip through our hands that ought to yet make it in!

I would like to request prayer for one of the men in prison who I have written about a number of times over the past years. You may remember me telling of how he just shines with the grace of God and the joy of the Lord. For a number of years now he has walked with God in the beauty of holiness and has been a real witness to men all around him. His testimony is one of the five that are even now at the publisher and will be coming out very soon. A couple of years ago now, he was moved to another prison and has continued to shine for God and holiness there.

Some time back he had a blood clot in his leg that broke out in the open in his ankle. Being diabetic it is not healing properly at all, and after seeing a podiatrist, he is under new treatment and is asking prayer for a healing touch. Would you please remember him in your prayers and ask others also to pray for him? He does not have a lot of time left in prison, and he is looking forward eagerly to getting out and coming to our church. We are certainly looking forward to it as well.

Here is another prayer request, and I will lay aside all misgivings of loading you down with too many requests when I realize that they come from God, not me. It has been about six years now since my former supervisor retired and was replaced. He continues to contact me once in a great while, and recently indicated that he would really like to get together for a visit. He told me that I had been the man who had influenced his life more than any other. Of course, I know full well that it was not me, but Christ shining through me. This is not the first time he has asked for this, and I do plan to make arrangements soon to visit. Would you please pray that God will anoint this visit to his eternal good? I have seldom seen a man immersed in the Calvinistic doctrines who was willing to give them up for clear Bible teaching. Of course, they feel they are teaching the Bible. But it is very evident in this man, at least, that he has seen and felt something that speaks to him beyond all of his other associates in that doctrine.

A year or two after he had retired (he is now volunteering at a county jail), we did go out to lunch together along with the Catholic chaplain who had served under him and is still with us. At that luncheon he confessed to us that for the last few years of his being there he had lost heart in the real purpose of a chaplain, and had just succumbed to the work load of it; which indeed it would be easy to do. He said that God had chastened him and he had experienced a revival of his personal relationship to the Lord, and he wanted to ask forgiveness. I did appreciate that, as such a condition as he confessed had been very obvious to us. So, again, please pray that our upcoming visit would be used of God for his soul's sake.

We are often made aware by one way or another, that we have perhaps as many needy souls among fellow staff workers as among the inmates. Every so often a door opens to speak to one of them. Recently one of the social workers who I have known for quite some time and often shared little tidbits of home life with, was assigned to work in the hospital. She hadn't been there long before she observed one of the nurses vaping. She reported it, and even though they removed the nurse, other staff members began to emotionally retaliate against her for reporting it. We have a very strong policy in the State against retaliation for being reported, but many of them are obviously disregarding the policy. When I was told this by the social worker's supervisor, I also learned that her husband had died during Covid, and I would guess them to be only in their late thirties or early forties. When I get a chance, I want to speak a few words of understanding to her as I know that valley all too well.

Just a little story about her: one day she told me that she has a dog that was just too much trouble as she has a five-year-old daughter. She decided that she needed to get rid of the dog, but knew she would have to prepare the little girl for the loss. She sat down with her and began to explain that she just could not keep up with her and the dog too. The little girl puckered up and said, "Then I'll have to go?"

We have also had two staff members recently go through a severe battle with cancer. We always make it a point to let them know that we are praying for them in our weekly prayer times as a group. We would be so glad of prayer that God would give us even more of a window into hurting souls, whether staff or inmates. You see, it is clearly stated in our employment conditions that we are chaplains to staff and officers as well as inmates. This means that on any day we are shut in with around five thousand souls all around us. Oh Lord, please give us more of them!

Thank you from our hearts once again for every prayer that goes up for us!

With love, William Cawman

┼┼┼

September, 2024

No sooner had the ink dried (so to speak) on the last letter, than the changes I spoke of, followed by the temporary hold, were re-instated with request that it happen as soon as possible. So we continued Sunday night services through August 11, planning to start the weekday services the next week, August 20, 21, & 22.

And if you remember I had requested prayer for the huge volume of work such changes entailed, taking all the names from the old modules and entering them in the new ones. Well, thank the Lord! One of the assistant superintendents who has been very helpful to us over and over, offered to do most of the typing of these names for us! Again, thank You, Lord! He still answers prayer in just His own very wonderful way!

Now it just so works out that the very first week of the new schedule and the opening of the new worship services in each facility, happens to be the very week my supervisor will be on vacation out of the country, so I will be left to do them all. On Wednesday, however, a volunteer is available to do the preaching, so I will just have the rest of the service that day.

I had spoken to the men and invited them to make us aware of any elements of worship they had been missing with the short time allotted on Sunday nights. I told them that we would not be open to anything not strictly taught in the Bible, such as drama or bizarre things such as playing with snakes or slaying in the spirit, but that we welcomed any input as to what would minister to them spiritually. Immediately a hand went up and the request was that we could have altar services and more prayer. Hallelujah! We will NOT deny that. Another suggestion was that we could have times of Scripture memorization and then quote them aloud in service. Needless to say, I was very pleased with the requests so far.

I am now home from the first day of the new schedule. It was a complete disaster! I was in the chapel waiting for them to call it out when a sergeant came down and asked me if an email authorizing the service had been sent. I told him that I was not in last week and so did not know what my supervisor had sent or not sent, but that it was on the appointment sheet and I had the roster with me. He went and reported it to the lieutenant and they said they could not run the service because they had received nothing regarding the change. They said that they knew that there was a meeting of all department heads the week before and that it had been discussed, but they had nothing in writing. I went to the phone and called the assistant superintendent and she said she would take care of it. Soon the sergeant and lieutenant came down again and said that they could not run the service because the appointment sheet called for over three hundred men from all three facilities to come to that chapel and they could not handle it.

I told them I could not understand where such an appointment had ever come from, but there was no use; they were not going to run the service; so that was that!

I soon got an email from the assistant superintendent saying that she had no idea where they pulled up the appointment sheet they were referring to. She apologized and I told her I would send her exactly what the appointment should be and hopefully we would not have that kind of trouble from there on. She assured me she would work for us.

I know that mistakes happen, but somehow, I sense more and more that the tide is turning against religious services. That morning for my Bible study only about a third of the men came, and that a half hour late, and they reported that it had not been called out on the units. The officer in charge of it told me he called to all areas on the radio, but then it is up to each tier officer as to whether he calls it out or not. Many times if he does, the inmates say he will wait a few minutes and then just call "Church!"

We never used to have such problems as this. But little by little the intercom systems by which they could announce it to everywhere have broken down and the state will not pay out the money to have it repaired, so it is up to each tier officer to announce anything. The morale is so low among the officers that administration is afraid to demand anything for fear of more retiring.

If it sounds like I am complaining, I would not deny it, but I am doing it to ask for prayer. There have been many moments lately when if I would give in to my feelings I would just turn in my badge and walk away, but then I see the faces of precious men that are walking in the light and wanting help and I just cannot do it. So please, please, help us pray. We are without a doubt facing the beginning waves of the takeover of the antichrist. I am committed to staying where God has put me until He releases me or calls me away.

Well, Wednesday the service went somewhat better; they finally called it out at 1:45. We knew when we put the services on the schedule for 1:00 pm that seldom if ever would we get started then, but we wanted to have as much time as we could. The men were very receptive and thankful for the longer service time and there were a number of testimonies, songs, and the message.

On Thursday my wife came in and we went to the third service. A good number came down and they called it out around 1:20. We again had a precious time clear until 3:15. Again we had a number of testimonies, a good season of prayer, my wife and I sang "Some Golden Daybreak," then I played a couple of verses of it on my trumpet and then we sang another song and had the message. I preached to them from Isaiah 35: "...the way of holiness." I spoke to them about how ridiculous it is that so many say there is no such a thing as living a holy life free from sin when that is exactly and specifically what Jesus came to do. I told them to reason with me for a bit. If there is no such a state this side of heaven where we can live a holy life without sinning, and yet we ask God for it; we have lost nothing. But if there is such a state and we do not ask for it, we have lost everything including heaven, for without holiness no man shall get there.

So I told them that holiness is the only way to heaven; it is the only way that makes sense; it is the only way to be truly happy on earth, it is the only way to have complete victory over sin; it is the only way to wage war against the gates of hell; it is the only way to please God; and it is the only way to make it safely through the perils of the midnight hour we are in.

I could see a progression in their reception of the truth where they may have had doubts about it when I started. You see, holiness really does make sense, doesn't it?

Please help us pray that Satan's multiple lies can be shown up for what they are and that many of these dear men can invite God to do all for them that He died to do. I cannot help but compare the present worthless "Christianity" so many are caught in with the atmosphere of this very country of South

Jersey in the early 1800s when holiness was the prevailing truth preached and lived. The very city in which the prison is located was a veritable hotbed of holiness around 1820-1850. Even when I was a small boy, there were little remnants of holiness churches scattered around us, but today our church and one other small skeleton congregation is all that is left. I would love to see God send another holiness revival and start it right in this prison!

If you remember the young man I told you about who broke into tears several times in a Bible study and then told me the next day it was because he was finally where God wanted him to be, I am happy to report that he becomes sweeter and more vibrant in his testimony every time I see him. He only has about a year left to serve and I so wish I could direct him to a godly church. Please help us pray to this end. The dearth of such as I just described in the paragraph above is more than painful. I know that there are churches not a few who need a pastor, but if anyone would feel God directing them to open a second church in NJ, we need it more than can be imagined. Most of the inmates when released are sent back to the communities they came from, and most by far come from an hour and a half north of our church, and beyond. Just think how this sounds: A Missionary to New Jersey! David Brainerd and Benjamin Abbott and Charles Pittman and R. G. Flexon are all gone home to their rewards now, and no one has arisen to fill their shoes. What a heritage we have had for where we are now!

Now I want to leave another prayer request, and one which would "seem" impossible except that the Word of God declares that nothing is impossible with God. It is this: the other day I was with the Islamic chaplain who is the only chaplain who has been here longer than I have. As we were talking, he began to say that he is so scared of what is coming on our country and the world that he has trouble sleeping at night. I hope that God is bringing conviction on him. I don't know what would happen if our imam would get saved, but I would certainly be willing to find out! Will you help pray for him also?

Thank you each one again for your prayers. As I travel about in our country it warms my heart to hear so many say that they are praying for us. Nothing you could do carries more important weight than that! Thank you again so much!

In the love of Jesus and those He died for,

William Cawman

16
"Great is Thy Faithfulness"

October, 2024

If you remember, I started last month's letter relating the tumultuous changes to our schedules of religious services. Now, one month later, we are even less settled than before. Even though the inmates were getting adjusted to the changes and we were having more time for services, the officers were not happy with having more work to do in the middle of the week instead of on Sundays. It seemed that the problem of officers opening cell doors and calling the men out for services was getting only worse.

On Wednesday, September 11, I was scheduled to have a worship service in facility two and then one in the minimum camp at 5:30. My supervisor went after lunch to a staff meeting of department heads and I was in my office around 4:00 pm preparing for the service in minimum camp. He called and I detected an unusual degree of agitation in his voice. He told me that at the meeting he was told that the officers are not happy with the services in the middle of the week because they said they do not have time to run them. My supervisor asked, "How come you have time to run the Muslim services?" The question was carefully avoided.

I had not had time to remove all the names from the old schedules and so they were still appearing on the daily appointment sheets and confusing the officers. My supervisor told me not to change anything as yet until we know what they are going to ask us to do.

Now, I think you will understand that sometimes with all of this obvious outright warfare against our religious services, I face the temptation to just walk away from it all; but then I think of the precious souls of these men and I just have to look to the One who called me here to begin with. That very day when my supervisor also felt so frustrated with the powers that are, I had a service in facility two and had asked if any of the inmates wanted to give a testimony. After several others, the man I have told you about who burst into tears in a Bible study months ago, and then told me he was so happy that he was finally where Jesus wanted him to be, arose and ever so humbly said to the men, "Men, I can hardly believe the change I feel. It seems that I can hardly remember ever thinking any other way than I am thinking now, because I am so happy with what God has done for me." I said to them, "Now, the reason for what he just said is that God told us that our sins and iniquities He would remember no more forever!" There was a round of applause with that.

How can I just walk away from hearts like this? I cannot, and I will not until God Himself leads that way.

I would like to share a prayer request with you. A man who has been with us for almost two years now is getting ready to leave. He was living the typical American life in another state, but for some time was deeply involved in secret internet pornography. He came to this state and was caught online with it because of carelessness in stepping over certain boundaries, and was sent to prison. He had been a member of a church along with his wife, but once he was found out, he just openly confessed it to everyone. The church said they no longer wanted him to attend, which made his wife very upset with the church.

For most of the time he has been here, his wife has stood by him and said she forgave him for it, and now he has been clean from it for four years and hates the thought of ever going back to it. But just as he is about to leave and go home, his wife called him and told him that she is starting divorce proceedings. It was a hard blow to him and he wanted to talk with me about it.

I asked him if this was a first marriage for both of them and he said that it was not only a first marriage, but that he was a virgin when he married her and has never been with anyone else. I pointed him to the Scriptures which clearly teach that the first marriage is until death, and he fully agreed with it. I then told him to write her a letter and humble himself in repentance and asking forgiveness, and in so doing, to avoid trying to demand anything of her. He said he could well see the wisdom of that and would do it.

Then I asked about his own spiritual walk and he told me that his love for Jesus is keeping the door closed on all sin. He told me that he has been spending several hours a day in communion with God and that he doesn't want to lose that when he gets out. I told him about the old song that says, "Take time to be holy!"

He said that the other day he was meditating on Psalm 47 where are these words: "O clap your hands, all ye people; shout unto God with the voice of triumph. For the Lord most high is terrible; he is a great King over all the earth. He shall subdue the people under us, and the nations under our feet. He shall choose our inheritance for us, the excellency of Jacob whom he loved. Selah. God is gone up with a shout, the Lord with the sound of a trumpet."

He became completely lost in the thought that God simply spoke the world into existence, but when He came down to deliver him, He shouted aloud his deliverance! He doesn't know how long he was just carried away up out of the prison with the thought, but suddenly an officer began shouting out on the tier floor and brought him back down to prison again.

Please help us pray for him and also for his wife, that God will soften her heart and bring them back together again to start a whole new life in Him and His sweet will.

It is mandatory that all staff members take some classes which are on the prison computers. You may wonder what the classes are? Well, they are man's supreme and laborious efforts to instruct us how to behave around each other. And it takes several hours to get through it all. As I had some time the other day, I figured I had better tackle some of them. I was right across the hallway from the assistant superintendent who is over us as chaplains. After an hour or so, I became so weary of it that I went over to her and said, "I am wading through the classes of non-uniformed staff training and I am finding it a very poor substitute for the Bible!" She laughed and agreed whole-heartedly with me. A little while later she came over and opened my door and said, "How's it going?" I said, "Blah, blah, blah!" Again, she laughed and agreed.

What a sad commentary on man's efforts to be good and make others be good, when all they would have to do is let Jesus come into their hearts and write the Law within them.

On the same line of thinking, I was recently in a meeting in another state and stopped in at a thrift store and picked up a few used books. One was a book I had heard a lot about: "The Case for Christ," by Lee Stroebel. I read a good portion of it and became so disgusted that I threw it aside and turned to something else to read. You might ask what was wrong with it? Well, it was what Jesus called "climbing up some other way," than going through the Door. The Bible says that with the heart man believeth. This poor writer traveled all over the world, consulting huge thinkers and gleaning information to the end that he could convince everyone else as well as himself that the Gospels were authentic and Jesus really lived. I wish I could have met him and invited him to humble himself and let Jesus come into his heart, and his erudite and gray-matter search would have ended immediately in glorious reality. Let me read from those with burning hearts, not overstuffed heads!

Now you might ask what that paragraph had to do with prison ministry. Nothing; nothing at all; I just put it in there at no extra charge.

An inmate came to me at the beginning of the service in facility one and with a pitiful look said, "Chaplain, I really need help. I am just totally helpless before alcohol. I've tried and tried to get the victory over it but I just keep falling back over and over. Can you help me?"

I told him that only Jesus could break that chain, but it would take more than just using Jesus as a crutch or a charm or an imagination. It was time to begin the service so I told him I would sit down with him soon and try to guide him to the Jesus who has power to deliver from any addiction. Please help me pray that I can lead him to the Fountain that cleanses from all sin.

We have had several deaths recently among staff and officers. One of our librarians died after a siege with cancer. I went to the funeral, but could not stay long as it was fast taking on ear-splitting sensuous "praise." So-called "praising" God without a trace of the indwelling Spirit of God borders too close to the demonic.

Then a well-liked officer after working a double shift last week, went home and went into the shower and his daughter found him dead. Please pray that these will be wake-up calls to all who are not ready for that moment we all shall come to.

Thank you each one again so much for your prayers.

William Cawman

November, 2024

I WANT TO START this letter by thanking any and all of you who are praying for us here in the prison. Here are a couple of bright spots from this month.

You may well remember the man I have written about a few times who about a year ago burst into tears several times during a Bible study and then told me the next day that it was because he was finally where God wanted him to be. Now I have heard in my life-long dwelling among the holiness people, several testimonies that professed a very high state of spiritual stature, but failed to ring that bell which gloriously accompanies a genuine walk with the Lord. This man had not learned even what to call his present state with God, but he is growing in his love and understanding of Jesus in a very noticeable way.

The other day I asked him to pray during a worship service. I wish all of you could have heard and felt that prayer! I was wishing I had a recorder to capture it for you. He started out and for several minutes just thanked the Lord for one thing after another. Here's a sample: "Thank You Jesus, for every trial You have allowed me to go through; it only brought me closer to You!" After a while he did ask for two things, and to the best of my memory they were both that those around him could go deeper with God; then he thanked Jesus for answering those two things. How much closer can one come to the Scriptural prescription: "Be careful for nothing; but in everything by prayer and supplication with thanksgiving let your requests be made known unto God"?

I could not truthfully tell you that there are not prayers prayed by these men as well as others, which are prayed to be heard of men. But the whole atmosphere surrounding his prayer was a definite communion with God. I am not sure that I have heard such a prayer anywhere else I have been.

Then I received a request for a Bible from an inmate I did not know. I took one and sat down with him and gave him the Bible and he immediately grasped it like a boy would grasp a chocolate chip cookie. I asked him how he was doing and he radiantly said, "Great!" I asked if he was finding God in prayer and what a fountain of affirmation came beaming out. He said, "My life has been wonderful since Jesus found me!" I asked him when that happened and he said that it was on August 16th, if I remember the day correctly.

He said that he had gone through a lot of depression in his life, but the moment Jesus found him it left and has not come back. He said that he has only two years to be locked up, and so I asked where his home was. He said it was in the very town our church is. I asked if he really wanted to go to a church that would match what he had found in God, and he enthusiastically said, "Yes!" I told him I would keep in contact with him about it.

I then asked if he liked to read. He said he did. I said I would bring him some good books and he seemed very excited about that. He said he had gone to the prison library and had taken out a few books and when it was time to return them he hadn't even started to read them as he was so taken up with reading the Bible. He hadn't had one of his own until I gave him one. He told me that the Bible is so interesting and gives him so much instruction in his walk with Jesus.

I went and told my supervisor about him and he was just then in the process of writing up a charge for an Odinist inmate who had gotten very unruly in the service and was going to be locked up for it. He was very glad that I had a better visit than what he had. I was too!

So you see, your prayers are not going unanswered; thank you and thank the Lord!

And now a couple of weeks later: after being away in a revival meeting, I returned to find my mailbox full of new requests for enrollment in studies and services. Among them I kept coming across the same inmate's name, and after reading all of his requests I gathered that he was highly confused, but deeply hungry. He was literally begging us to help him find God. The last one that came before I had a chance to call him down was different. It stated that he had found Jesus and wanted to be removed from all the other religions he had tried and just be a Christian.

On the morning of October 25, 2024, I finally had an opportunity to visit with him and he immediately launched into this conversation: "Chaplain, not many people will believe me when I tell them this, but Jesus saved me!" He looked me right in the eye and said emphatically, "Jesus saved me!"

He sat before me with dreadlocks almost to his waist and arms that were plastered with tattoos, but his testimony was clear! He then began to tell me his life's story. He was born into a very dysfunctional and wicked home life, and was abused by family members from earliest childhood. He followed the pattern and had the first of his thirteen children that he knows about at the age of fourteen. That son, now twenty-eight, is also in another facility of the same prison. Do you remember what God said to Moses? "The LORD, The LORD God, merciful and gracious, longsuffering, and abundant in goodness and truth, Keeping mercy for thousands, forgiving iniquity and transgression and sin, and that will by no means clear the guilty; visiting the iniquity of the fathers upon the children, and upon the children's children, unto the third and to the fourth generation." Certainly God is not of such a nature that He punishes children for the father's sins, but He is only saying that when He comes to visit the child, He will find the sins of the father perpetuated in the children. How God's Word is so dramatized in real life!

As he grew older, he knew nothing of employment except to use and deal drugs, until he was just a wreck of Satan in every area of his life. But listen: "Jesus saved me! He broke every addiction immediately and I have no desire for the old life anymore." I asked him when this happened and he said it was two weeks ago, and that sins of every kind had no more power over him.

Without a doubt God always moves according to His own Word, for His Word is Him! He has promised: "There hath no temptation taken you but such as is common to man: but God is faithful, who will not suffer you to be tempted above that ye are able; but will with the temptation also make a way to escape, that ye may be able to bear it." Now it is obvious that this man has been addicted way beyond his power to control, and also that he is not fully responsible for even being addicted, as he was led into it almost without a choice. Perhaps he fits the category spoken of in 2 Tim. 2:26 "And that they may recover themselves out of the snare of the devil, who are taken captive by him at his will."

Another old song says: "I know not how the Spirit moves, convincing men of sin; revealing Jesus through the Word, creating faith in Him..." but like the man in John's gospel chapter nine, it is not necessary to know all the factors involved, but this much he knew, and this man knows: "Jesus saved me!"

Isn't this marvelous evidence that God is not finished preparing His bride for His soon coming? Doesn't it just make you want to hug up to Him, not only in love, but in working together with Him, that He might see even yet the travail of His soul and be satisfied?

Now another side to all of these recent victories has come to light. Two of our chaplains, the supervisor for one, have encountered to their utter shock, the antichrist tidal wave that is sweeping over the world. Our supervisor was teaching in his Bible study that Jesus is truly God. Voices began to protest loudly and one man just got up and walked out! A couple of days later I went to the same group for their worship service and I could feel a dark presence still lingering over the group.

The supervisor told us about it and said he feels the need of starting up a class of introduction to Christianity, where we could begin to combat this and teach correctly. The other chaplain mentioned this to his group and told them that the classes would teach us that Jeus is truly God. A strong voice spoke up and said, "No He's not!"

There is a strong undertone of undermining the authenticity of Scripture and of the Deity. We met together and laid plans to start such a class and then the supervisor said, "Now, let's pray; because we are going to buck right up against strong opposition teaching these truths. But if we aren't going to teach God's Word as authoritative, what are we going to teach?" After prayer, he asked us to carry this request to our connections outside and ask for prayer. That is what I am doing right here! Please help us pray! And we may as well be aware that these demonic and blasphemous teachings are cropping up all across our land which was once founded upon the inerrant Word of God. For certain, the Muslims are responsible for some of it, but it is also stemming right out of the pit of heart corruption that has swept away the fear of God from our country. We are definitely encountering that "…how great is that darkness" that Jesus said would come if the Light goes out.

Another bright spot recently is that a man who has spent years in prison and has just played around with God and even after definite touches of God on his heart, has failed to settle with God, sent me a letter filled with victory over sin and spiritual failure. The Hound of Heaven has followed him for years, and hopefully this time he has turned to never go back into sin again. Please pray for him.

It is so gloriously evident that in the very face of the rapidly encroaching night of sin, God is still gathering souls into His kingdom. I often wonder who will be the last one in before He closes the door on the Ark.

Now let me tell you a story that should make you ever so grateful if you do not have one like it! I just visited with a forty-four-year-old who says he grew up in a home with no religious influence whatsoever. His mother killed herself when he was young and then his father died, leaving him with no family at all that will have anything to do with him. He does have a fourteen-year-old daughter who never contacts him. He has never married, as his life consisted completely in drugs and alcohol and drink. Half-way through life his body is wrecked by all the abuse and he has no pleasant memories of the past. And yet, he is a living man with an eternity bound soul. Such is the reward handed out to the choice to favor self instead of God.

I tried to point him to the better way that can only be found in full surrender to Jesus. I trust he understood; he said he did; and we had prayer together, after which he crossed himself. Perhaps there is some Catholicism in his past life. I was so painfully reminded of the pathetic and tragic product of a life given to self and Satan. If God brings him to you in prayer, please pray; I would love to see him come out into the glorious liberty of a child of God.

Another one of our teachers has died. She was a very influential staff member and highly liked, but died as a result of a car accident a few days before. It has hit the education department very hard, so pray that there will be some serious thinking among the rest as well as the inmates as a result of it.

It is rather touching that the prison puts a plaque in the window of the control center for each of the officers who passes away. It has their badge with black tape over it and says, "End of Watch." It is, and should be, a stark reminder of the uncertainty of life.

God alone knows how much longer any of us have to work where He has called us, but the darkening night calls loudly to us to be at our very faithful best for Him.

Thank you each one for praying,

William Cawman

December, 2024

TWENTY-FIVE YEARS AGO this month the first of these letters was sent out. There has been one every month from then on and many prayers have ascended to God and many answers have come back, but it is very evident that God is not finished working among these men. Thank you, each and every one, for your continued prayers for us.

Last month I told you the start of a story that I pray will not end. I told you about the man who had sent many very confused requests, pleading for a chaplain to help him find God. I will not here repeat the part I told you of this miracle again, but I do want to give you some details that have come up since.

The very next day after I had at his request removed him from all other religions and signed him up for the Christian studies and services, he appeared in class with a radiant face (still beaming among the dreadlocks!). It was not long until he wanted to share what God had done for him with the class. The other men rejoiced greatly. Then the next day in the worship service, he again arose to share the joy he was finding. I will try to recall as nearly as I can the details he told, but once again in both testimonies, he kept bursting out with "Jesus saved me!" I love that kind of salvation!

He said he was a Muslim as well as a member of the gang called "Bloods." They are a very violent gang, and in order to become one a person must give and receive at least forty stiches. On top of that, he was hopelessly addicted to every sin Satan has in his catalogue. He was chronically using drugs and when not in prison smoking and drinking and fornicating all the time.

He said that suddenly, in this most pitifully hopeless condition, Jesus appeared to him in a dream and began to pull something huge out of him. He could actually see Him doing it, and it was a tremendously difficult extraction. When he woke up, he instantly knew that he was completely delivered from every bit of it. Not a single sin had any attraction to him. He said he went out into the courtyard and witnessed boldly to all the other gang members that he was totally finished with all their activities and was no longer one of them because Jesus had saved him. Note: a person does not leave this gang without severe repercussions; but thank God for the shelter of the Blood!

After he had testified, I preached to them that day from Jude's words: "Beloved, when I gave all diligence to write unto you of the common salvation, it was needful for me to write unto you, and exhort you that ye should earnestly contend for the faith which was once delivered unto the saints." His face lit up over and over, showing that he comprehended the truth, even though I would suppose he had never heard it before. Isn't it marvelous as to how God can get His Word through to the most ignorant soul, as long as His Spirit is dwelling within them?

On the way out the door, he shook my hand and said with deep joy: "All I want now is Jesus!"

I just have to rejoice that I had nothing to do with this marvelous conversion except to witness it. The Holy Spirit did this all by Himself! Doesn't that just give us a window into what He is doing all around the world as He continues to prepare a Bride for Jesus right in the face of the wrath of the antichrist? Hallelujah for the Holy Spirit and the Blood of Jesus! Listen to this glorious uniform resumé of every single one of the Bride of Christ: "These are they which came out of great tribulation, and have washed their robes, and made them white in the blood of the Lamb." Oh, I want to be among them, don't you?

Now, after being away in a revival meeting for ten days, I returned and found him just as happy and victorious as the Life of Christ within can make one. He said that he has been receiving many threats from former gang members, but he has no fears because he now belongs to Jesus. Then he pointed to his arms and said, "As soon as I get out of here these tattoos are coming off!" "...yea, what revenge..." Scripture says, is one of the marks of a new birth.

Another week went by and I received a request from his cell mate. "My bunky [inmate's name we're talking about] has mention my name and have said a few prayers for me as well. I'd like very much to join this service." One more mark of a genuine conversion!

For several months now, the Native Americans (Indians) have been having a weekly meeting, and I haven't paid much attention to it. But my supervisor was going to be away on the day it is held and so he asked me if I could sit in with them. I agreed. It so happened (so we say when God is ordering our steps) that his plans changed and he was not gone, but I didn't know it until I got there. I went to the cabinet to get the bag of whatever they use to take it to them and it was not there, and then I noticed that my supervisor had signed in. I went to visit with an inmate and sent him a note that I was there. He wanted me to come as soon as I could to see what the ceremony entailed in case he was ever absent.

When I finished the visit, I went over to facility one and went out the back door into the yard which is used for nothing else and found him sitting in a chair in the chilly breeze. There was a ring of "Native Americans" of which I am confident not one in five has a drop of Indian blood in him, and they had a sheet spread on the ground and were reading something from a book. Each one in turn would leave the ring and come over to my supervisor who would light their smoke pipe for them and then they would go over and face the sun, then tap the earth, as they puffed out quantities of smoke from a combination of tobacco and kinnikinic.

Of course, since tobacco products are not allowed in the prison, these items had to be secured and provided by the chaplain. I am very glad that the government recognizes and promotes freedom to worship according to one's belief, because that protects us as well, but that does not change the fact that one cannot serve Christ and Belial. When we got back inside, I wasted no time in telling my supervisor that when it is simply a staff member needed to sit in on a service, I had no objection, but that I could not provide their smoke for them or light their pipes. He made no objection about relieving me of that function!

We have never replaced the part-time chaplain that retired at the end of last year, but now one has been interviewed and will most likely be approved to come on board with us. It will be the first female chaplain we have had in all the years I have labored here. We'll see how that works!

I am working towards getting a group together for Christmas in the prison. I would like to have a special Christmas service in each facility the week before Christmas. I know better than to try it Christmas week, as many of the officers will be taking off and custody will be stretched to the limit. I want to have a service each afternoon for Tuesday, Wednesday, and Thursday of that week, thus covering each of the facilities. We may have to figure out a time for one in the minimum camp also. The men are already looking forward to those services. Please help us pray that they will be anointed with God's presence.

I want to make another special request for prayer. The supervisor of the state chaplains for New Jersey is retiring at the end of this year. Even though he does not even come close to living an exemplary Christian life, he has been very supportive and favorable to our sincerely held religious beliefs, and has done much to keep the door open for us. It is very critical as to who replaces him. Please help us pray that God will plant the right man in this position so that we can continue this ministry without restrictions.

I do not know why I never noticed this so definitively before, after laboring among these men for over twenty-six years, but lately I have asked groups of inmates how many of them were raised or had been on a farm. I discover that hardly two or three in a whole class knows anything except inner city life. Doesn't that tell us pretty clearly where the majority of crimes develop? We rarely get a farm boy, or even a country boy in prison. That fact sets the mind to work, doesn't it?

A few days later, and what a precious day it was—November 26. The man I wrote about above came to Bible study in the morning along with his "bunky." I thought since they as well as a couple of others were fairly new in Jesus that I would just leave our regular Bible study for later and give them very simply the whole plan of salvation from the first "breath of life" to the complete infilling of the Holy Spirit. They sat there like two hungry birds just soaking it in and, all glory be to God and His Word, they seemed to understand everything I told them. The further we went the nearer God's presence came until at last I could hardly get the class dismissed for count time.

Then I went to another facility for their weekly worship service. Being Thanksgiving week, we sang a couple of thanksgiving songs and then I just opened it up for them to say what they were thankful for. I wish you could have been there! God's presence just settled down until it seemed everyone felt it. I will try to give you the gist of a couple of the testimonies. One man said, "I thank God because I am forty-four years old and I just found Him! Now I don't ever want to lose Him!" Another said, "I thank God because when I came to prison twenty-three years ago I could not read, until someone gave me a Bible, and I could read it!" I wish I had more room to tell you more of them, but there was no question that God was honoring it and His presence was deep and precious. Days like this one are worth it all!

Please pray for the special Christmas services we are planning for the week before Christmas. A group will be going in with us for the services and we pray that the Gift of Christmas will enter many hearts.

–William Cawman

And so, another four years of God's faithfulness in answering your prayers has closed, and the future is just as bright as the promises of God! Amen!

www.ingramcontent.com/pod-product-compliance
Lightning Source LLC
Chambersburg PA
CBHW070608170426
43200CB00012B/2621